Democracy, Law and Religious Pluralism in Europe

In contrast with the progressive dilution of religions predicted by traditional liberal and Marxist approaches, religions remain important for many people, even in Europe, the most secularised continent. In the context of increasingly culturally diverse societies, this calls for a reinterpretation of the secular legacy of the Enlightenment and also for an updating of democratic institutions.

This book focuses on a central question: are the classical secularist arrangements well equipped to tackle the challenge of fast-growing religious pluralism? Or should we move to new post-secular arrangements when dealing with pluralism in Europe? Offering an interdisciplinary approach that combines political theory and legal analysis, the authors tackle two interrelated facets of this controversial question. They begin by exploring the theoretical perspective, asking what post-secularism is and looking at its relation to secularism. The practical consequences of this debate are then examined, focusing on case-law through four empirical case studies.

This book will be of interest to students and scholars of political theory, philosophy, religion and politics, European law, human rights, legal theory and socio-legal studies.

Ferran Requejo is Professor of Political Science and Director of the Research Group on Political Theory and of the MA programme on Diverse Democracies at the Universitat Pompeu Fabra in Barcelona.

Camil Ungureanu is Lecturer in Political Theory and Director of the MA programme on Political Philosophy at the Universitat Pompeu Fabra in Barcelona.

Routledge Advances in European Politics

1 **Russian Messianism**
Third Rome, revolution, Communism and after
Peter J.S. Duncan

2 **European Integration and the Postmodern Condition**
Governance, democracy, identity
Peter van Ham

3 **Nationalism in Italian Politics**
The stories of the Northern League, 1980–2000
Damian Tambini

4 **International Intervention in the Balkans since 1995**
Edited by Peter Siani-Davies

5 **Widening the European Union**
The politics of institutional change and reform
Edited by Bernard Steunenberg

6 **Institutional Challenges in the European Union**
Edited by Madeleine Hosli, Adrian van Deemen and Mika Widgrén

7 **Europe Unbound**
Enlarging and reshaping the boundaries of the European Union
Edited by Jan Zielonka

8 **Ethnic Cleansing in the Balkans**
Nationalism and the destruction of tradition
Cathie Carmichael

9 **Democracy and Enlargement in Post-Communist Europe**
The democratisation of the general public in fifteen Central and Eastern European countries, 1991–1998
Christian W. Haerpfer

10 **Private Sector Involvement in the Euro**
The power of ideas
Stefan Collignon and Daniela Schwarzer

11 **Europe**
A Nietzschean perspective
Stefan Elbe

12 **European Union and E-Voting**
Addressing the European Parliament's internet voting challenge
Edited by Alexander H. Trechsel and Fernando Mendez

13 **European Union Council Presidencies**
A comparative perspective
Edited by Ole Elgström

14 **European Governance and Supranational Institutions**
Making states comply
Jonas Tallberg

15 **European Union, NATO and Russia**
Martin Smith and Graham Timmins

16 **Business, the State and Economic Policy**
The case of Italy
G. Grant Amyot

17 **Europeanization and Transnational States**
Comparing Nordic central governments
Bengt Jacobsson, Per Lægreid and Ove K. Pedersen

18 **European Union Enlargement**
A comparative history
Edited by Wolfram Kaiser and Jürgen Elvert

19 **Gibraltar**
British or Spanish?
Peter Gold

20 **Gendering Spanish Democracy**
Monica Threlfall, Christine Cousins and Celia Valiente

21 **European Union Negotiations**
Processes, networks and negotiations
Edited by Ole Elgström and Christer Jönsson

22 **Evaluating Euro-Mediterranean Relations**
Stephen C. Calleya

23 **The Changing Face of European Identity**
A seven-nation study of (supra) national attachments
Edited by Richard Robyn

24 **Governing Europe**
Discourse, governmentality and European integration
William Walters and Jens Henrik Haahr

25 **Territory and Terror**
Conflicting nationalisms in the Basque country
Jan Mansvelt Beck

26 **Multilateralism, German Foreign Policy and Central Europe**
Claus Hofhansel

27 **Popular Protest in East Germany**
Gareth Dale

28 **Germany's Foreign Policy Towards Poland and the Czech Republic**
Ostpolitik revisited
Karl Cordell and Stefan Wolff

29 **Kosovo**
The politics of identity and space
Denisa Kostovicova

30 **The Politics of European Union Enlargement**
Theoretical approaches
Edited by Frank Schimmelfennig and Ulrich Sedelmeier

31 **Europeanizing Social Democracy?**
The rise of the party of European socialists
Simon Lightfoot

32 **Conflict and Change in EU Budgetary Politics**
Johannes Lindner

33 **Gibraltar, Identity and Empire**
E.G. Archer

34 **Governance Stories**
Mark Bevir and R.A.W. Rhodes

35 **Britain and the Balkans**
1991 until the present
Carole Hodge

36 **The Eastern Enlargement of the European Union**
John O'Brennan

37 **Values and Principles in European Union Foreign Policy**
Edited by Sonia Lucarelli and Ian Manners

38 **European Union and the Making of a Wider Northern Europe**
Pami Aalto

39 **Democracy in the European Union**
Towards the emergence of a public sphere
Edited by Liana Giorgi, Ingmar Von Homeyer and Wayne Parsons

40 **European Union Peacebuilding and Policing**
Michael Merlingen with Rasa Ostrauskaite

41 **The Conservative Party and European Integration since 1945**
At the heart of Europe?
N.J. Crowson

42 **E-Government in Europe**
Re-booting the state
Edited by Paul G. Nixon and Vassiliki N. Koutrakou

43 **EU Foreign and Interior Policies**
Cross-pillar politics and the social construction of sovereignty
Stephan Stetter

44 **Policy Transfer in European Union Governance**
Regulating the utilities
Simon Bulmer, David Dolowitz, Peter Humphreys and Stephen Padgett

45 **The Europeanization of National Political Parties**
Power and organizational adaptation
Edited by Thomas Poguntke, Nicholas Aylott, Elisabeth Carter, Robert Ladrech and Kurt Richard Luther

46 **Citizenship in Nordic Welfare States**
Dynamics of choice, duties and participation in a changing Europe
Edited by Bjørn Hvinden and Håkan Johansson

47 **National Parliaments within the Enlarged European Union**
From victims of integration to competitive actors?
Edited by John O'Brennan and Tapio Raunio

48 **Britain, Ireland and Northern Ireland since 1980**
The totality of relationships
Eamonn O'Kane

49 **The EU and the European Security Strategy**
Forging a global Europe
Edited by Sven Biscop and Jan Joel Andersson

50 **European Security and Defence Policy**
An implementation perspective
Edited by Michael Merlingen and Rasa Ostrauskaitė

51 **Women and British Party Politics**
Descriptive, substantive and symbolic representation
Sarah Childs

52 **The Selection of Ministers in Europe**
Hiring and firing
Edited by Keith Dowding and Patrick Dumont

53 **Energy Security**
Europe's new foreign policy challenge
Richard Youngs

54 **Institutional Challenges in Post-Constitutional Europe**
Governing change
Edited by Catherine Moury and Luís de Sousa

55 **The Struggle for the European Constitution**
A past and future history
Michael O'Neill

56 **Transnational Labour Solidarity**
Mechanisms of commitment to cooperation within the European Trade Union Movement
Katarzyna Gajewska

57 **The Illusion of Accountability in the European Union**
Edited by Sverker Gustavsson, Christer Karlsson, and Thomas Persson

58 **The European Union and Global Social Change**
A critical geopolitical-economic analysis
József Böröcz

59 **Citizenship and Collective Identity in Europe**
Ireneusz Pawel Karolewski

60 **EU Enlargement and Socialization**
Turkey and Cyprus
Stefan Engert

61 **The Politics of EU Accession**
Turkish challenges and Central European experiences
Edited by Lucie Tunkrová and Pavel Šaradín

62 **The Political History of European Integration**
The hypocrisy of democracy-through-market
Hagen Schulz-Forberg and Bo Stråth

63 **The Spatialities of Europeanization**
Power, governance and territory in Europe
Alun Jones and Julian Clark

64 **European Union Sanctions and Foreign Policy**
When and why do they work?
Clara Portela

65 **The EU's Role in World Politics**
A retreat from liberal internationalism
Richard Youngs

66 **Social Democracy and European Integration**
The politics of preference formation
Edited by Dionyssis Dimitrakopoulos

67 **The EU Presence in International Organizations**
Edited by Spyros Blavoukos and Dimitris Bourantonis

68 **Sustainability in European Environmental Policy**
Challenge of governance and knowledge
Edited by Rob Atkinson, Georgios Terizakis and Karsten Zimmermann

69 **Fifty Years of EU–Turkey Relations**
A Sisyphean story
Edited by Armagan Emre Çakir

70 **Europeanization and Foreign Policy**
State diversity in Finland and Britain
Juha Jokela

71 **EU Foreign Policy and Post-Soviet Conflicts**
Stealth intervention
Nicu Popescu

72 **Switzerland in Europe**
Continuity and change in the Swiss political economy
Edited by Christine Trampusch and André Mach

73 **The Political Economy of Noncompliance**
Adjusting to the single European market
Scott Nicholas Siegel

74 **National and European Foreign Policy**
Towards Europeanization
Edited by Reuben Wong and Christopher Hill

75 **The European Union Diplomatic Service**
Ideas, preferences and identities
Caterina Carta

76 **Poland within the European Union**
New awkward partner or new heart of Europe?
Aleks Szczerbiak

77 **A Political Theory of Identity in European Integration**
Memory and policies
Catherine Guisan

78 **EU Foreign Policy and the Europeanization of Neutral States**
Comparing Irish and Austrian foreign policy
Nicole Alecu de Flers

79 **Party System Change in Western Europe**
Gemma Loomes

80 **The Second Tier of Local Government in Europe**
Provinces, counties, départements and Landkreise in comparison
Hubert Heinelt and Xavier Bertrana Horta

81 **Learning from the EU Constitutional Treaty**
Democratic constitutionalism beyond the nation-state
Ben Crum

82 **Human Rights and Democracy in EU Foreign Policy**
The cases of Ukraine and Egypt
Rosa Balfour

83 **Europeanization, Integration and Identity**
A social constructivist fusion perspective on Norway
Gamze Tanil

84 **The Impact of European Integration on Political Parties**
Beyond the permissive consensus
Dimitri Almeida

85 **Civic Resources and the Future of the European Union**
Victoria Kaina and Ireneusz Pawel Karolewski

86 **The Europeanization of National Foreign Policies towards Latin America**
Lorena Ruano

87 **The EU and Multilateral Security Governance**
Sonia Lucarelli, Luk Van Langenhove and Jan Wouters

88 **Security Challenges in the Euro-Med Area in the 21st Century**
Mare nostrum
Stephen Calleya

89 **Society and Democracy in Europe**
Oscar W. Gabriel and Silke Keil

90 **European Union Public Health Policy**
Regional and global trends
Edited by Scott L. Greer and Paulette Kurzer

91 **The New Member States and the European Union**
Foreign policy and Europeanization
Edited by Michael Baun and Dan Marek

92 **The Politics of Ratification of EU Treaties**
Carlos Closa

93 **Europeanization and New Member States**
A comparative social network analysis
Flavia Jurje

94 **National Perspectives on Russia**
European foreign policy in the making
Maxine David, Jackie Gower and Hiski Haukkala

95 **Institutional Legacies of Communism**
Change and continuities in minority protection
Edited by Karl Cordell, Timofey Agarin and Alexander Osipov

96 **Sustainable Development and Governance in Europe**
The evolution of the discourse on sustainability
Edited by Pamela M. Barnes and Thomas C. Hoerber

97 **Social Networks and Public Support for the European Union**
Elizabeth Radziszewski

98 **The EU's Democracy Promotion and the Mediterranean Neighbours**
Orientation, ownership and dialogue in Jordan and Turkey
Ann-Kristin Jonasson

99 **New Democracies in Crisis?**
A comparative constitutional study of the Czech Republic, Hungary, Poland, Romania and Slovakia
Paul Blokker

100 **Party Attitudes Towards the EU in the Member States**
Parties for Europe, parties against Europe
Nicolò Conti

101 **The European Union and Occupied Palestinian Territories**
State-building without a state
Dimitris Bouris

102 **Portugal in the European Union**
Assessing twenty-five years of integration experience
Laura C. Ferreira-Pereira

103 **Governance and European Civil Society**
Governmentality, discourse and NGOs
Acar Kutay

104 **The EU, Migration and the Politics of Administrative Detention**
Edited by Michela Ceccorulli and Nicola Labanca

105 **Political Representation in the European Union**
Democracy in a time of crisis
Edited by Sandra Kröger

106 **New Approaches to EU Foreign Policy**
Edited by Maciej Wilga and Ireneusz Pawel Karolewski

107 **Democracy, Law and Religious Pluralism in Europe**
Secularism and post-secularism
Edited by Ferran Requejo and Camil Ungureanu

108 **Contemporary Spanish Foreign Policy**
Edited by David Garcia and Ramon Pacheco Pardo

Democracy, Law and Religious Pluralism in Europe

Secularism and post-secularism

Edited by Ferran Requejo and Camil Ungureanu

Routledge
Taylor & Francis Group
LONDON AND NEW YORK

First published 2014
by Routledge
2 Park Square, Milton Park, Abingdon, Oxon OX14 4RN

and by Routledge
711 Third Avenue, New York, NY 10017

Routledge is an imprint of the Taylor & Francis Group, an informa business

British Library Cataloguing in Publication Data
A catalogue record for this book is available from the British Library

Library of Congress Cataloging in Publication Data
Democracy, law and religious pluralism in Europe: secularism and post-secularism / edited by Ferran Requejo and Camil Ungureanu.
pages cm. – (Routledge advances in European politics)
Includes bibliographical references and index.
1. Secularism–Europe. 2. Secularism–Political aspects–Europe. 3. Postsecularism–Europe. 4. Postsecularism–Political aspects–Europe. 5. Religious pluralism–Europe. 6. Religious pluralism–Political aspects–Europe. 7. Religion and politics–Europe. I. Requejo Coll, Ferran. II. Ungureanu, Camil.
BL2765.E85D46 2014
201'.5094–dc23 2014006374

ISBN: 978-0-415-82833-8 (hbk)
ISBN: 978-1-315-75880-0 (ebk)

Typeset in Times New Roman
by Wearset Ltd, Boldon, Tyne and Wear

Contents

Contributors

Bernard Gagnon is Professor in Ethics at the University of Québec at Rimouski (*UQAR*), Canada, and Researcher in Contemporary Political Theories. He is a member of the research group Ethos and researcher at the Centre de recherche interdisciplinaire sur la diversité et la démocratie. His publications include: *Concilier diversité et démocratie. Essais de théorie politique* (P.I.E. Peter Lang 2014); *La diversité québécoise en débat. Bouchard, Taylor et les autres* (Québec Amérique 2010); *La philosophie morale et politique de Charles Taylor* (Les Presses de l'Université Laval 2002).

Daniel Gamper is Associate Professor of Philosophy at the Universitat Autonòma de Barcelona (UAB), Spain. His main fields of research include ethics and contemporary political philosophy.

Marisa Iglesias is Associate Professor of Legal Philosophy at Universitat Pompeu Fabra (Barcelona), Spain, and has been Researcher or Visiting Scholar at the European Humanities University of Minsk, Oxford University, the Law Faculty of Puerto Rico University and the Global Law School of New York University. Her publications include *Facing Judicial Discretion: Legal Knowledge and Right Answers Revisited* (Kluwer 2001); *Globalisation, Democracy and Citizenship – Prospects for the European Union* (Duncker & Humblot 2003); *Poverty and Humanity: Individual Duties and the Moral Point of View* (Duncker & Humblot 2006).

Cécile Laborde is Professor of Political Theory at University College London, UK. She has published extensively in the areas of republicanism and toleration, theories of law and the state, and global justice. Her last book is *Critical Republicanism. The Hijab Controversy in Political Philosophy* (Oxford University Press 2008). She is the Director of UCL's Religion and Political Theory Centre. She is currently writing a book for Harvard University Press, entitled *Liberalism's Religion.*

Cristina Lafont is Professor of Philosophy at Northwestern University, USA. She is the author of *Global Governance and Human Rights* (Spinoza Lecture Series, van Gorcum 2012); *Heidegger, Language, and World-disclosure* (Cambridge University Press 2000); *The Linguistic Turn in Hermeneutic*

Philosophy (MIT Press 1999); and co-editor of the *Habermas Handbuch* (Metzler Verlag 2012). Some of her recent articles include "Deliberation, Participation and Democratic Legitimacy: Should Deliberative Minipublics shape Public Policy?" *The Journal of Political Philosophy*, doi: 10.1111/jopp.12031; "Religion and the Public Sphere. What are the Deliberative Obligations of Democratic Citizenship?" in C. Calhoun, E. Mendieta and J. Van Antwerpen, eds, *Habermas and Religion,* Polity Press, 2013, 230–248.

John Loughlin is a Fellow of the St Edmund's College, Cambridge, and a Senior Fellow of the Department of Politics and International Studies of the University of Cambridge, UK. He is Director of the Von Hugel Institute at St Edmund's College, UK. He has published widely on territorial politics and, more recently, on religion and politics. The French Government appointed him an Officer in the Ordre des Palmes Académiques and the University of Umea in Sweden awarded him an honorary doctorate – both honours being awarded because of his research on European politics. He is a Fellow of the Royal Society of Arts, of the Royal Historical Society, of the European Society of Sciences and Arts and of the Academy of Social Sciences. In 2014 he was admitted as a Fellow of the Learned Society of Wales, UK. He has held Visiting Professorships and Fellowships in many universities including Oxford, Cambridge, Princeton, Paris, Brussels and Umea, Sweden. In 2013 he held the Ganshof van der Meersch Chair of the Wiener-Anspach Foundation at the Université Libre de Bruxelles which is awarded to an academic from the Universities of Oxford and Cambridge, UK.

Javier Martínez-Torrón is Professor of Law and Director of the Department of Law and Religion, Complutense University (Madrid), Spain. Vice-President of the Section of Canon Law and Church–State Relations of the Spanish Royal Academy of Jurisprudence and Legislation. Former member of the OSCE/ODIHR Advisory Council for Freedom of Religion or Belief (2005–2013). Member of the Spanish Advisory Commission for Religious Freedom within the Ministry of Justice (since 2002). His research on law and religion issues is characterized by a predominant interest in international and comparative law.

Paolo Monti is Postdoctoral Researcher at Università Cattolica del Sacro Cuore, Milan, Italy. He has been Visiting Researcher at Notre Dame University and at the Department of Bioethics of the NIH, USA. Among his recent publications are the essays "On the Rationality of Social Practices" (2012) and "A Postsecular Rationale? Religious and Secular as Epistemic Peers" (2013). His research focuses primarily on the epistemology of social practices and the ethics of citizenship.

Ferran Requejo is Professor of Political Science at the Universitat Pompeu Fabra (Barcelona), Spain, where he is Director of the Research Group on Political Theory and has been Director of the MA on Political Philosophy and the MA on Diverse Democracies. In 1997 he was awarded the Rudolf

Wildenmann Prize (research, ECPR), in 2002 he received the Ramon Trias Fargas Prize, and in 2006 the Spanish Political Science Association Prize to the best book (*Multinational Federalism and Value Pluralism,* Routledge 2005). He is currently member of the National Transition Advisory Council (Catalan Government) and has been member of the *Spanish Electoral Board* (2004–2008). He is furthermore a regular contributor to the newspapers *La Vanguardia* and *Ara* (Barcelona) and other Catalan, Spanish and international media. Among his recent books are: *Federalism, Plurinationality and Democratic Constitutionalism* (Routledge 2012); *Federalism beyond Federations* (Ashgate 2011; with K.J. Nagel); *Federalism and Plurinationality. Theory and Case Analysis* (Routledge 2011); *La legitimidad en las democracias del siglo XXI. Un giro hegeliano* (Lap Lambert 2011); *Political Liberalism and Multinational Democracies* (Routledge 2010). More information in www.ferranrequejo.cat.

Camil Ungureanu is Lecturer in Political Theory at the Universitat Pompeu Fabra, Spain. He published with journals like *European Journal of Political Theory*, *Journal of Political Philosophy*, *Human Studies*, *European Legacy*, etc. He also co-edited *Law, State and Religion in the New Europe*: *Conflicts and Dilemmas* (Cambridge University Press 2012; with L. Zucca); *From the Nation-State to the Postnational Constellation: Jürgen Habermas' Theory of Law and* Democracy, vol. I–II (Ashgate 2011; with K. Günther and C. Joerges); *Religion in European Cinema* (Routledge 2014; with C. Bradatan). At present he is working on the book *Democratic Theory and Religion* (Routledge 2015).

Lorenzo Zucca is Reader in Jurisprudence. He holds the degrees of Maitrise from Paris 2 Assas, DEA from Paris 1 Sorbonne, France, Mjur from The University of Oxford, UK and a PhD from EUI, Florence, Italy. He is the author of *Constitutional Dilemmas: Conflicts of Fundamental Legal Rights in Europe and the USA* (Oxford University Press 2007) and of *A Secular Europe: Law and Religion in the European Constitutional Landscape* (Oxford University Press 2012). He is currently working on a new project entitled Secular Globe, which deals with global religious conflicts and transnational legal ways of dealing with them.

1 Uses and abuses of postsecularism

An introduction

Camil Ungureanu

The relative decline of church-going in Europe notwithstanding, the secularist worldview and ideology which is hostile to religion and predicts its disappearance has become increasingly implausible (Berger 1999; Bhargava 2006, 2007; Taylor 2007a). Religion is, globally, on the rise (Norris and Inglehart 2004); and even in the most secularized continent, Europe, religious and quasi-religious experiences remain important for many of its inhabitants, often in heterodox, transformed and disguised forms (Davie 2000; Casanova 2006). In Europe, there has been a growing pluralization of deep preferences and values – a process involving multiple factors that are difficult to reconcile. Various religious communities resulting largely from immigration have become ever-more assertive in the public sphere; majority churches have been reaffirming their influence on politics and law-making in new ways – namely, by the use of technology and transnational lobbying. Additionally, in several European societies the interest in (individualized) spiritual-religious experiences has grown beyond established institutions. The film director Bruno Dumont conveys this mood: "one must recover words like 'grace,' 'holiness,' for the profane world, we should not simply grant organized religion a monopoly over this language. I desire a sacred humanism, indeed a spiritual life, transcendence, but without God or the Church" (Smith, D. 2010).

This multifaceted pluralization, which is pulling in different directions, has generated new cultural-religious "wars" (Dworkin 2013; Nussbaum 2013) and – by way of reaction – innovative proposals that aim at overcoming deep divisions in pluralist societies. A new wave of philosophers and social theorists has, in the past decade, questioned the secularist opposition between religion vs. modernity, faith vs. reason, and looked for a new common ground shared by atheists and faithful alike. Jürgen Habermas, Charles Taylor, John Caputo, Jacques Derrida, Ronald Dworkin, Thomas Nagel, Jean-Luc Nancy, Gianni Vattimo, José Casanova, Peter Berger, Rajeev Bhargava, Partha Chatterjee, Bruno Dumont, Michael Haneke – to name but a few – form a complex constellation of contemporary thinkers and artists who search for alternatives beyond religious conservatism and a secularism which is hostile to religion (Bradatan and Ungureanu 2014). Self-declared atheists (Habermas, Dworkin) and unorthodox believers (Taylor, Caputo, Vattimo) take religion seriously in contrast to the celebrators of the self-sufficiency of secularist reason, including the supporters of the philosophical program of the naturalization of reason by means of neo-Darwinian evolutionism and neuroscience (Dennett 2010; Requejo Chapter 11 in this volume; for criticism, see Habermas 2008a; Nagel 2012; Dworkin 2013).

The debate between naturalists and their critics remains inconclusive. The critics of the *complete* reduction of consciousness and moral-religious practice to adaptive mechanisms resort to public reason and other philosophical resources to posit a more interactive role of religion in modernity – a role that some of them call "postsecular."[1] Habermas' principle of translation from religious into secular language, and Rawls' "overlapping consensus" and "proviso" are premised on the belief in the reconciling powers of reason and the positive contribution of religion to democracy (see, especially, Chapters 3, 5 and 6 of this volume). In turn, other "postsecular" authors distance themselves from the rationalist approach, and either reflect on secular traditions and varieties of secularism from the perspective of religious history and political theology (De Roover *et al.* 2011; Loughlin, Chapter 4 in this volume) or retrieve notions of faith and transcendence – which are usually placed under the heading of religion – for the general understanding of ethics and politics (Derrida 2002; Taylor 2007a; Dworkin 2013; see Gagnon, Chapter 6 in this volume). For example, Dworkin's last book, *Religion without God*, advances a project of reconciliation based on the claim that religion is essentially faith in the objectivity of value (moral, aesthetic, etc.). From the perspective of Dworkin's religious atheism, "(w)hat divides godly and godless religion – the science of godly religion – is not as important as the faith in value that unites them" (Dworkin 2013: 29).

The differences between the rationalist and non-rationalist versions of postsecularism are often quite stark; yet the two versions share the conviction that religion cannot be simply dismissed as obsolete and irrelevant; instead, it can be a powerful source of moral values and experiences – of faith, forgiveness, responsibility, guilt, solidarity, gift-giving, sacrifice, transcendence, mystical insight and conversion – that a secularism focused exclusively on a self-sufficient reason is unable to account for.

The chapters of this volume tackle various theoretical and practical aspects of the current secularism/postsecularism debate, with a focus on an increasingly pluralistic Europe. The contributors represent a plurality of standpoints on this theoretical debate (Part I), and its practical relevance (with a focus on legal aspects (Part II)). Some of the authors are sympathetic towards the term "postsecular" or to an equivalent of it – that is, open or contextual secularism or secularity, etc. (Cecile Laborde, Chapter 2; Cristina Lafont, Chapter 3; Daniel Gamper, Chapter 9; and Camil Ungureanu and Marisa Iglesias, Chapter 10). Others are either critical of it, or they overlook it, opting for "secular" as designating the modern constitutional theory and the modern state, and look for alternative practical solutions at odds with secularism as a standpoint that excludes religion from the public sphere (Javier Martínez-Torrón, Chapter 7; Lorenzo Zucca, Chapter 8; and Ferran Requejo, Chapter 11). Critical reactions to postsecularism should come as no surprise: like other "post" terms – postmodern, poststructural, post-national, post-sovereign, post-human – the use of "postsecular" invites *prima facie* scepticism. However, I submit that, once properly circumscribed and severed from inflationary definitions, this term can be helpful in identifying a significant trend in philosophy and socio-legal theory.[2]

I shall start by characterizing the notion of "postsecular," and by eliminating inflationary uses (namely, the notion of a new post-secular society). Postsecularism is not opposed to the secular per se, or to modern constitutionalism, but to the secularist worldview or ideology which is dismissive of the relevance of religious practice and imagination (Bottici and Challand 2013). I shall then introduce two types of postsecularism: first, there is a rationalist post-secularism (e.g., Habermas), which envisages an interactive relationship between reason and religion mediated by processes of translation. Second, there are non-rationalist understandings of the postsecular that retrieve the relevance of faith and transcendence of ethical–political theorizing (e.g., Dworkin 2013). I shall move on to consider some of the practical consequences of the secularism–postsecularism debate at the legalconstitutional level. More specifically. I shall reflect on a hotly-debated issue that permeates, explicitly or implicitly, the chapters of this book: Should religion in a pluralist society be deemed special? Should religion enjoy special protection and status, and benefit from specific exemptions?

The idea of a postsecular constellation

Is postsecular talk simply a passing fashion in social theory and philosophy (Bader 2012), often used to get access to research grants? Bader may be right about the term "postsecular" itself. Its prominence in philosophy, social theory and sociology notwithstanding, the meaning of "postsecular" has sometimes been vague, and its importance exaggerated. "Postsecularism" has been interpreted as referring either to a new age or to a new type of society coming after the secular one. According to this view, advanced by philosophers as different as Habermas, Caputo or Vattimo, in a postsecular age/society, religion plays a fundamental role in the social–political sphere, and individuals are able to overcome divisions between reason and faith. Habermas, for one, speaks of a new "postsecular society" in which religious and non-religious citizens engage, predominantly in the social–public sphere, in a process of mutual learning and reconciliation through dialogue and reason-exchanges. For Habermas, (non)religious citizens are able to attain agreements and enrich "public reason" by means of rational dialogue understood, in large part, as leading to translations from the sacred language into the secular one.[3]

Caputo's image of a "secular age" severs it from Habermas' rationalism. By developing Derrida's deconstructive reading of religion, Caputo interprets the end of the secular age as the abandonment of the belief in the death of God and of religion as proclaimed by the likes of Feuerbach and Marx (Caputo 2001). For Caputo, we have entered a new postsecular age characterized by "the death of God," namely by a shift in focus away from God as Reality and Truth to God as

Love (Caputo 2001). Like Derrida and Vattimo, Caputo argues that the deconstruction of the question of the existence of God, namely the onto-theological critique of religion, has a liberating political–religious impact: bracketing the question of the Reality of God opens up the possibility of experiencing God as passionate, impossible love beyond the Church's absolute certainties and rigid institutional hierarchies.

These divergent uses of postsecularism are, from a socio-theoretical perspective, unconvincing. They are based on an inflation of the meaning and the relevance of postsecularism. On the one hand, speaking of a postsecular age/society is premised on the false assumption that Western societies have become secular. However, in Europe, religion has played an important role in society and in politics, even when the gigantomachia between capitalism and communism eclipsed it between World War II and the fall of the Berlin Wall. And, as various commentators have noted, the image of the neutral-secular European state is, largely, a myth.

On the other hand, Habermas' rational agents are, at worst, fictional and, at best, a minority (Requejo 1991). In any case, people who are inspired by and learn from religious traditions and models do not represent a novelty that would justify speaking of a new society. Likewise, religious people willing and able to bracket the question of the (non)existence of God, so as to cultivate a post-Kierkegaardian impossible love, are far from representing the common religious believer. Instead, they constitute a restricted group of philosopher-believers – be they post-Heideggerian deconstructivists influenced by Derrida and Caputo, or hermeneuts influenced by Vattimo – rather than the *differentia specifica* of a new epoch. As a result, the term "postsecular" does not plausibly describe the coming of a new age/society after the secular one. More convincingly, the "postsecular" refers to a trend whose roots can be traced back to one (post-)Enlightenment reaction to modern secularism and its radical challenge to the dominance of religion in society (Taylor 2007a).

This postsecular trend pertains to the very development of modernity and late modernity; it emerges as a dissatisfaction with the influential tradition of militant atheism and rationalist secularism built on the Manichean opposition between reason and faith, emancipation and religion, and is represented by Rousseau, Kant, Novalis, Hegel or Herder. In contrast to secularism, postsecularism regards the relation between religion and modernity as one of tension *and*, at the same time, as a positive-sum game of mutual interaction and transformation; from this perspective, experiences of transcendence, conversion, faith, transfiguration and sacrifice are not seen as the monopoly of the Church or other religious institutions, but can be vital for heterodox believers and even for atheists as well. The current age is thus not postsecular, but is one of accelerated pluralisation in all societal fields. In particular, Europe is neither Christian, nor postsecular, nor secularist: it is plural. Together with forms of militant atheism, secularism and religious conservatism, postsecularism is one trend in an on-going dynamic of pluralization.

Postsecularism also raises the suspicion that it rejects the secular per se. But this is not necessarily so. It is true that conservative forces can instrumentalize postsecular rhetoric, yet postsecularism is opposed not to the secular, but to secularism as a worldview and an ideology that is dismissive of religion. "Secular" and "secularization" refer to the modern socio-historical process of separation and differentiation between various spheres of society (state, law, the arts, etc.) from both theology and religion. In turn, secularism is a normative view that can take simplistic ideological forms (e.g., Stalinism) but also sophisticated philosophical ones (Feuerbach, Marx, the earlier Habermas, Daniel Dennett, etc.). Secularism incorporates a fighting creed: it is a militant set of ideas and practices aiming not only at separation and differentiation between religion and other societal spheres (i.e., politics, law), but at dismantling religion as a premise of a free, emancipated society. For secularists, the relation between religion and modernity is a zero-sum game – namely, one of mutual exclusion; the proclamation of God's death means that religion is irrelevant for dealing with current ethical and socio-political issues. These issues are to be made sense of by means of what Taylor calls, in his *A Secular Age*, "exclusive humanism" and "immanent frame" (Taylor 2007a).

The postsecular is not the overcoming of secular modernity and modern constitutionalism; it designates a complex center between, on the one hand, a secularist worldview and militant atheism, and conventional religion and a renewed religious conservatism–fundamentalism, on the other.[4] "Postsecular" describes a series of discourses and practices that cannot be circumscribed and defined in essentialist terms; instead, a more fruitful strategy to characterize it is in terms of "family-resemblances" (Wittgenstein 2009). In *Philosophical Investigations* (§66), Wittgenstein famously considered the case of games, and asked whether we called "games" ... [to] look and see whether there is anything common to all ... the result of this examination is: we see a complicated network of similarities overlapping and criss-crossing: sometimes overall similarities." This famously characterized them as "family resemblances" (§67).[5] When applied to "postsecularism," this conceptual strategy has the merit of better accommodating the ever-growing variety of spiritual–religious experiences and their continuous transformations; it also has the advantage of admitting the relevance of borderline cases, whose appurtenance to a specific category can be elusive and controversial.[6] The *postsecular constellation* is made up of "families" of representative thinkers and artists organized around emblematic or star figures.[7] For example, Habermas, Derrida and Vattimo are school-makers and founders of different families of conceptions of religion in modernity – families of deliberativists, hermeneuts or deconstructivists. Notwithstanding differences and even oppositions between them, they are all members of a broader constellation in virtue of their rejection of secularism and of their search for a cooperative relationship between reason and religion in contemporary democracies. In sum, the "postsecular" describes a constellation of discourses and practices – philosophical, socio-theoretical, artistic, social and political, etc. – that are premised on the search for a complex, open and interactive relationship between modern reason and religion, as well as on retrieving in non-dogmatic, non-authoritarian, creative, and heterodox ways the salience of faith, sacrifice, transcendence, mystical insight, transfiguration, conversion and sacrifice, beyond the self-complacencies of both conventional religion and militant atheism (see, especially, Lafont, Loughlin, Monti and Gagnon in Chapters 3, 4, 5 and 6 of this volume).[8]

Let me deal with two opposing theoretical versions of postsecularism (rationalist/non-rationalist) before moving on to legal–constitutional aspects of the postsecular–secular debate.

Public reason postsecularism

There are least two versions of postsecularism challenging the secularist dichotomy between reason and religion – rationalist and non-rationalist. Consider Habermas' perspective, which has largely been responsible for the current vogue of the term "postsecular." In the 1970s and 1980s, Habermas advanced a post-Marxist version of secularism that ruled out the presence and relevance of religion in a post-class emancipated society. However, some fifteen years ago, Habermas initiated a postsecular "turn" motivated by empirical and conceptual-normative concerns, as well as by his interest in the historicity of modern reason. For Habermas, modernized religion – namely a religion that grants recognition to human rights, scientific achievements and its separation from the state – can work as a prop for current disaffected democracies (Habermas 2006b, 2008a, 2010, 2011). Habermas' claim regarding the capacity of religion to inject moral "blood" into an impoverished democratic practice is premised on the distinction between two layers of the public sphere – the political and the social. For Habermas, politics and law-making should be rigorously neutral with respect to religion: a "wall of separation" is required, given that any privileged relationship with a specific religious community leads to discrimination. However, if religion cannot directly shape decision-making in the formal public sphere, it can do so indirectly by means of its impact on the social public sphere (civil society, mass-media, etc.).

Religious values can legitimately influence commonly binding decisions once citizens translate them into secular norms and reasons at the level of the social public sphere. Translation implies bracketing the reference to religious absolutes – God, the Holy Book, dogmas – in order for communication to enter the terrain of fallible dialogue based on reason–exchange between equally positioned, informed and sincere participants. Translations are not, for Habermas, literal: they are not meant to display fidelity to particular traditions. Translation and deliberation lead to convergence towards rational reconciliation and secular consensus (the "same perspective") beyond particular traditions and contexts (Habermas 2006b). In Habermas' teleological view, translation is able to retrieve the seeds of moral truth contained in the *plurality of religious voices*; in so doing, it contributes to the gradual constitution of the *unity of secular reason*.

Habermas' postsecular "turn" has the virtue of mitigating the exclusivist consequences of his earlier secularism, but it is unable to adequately consider pluralism. I think that Habermas fails to prove that dialogue and translation guarantee linear progress towards a pure and unitary reason. As he acknowledges, communicative practices are embedded in and interpreted on the basis of ultimately non-reconciling religious traditions: Christian, Islamic, Hindu, Confucian, Buddhist, together with their myriad trends.[9] Religious traditions are non-reconcilable, and there are no convincing criteria for ordering them hierarchically on a value scale. If this is so, then it is hard to see how translations could aim towards the "same perspective" espoused by religious and non-religious citizens at the level of ideal consensus. For instance, a minority or an immigrant group can gradually produce a new interpretation of the principles of political justice by drawing on their religious tradition. In time, they can form a majority that triggers a shift in existing democratic practice. Nonetheless, as religious traditions can neither be reconciled nor placed on a hierarchical scale, such shifts cannot be accounted for by an image of linear progress whereby reason gradually converts the plurality of religious and non-religious voices into unity (for a more detailed treatment of the concept of translation, see Lafont, Monti and Gagnon, in Chapters 3, 5 and 6 of this volume).

Translations are incapable of taking *the edge of singularity* of religious traditions so as to transmute the plurality of religious voices into the unity of reason. Derrida's deconstruction of metaphysical dichotomies (rational and empirical, reason and imagination, philosophy and rhetoric, argument and practice, universal and singular) that are still at work in Habermas is useful: the process of translation is not simply one of the gradual passage from singular to universal – namely, a teleological process whereby the particular "melts away" or is absorbed under the light of reason, but is one of open dialectic. Translations – or, better, *embedded interpretations* – are complex processes of passage from one discursive experience to another in specific practical contexts. Embedded interpretations are not simply a matter of exchanging reasons, or of bringing a discourse to reason; instead, they involve an open dialectic between argument and rhetoric, reason and religious imagination, argumentative exchange and practical experiences, reason and faith.

Consider a well-known example – the South African transition from a criminal-authoritarian regime to democracy. Under the influence of religious figures like Desmond Tutu – the president of the *Truth and Reconciliation Commission* – values incorporated and "codified" within the Christian tradition (forgiveness, confession, reconciliation) played a significant role in a transition to a democratic regime marked by the fear of civil war and violence. In this complex process,[10] the requirements of (penal) justice were curtailed in favour of forgiveness, public confession and reconciliation. Yet the fact that these values were severed from the appeal to the divinity of Christ or the "absolute truth" of the Bible did not turn them into "pure" reasons; their novel interpretation and usage in a concrete practical context did not erase the trace of the original Christian script. They contributed to bringing about a "post-Christian" solution to a political dilemma – namely, balancing between justice, efficiency and peace – and not a secular political practice governed by neutral rational norms. The "Christian values" of forgiveness, confession and reconciliation were *believed in*; as such, they were creatively interpreted and experienced in a new context, they were not – in accordance to Habermas' teleological concept of translation – "brought to reason" (or closer to pure reason) through deliberation.

The quest for moral truth and fair solutions is an experiential enterprise in singular practical contexts; the explicit exchange of reasons is just one dimension of it. The success of the proposed solution was not guaranteed; opting for it, and bringing it about was also a matter of having faith in specific values drawn from Christianity. The relative convergence with respect to a solution was one of experiencing together a singular political drama: when reason-exchanges played a role, they did not occur in the abstract; reasons themselves were generated and shaped within a context of "living actually." By forsaking the teleological view, the dialectic between reason and faith/religion can be conceived differently, as more open and closer to practice.

The semantic contents and experiences inherent in religious practice are not "empirical" or "accidental" impurities to be filtered out by means of translation and deliberation. In contrast, they are constitutive of morality, religion and democracy. In particular, democratic practice is not a quest for pure neutrality (Habermas). Political forces do not aspire to impartiality, but they engage – with their specific interests, value commitments and beliefs – in the political battle of *producing* and, at the same time, *representing* the "people," "general will" and "popular sovereignty." These notions, which are central to democracy, are not merely rational concepts: "people," "general will" and "popular sovereignty" are not transparent and unambiguous political facts either, but contested idealizations. The struggle over their construction and representation is a struggle over faith, belief and imagination as well. Partisanship in commitments and beliefs is an intrinsic part of the democratic struggle, and here religion can play a significant role.

Under the influence of religious practice, political forces representing majorities or minorities can interpret and rank rights and duties differently, even when they face similar political circumstances. There are a variety of embedded interpretations that can result from the fact that ultimately non-hierarchizable and non-reconcilable value frameworks affect the interpretation and prioritization of rights and duties. Crucially, this comes into play when rights and duties conflict and one must decide which one should be given the upper hand.[11] One religion's ethics may put the emphasis on individual responsibility, while another religion's ethics may put it on community and solidarity, and yet another on ecological principles. Under the influence of the former, a majority may be more willing to grant less importance to a social, economic or ecological right in cases of conflict with a civil or political right. If neither the constitution nor a majority of democratically elected representatives support universal access to health care, then the right to health care, regardless of income, could be reduced to a minimum. In contrast, in times of scarcity, another majority, under the influence of different religious ethics, may prefer to chip off the liberal principle of liberty as non-interference in order to provide a socio-economic or an ecological right. The place of value traditions may seem less obvious regarding welfare and capital gains than genetics, abortion, ecology, etc., but they influence people's sense of what the community owes to its less fortunate members and their sense of how tolerable the gap between rich and poor is, what our duties are towards the environment and future generations, or of what their attitudes towards immigrants should be.

That there is a more pluralistic interaction between public reason and religion that Habermas is willing to admit does not mean that the border between them is, as a matter of principle, blurred. A good deal of the rationales invoked in political and legal discourse are clearly not religious. The rationale for public safety on roads is, generally speaking, non-religious, while the argument that God requires that children should not be sent to state schools until they are sixteen is religious. The rationale for proportional or majority electoral systems is non-religious, while claiming that premarital sex and homosexuality represent a sin condemned by the Holy Book is clearly religious. Nonetheless, not all cases are so clear-cut. While values like forgiveness, solidarity, responsibility, compassion, and many others are not essentially religious, religious traditions interpret them and give them varying importance – something that can significantly shape political practice. However, detaching these values from absolute truths and dogmas, integrating them into the logic of democratic dialogue, and even imagining an ideal consensus cannot guarantee the erasure of the "trace" (Derrida) of their embeddedness in specific religious traditions (see also Gagnon, Chapter 5, discussing the differences between Habermas and Taylor on the concept of translation).

In short, public reason postsecularism, in its most influential versions, has the merit of taking into consideration the historicity of reason as well the possibility of a positive interaction between religion and democracy in late modernity. While we cannot reproduce here the complexity of the debate around Habermas' work, his view remains too much under the spell of Kant's teleological view of reason. In spite of its merits, Habermas' rigidly rationalistic concept of translation and deliberation fails to consider the diversity of embedded communicative exchanges that occur between atheists, non-believers, and believers in pluralistic democracies.

Postsecularism beyond public reason?

There is a second version of postsecularism that challenges in a different way the secularist opposition between faith and reason. Notwithstanding his revisiting of secularism, Habermas sees himself as a "guardian" of the domain of reason; he claims to be able to keep it at bay, by means of post-metaphysical thinking (Habermas), from the intruding forces of faith, transcendence and metaphysics. However, various analytical and continental philosophers (Wolterstorff, Weithman, Dworkin, Levinas, Nancy, Derrida, Vattimo, Bhargava, Balagangadhara, etc.), have advanced a more substantive challenge to secularism – namely, one that reflects on the relevance of political theological traditions for the varieties of secular regimes, and retrieves the experience of faith, transcendence, the holy and the mystical for ethics and political philosophy in general.[12] These endeavors often enter the domain of the philosophy of religion as well, and advocate a more substantial transformation of religious discourse and experience, not least by taking into account radical pluralization, *differance*, and otherness.[13]

It is impossible to deal seriously with these various endeavours within the limited space of an "Introduction." However, let me briefly present one such recent enterprise – namely, Dworkin's plea for "religious atheism" (Ungureanu 2014). In his last book *Religion without God* (2013), Dworkin does not abandon the claims of public reason, yet he connects them with a head-on engagement with themes such as faith, transcendence, immortality, metaphysics and God. In so doing, he provides a nuanced post-Kantian attempt to *reconcile* Enlightenment and religion. Dworkin does not make a single reference to Immanuel Kant's project on religion, yet his book bears his imprint. He carries on Kant's reflection on a universal and rational faith/religion, even if he dilutes his stiff rationalism, and adds a Romantic sensibility for the "mysterious." Kant asked: "How is it possible to think about religion within the boundaries of reason alone?" By way of response, Kant claimed to retrieve a rational, timeless and universal core of faith/religion by piercing through the shell of historical faiths/religions (Kant 2001).

Not unlike Kant, Dworkin is concerned with the question of the universal essence of faith, and the distinction between two strata of religion. Dworkin distinguishes between two such strata – one that is fundamental and universal, and another that is "superficial" and "accidental." Common knowledge notwithstanding, his claim is that belief in God is the superficial and external stratum of religion, not its essential one. God is an "accident": true, the majority of religious people believe in it; yet other people who are, for Dworkin, religious, do not. Here Dworkin's intriguing claim is that, in spite of their self-understanding, many atheists *are* religious. This is in virtue of their belief in what Dworkin considers to be religion's essence. This essence is both independent from and more profound than theistic beliefs, and is made up of two elements: faith in full independence and objectivity of values; and faith in the objective beauty of nature.

To better grasp Dworkin's view of the universalizing faith in value, consider a continuum whose extremes are Kant's view of moral and rational faith and S. Kierkegaard's conception of faith as an experience of absolute singularity. On this continuum, Dworkin is closer to Kant. Kant placed universal faith (i.e., the essence of religion) *within* the domain of reason and rational morality, and ultimately justified it by means of our participation in the noumenal world. The essence of faith/religion is, for him, rational and moral (Kant 2001). In contrast, Kierkegaard's Abrahamic "model" of faith in God conceives it as "irrational" and "mad." The belief in *das ganz Andere* is at the core of Abraham's readiness to sacrifice his son Isaac; as such, it is rigorously at loggerheads with moral-universal norms.

In turn, for Dworkin, faith is understood as belief in objective values in morality and science: "(t)he religious attitude … insists on the full independence of value: the world of value is self-contained and self-certifying" (Dworkin 2013: 16). Dworkin admits that this view of moral values is circular; however, he also points out that in science we encounter a similar circularity, as we have to rely on faith in some fundamental truths and axioms (e.g., that the external world exists; basic mathematical axioms, and so on) (Dworkin 2013: 16–17). Here, Dworkin does not propose a mere conceptual or transcendental argument for faith. In the final analysis, faith represents a kind of existential affirmation of values in relation to our moral and natural world – an affirmation of their rationality and objectivity. As Dworkin claims:

> (t)his kind of faith is not just passive acceptance of the conceptual truth that we cannot justify our science or our logic or our values without appealing to science or logic or value. It is a positive affirmation of the reality of these worlds and of our confidence that though each of our judgments may be wrong, we are entitled to think them right if we have reflected on them responsibly enough.
>
> (Dworkin 2013: 19)[14]

In short, Dworkin's faith is neither strictly speaking rational (Kant), nor "irrational" (Kierkegaard): it does not depend on faith in a specific god, but it is a reasonable belief in objective and independent value – in the rationality of the worlds we live in. This faith is universalizable, and could appeal to and reconcile believers and atheists alike.

How persuasive is Dworkin's "religion without God"? Dworkin's understanding of religion and values runs into significant difficulties. His view is *ahistorical*, as it does not take into account the plurality of religious experiences, and is tributary to questionable metaphysical dichotomies. Dworkin affirms the "radical independence of value from history" (Dworkin 2013: 22), echoing Kant's notion of pure reason as completely independent of history. Yet history, driven out through the door, comes back in through the window. Dworkin injects a historically modern understanding of value into religion in general. According to Dworkin, having a religious attitude means that "(e)ach person has an innate and inescapable responsibility to make his life a successful one: that means living well ..." (Dworkin 2013: 10). This is, however, a problematic overgeneralization. Dworkin projects a combination of modern individualism and universalism into religious experiences regardless of circumstances and historical period.

His view of two strata of religion is also residual of an old metaphysical–hierarchical scheme (essence/accident; universal/particular) that is in need of questioning. For all their differences, Kant, Marx, Freud, Durkheim, Frazer, Cassirer, Levi-Strauss, Bourdieu and Dworkin, have in common this dualistic metaphysical scheme. They all claim to have unearthed the secular essence of the religious phenomenon: in turn, this essence is considered to be moral reason, sexuality, economic interests, society, natural forces, ethical values, structure, and interest (material/symbolic). It is true that religious experience has been deeply connected with morality, power, sex, natural forces, society and economic interests. But this foundationalist approach runs into the insurmountable difficulty of demonstrating that the variety and complexity of religious phenomena can be ultimately reduced to or derived from something that is its ultimate *Grund.* The philosopher places himself/herself in a dubiously privileged position: while the universal essence is hidden to participants, the philosopher claims to have a totalizing view and a special access to the ultimate foundation of religion. Consider what seems the most fundamental experience for a Buddhist – the experience of *nirvana.* This is what is ultimately essential for a Buddhist. What, then, is the evidence for the claim that the essence of Buddhism is the belief in objective value, since Buddhists themselves maintain that their most fundamental experience is one of extinction (*nirvana*) – an experience whereby values and differences in values are all overcome as pertaining to the illusory domain of *maya*?[15] Dworkin's generalization seems a misunderstanding of such religious experiences rather than the expression of what is fundamental in them.

Overall, Dworkin's argument about faith in objective value is questionable. Apart from the difficulties in his attempt to define religion, it is unclear why we need faith in fully independent and objective values. Even if one accepts – as I tend to do – that there is an element of faith or belief in the projections and idealizations that are inherent in our pursuit of democratic justice, moral truth, and a better life, it is unconvincing to claim that we need *ultimate* transhistorical idealizations (*the* objective value, *the* right way to life, etc; see also my critique of Habermas' idealizations, pp. 6–8). Dworkin is, in the final analysis, a nostalgic post-Kantian metaphysician. Kant's faith in the kingdom of ends turns, for him, into faith in ultimate, objective values. However, an approach that grants importance to intersubjectivity and history, and that envisages faith, transcendence and idealizations not as necessarily universal and ultimate but as embedded in concrete contexts, could be more appealing. This search would neither depend on the fiction of an abstract faith – a ghost hovering above historical practices, nor on faith in the existence of a divine creature.

In sum, the debate about the relevance of postsecularism beyond the discourse of conventional religion and rationalistic theorizing cannot be settled within the limited scope of this "Introduction." However, the interrogations posed by authors like Dworkin open up a field of debate that will bear new and fascinating fruits in the years to come (see Gagnon on Taylor's treatment of transcendence, Chapter 6 of this volume; and Loughlin's view of the continuous relevance of political theology, Chapter 4 of this volume).

Is religion special? The legal–constitutional debate

Part II of this volume deals with legal–practical implications of the current debates both at the level of the European nation-states (e.g., Zucca, Chapter 8) and of the European Court of Human Rights (ECtHR) (Martínez-Torrón, Chapter 7; Gamper, Chapter 9; and Iglesias and Ungureanu, Chapter 10). Is postsecularism a sort of Trojan Horse of conservatism, i.e., a tool for maintaining the privileged status of majority religion in contemporary democracies? Does postsecularism lead to granting special protection to religion in legal–constitutional terms? What is the role of the ECtHR in balancing inter-state and infra-state (non-)religious pluralism?

Historically speaking, majority religion has often enjoyed privileged treatment from the modern state. The purely secular and neutral European state is a fiction: European states have generally developed a separation-and-privilege approach towards the main Church/churches (Ferrari 1997). Even if sometimes implicitly, the puzzle of whether religion could legitimately enjoy a special status in European states permeates the chapters of the present volume (see, most explictly, Laborde, Chapter 2 and Gamper, Chapter 9 in this volume on the question of religious exemptions). Given the variety of postsecular views, it is difficult to give a general answer as to their relation to practice. The postsecular rhetoric of the positive contribution of religion to democracy and dialogue between state and religious institutions has been increasingly used to preserve the status quo (see, for instance, the Lautsi "affair," the stem cell research debate in Italy, or the current abortion debate in Spain). Given the level of influence and organization of majority religious institutions, the goodwill rhetoric of dialogue can serve to strengthen their privileges and power. However, the most important "postsecular" authors – Habermas, Dworkin, Taylor, Derrida, Bhargava – understand that they are at odds with the current privileged majority religion–state relationship, and require a more sustained consideration of pluralism by political and religious institutions alike. Generally speaking, these authors do not espouse a uniform model which is valid in all circumstances, and that is based on the image of a "wall of separation" between state and religion, but build a more contextual and open understanding of the secular state (see especially Laborde, Chapter 2; Loughlin, Chapter 4; Martínez-Torrón, Chapter 7; Zucca, Chapter 8; Gamper, Chapter 9; and Iglesias and Ungureanu, Chapter 10 in this volume).

At the theoretical level, there are different argumentative strategies for regarding religion as special: (1) The first strategy is connected to the very origins of liberal thought as a reaction to religious wars in sixteenth-century Europe. The concern is that granting religion a special status is required in the interests of maintaining peace. Yet the argument of peace is hardly convincing nowadays: there is no clear-cut empirical relation between granting religion protection and the preservation of peace; (2) the second argument grounds the special right of religion in the belief in God or Transcendence. This argument has been supported either by (Christian-)conservative or communitarian thinkers. In his *Democracy's Discontent*, Michael Sandel develops a critique of liberalism, and a defence of the special status of religious freedom. According to Sandel, members of a religious community develop a special sense of duty rooted in their belief in God. "Imperative" and unchosen duties are not accounted for by the individualist-cum-voluntarist liberal narrative. I think that Sandel is right to criticize an exclusively voluntaristic view of duty; still, the conclusion that religion should enjoy special protection does not obtain. Religious freedom cannot be only about Transcendence and God (or about theistically understood religions), since atheists can have duties and convictions that are equally imperative. Consider pacifism, deep ecology, and even kinds of vegetarianism.

Non-religious "imperative" convictions have, in effect, found their place in legal decision-making in Western democracies. For instance, during the Vietnam War, the US Supreme Court granted a pacifist–atheist (Daniel Andrew Seeger) an exemption on account of his conscientious objection. The Supreme Court argued that "… (a) sincere and meaningful belief which occupies in the life of its possessor a place parallel to that filled by the God of those admittedly qualifying for the exemption comes within the statutory definition"[16] (for a detailed discussion of the Seeger case, see Laborde, Chapter 2 in this volume). Furthermore, taking God and Transcendence as essential to religion is questionable, since it is based on the generalization of the model of monotheistic religions. There are religious conceptions which are either not centred on God (e.g., Buddhism and Confucianism – especially in certain formulations), or do not make a distinction between immanence and Transcendence; (3) a third argumentative strategy takes religion as based on deep beliefs or preferences. Again, this strategy is clearly objectionable, as religion does not have the monopoly over what is deep in one's life.

The failure of these strategies leaves us with a dilemma (Dworkin 2013). In a pluralistic democracy special protection cannot be granted only to theistic religions; it cannot be extended either to "to all passionately held convictions" – namely, to what Dworkin takes as religion in a broad sense. Such an extension would entail protecting too large an array of eccentric and/or unfair "imperative" convictions and duties (e.g., racism). This results in a conundrum: the protection of a distinct moral right to freedom of choice about religious practice cannot be limited to godly religions; however, a government cannot protect all the convictions that fall under a broader understanding of religion, including deep, passionate beliefs.

How is it possible to solve this dilemma? Dworkin's way out of it is a "radical approach" that entails a significantly different reading of national and international legal documents concerning religion (Dworkin 2013: 133). Dworkin argues that political liberty has two components: the right to ethical independence and a special right to particular liberties – e.g., freedom of speech; the right to due process and a fair trial – (Dworkin 2013: 130). The special right of religion (government must not constrain religion in any way, except in an extraordinary emergency) should be replaced by a general right that limits the reasons government may offer for any constraint on a citizen's freedom at all. The right to ethical independence is defined as follows: "government must never restrict freedom just because it assumes that one way for people to live their lives … is intrinsically better than another" (Dworkin 2013: 130). The two strategies to provide a restrictive definition of legally relevant convictions, i.e., *functional* – in terms of their intensity and sincerity – and *substantive* – in terms of their worth – fail. Governments in pluralist societies should neither assess the sincerity of a belief nor its worth: one's values should be a matter of individual choice. It follows that granting special protection and exemptions from general rules to religion (consider the *peyote* case[17] and the 1993 Religious Freedom Restoration Act) is not acceptable. In a liberal-pluralist society freedom cannot be restricted on account of privileging specific values: the general right to ethical independence will do. In short, Dworkin's religious atheism based on an opening up of the concept of religion does not lead him to argue for the special status of religion; quite the contrary, "religious atheism" leads him to advocate a radical secularization of the state in conditions of deep pluralism of beliefs – namely, doing away with any remnant of the notion that religion should enjoy special state protection.

I am persuaded that, in contemporary Western democracies, there should *not* be a special right of religion. Postsecularism – if it is convincing at all – entails the recognition of the worthiness of a variety of deep beliefs, religious and non-religious alike. It is a positive development in all Western democracies that courts – both at state and beyond the state level – have, albeit often reluctantly, started to take more and more into account non-religious convictions as a reason for granting exemptions from general rules. In *Torcaso v. Watkins*, for instance, the concept of religion is extended so much that it comprises secular humanists;[18] likewise, the so-called religious article (art. 9) of the European Convention of Human Rights is, in fact, dedicated to non-religious manifestations.[19] Starting in particular from the landmark *Kokkinakis v. Greece* case (1993), the ECtHR has been emphasizing the importance of the protection of pluralism in a democratic regime. This positive trend will hopefully gain in importance and will lead to a diluting of the exclusive privileges of majority religious institutions (for the difference between a privileged and a special relation between state and religion, see Iglesias and Ungureanu, Chapter 10 in this volume).

However, Dworkin unconvincingly argues that the only way out of the dilemma is strictly individualistic (for a defence of exemptions, see Laborde, Chapter 2 and Gamper, Chapter 9 in this volume). Dworkin's radical-individualistic solution (resonant in practical terms of Barry's vitriolic *Culture and Equality* (2001)) that rejects any religious–cultural exemptions is, I think, questionable. Dworkin's dichotomist option between (religious) majoritarianism and atomized individualism is too crude; in between there is a social space of deep value practices that is relevant for policy- and law-making. Deep experiences and collective beliefs in worthwhile values have been and should continue to be sometimes reflected in law making. Consider the famous *peyote* case. If peyote puts at "serious risk" (Dworkin 2013: 136) the member of the Native American Church, as Dworkin (amongst others) argues, then he is right to reject granting a religious exemption. But one can imagine granting a *legitimate* exemption if usages of something like peyote in ceremonies by a traditional community is rigorously limited so that no significant harm is likely to happen. The general right to ethical independence would not suffice to justify such exemptions from general rules.

Values that are generally worth pursuing (protecting the environment; improving general welfare; helping the poor; supporting some cultural enterprises and institutions) are not always a matter of simple individual preference, and the law cannot ignore this. Is not the political–legal battle in democracy often about such values? Even in the absence of consensus regarding such values, legal and political rules and policies that entail some relative limitation of individual freedom could be legitimately developed with respect to certain value issues of general significance. Likewise, courts need sometimes to make evaluations when it comes to petitions of exemptions from military service, hospital practices, and so on. True, there is an intrinsic difficulty in determining which conviction is deep, salient and worthy as a reason for granting exemptions for general rules. There is no ultimate and unique criterion for granting exemptions, just as there is no final criterion to decide what religion is. Yet only a nostalgic metaphysician would look for absolute and transhistorical criteria. Given changes in any society, the criteria for determining when exemptions should be granted are not cast in stone; in addition, there will always be borderline cases: think of controversies concerning Scientology – is it a religion or a lucrative business wrapped up in shallow spiritualist claims? (For a discussion of Scientology in the UK, see Zucca, Chapter 8 in this volume). However, the active belief in God of a long-term member of Christian Action cannot have the same weight in deciding on an exemption from the draft as membership in the Church of the Flying Spaghetti Monster.[20] In muddling through the labyrinth of practice, judges will sometimes have difficulties in distinguishing between significant deep beliefs. But is this not preferable to denying societal complexity?

Acknowledging and taking into account this complexity does not necessarily entail a case-by-case approach.[21] The circumstantial approach would undermine a minimal legal consistency. In contrast, there is a need for a passage from exclusive religious tests based on the questionable belief that religion is special, to cultural–religious ones taking into account religious and non-religious deep convictions (Renteln 2004; Eisenberg 2010). These tests – as developed in various ways in the US and Canada – would incorporate substantial and functional criteria for assessing the relevance of specific beliefs. While not cast in stone, these criteria are general enough to avoid falling into an ad hoc, case-by-case approach.

In sum, the practical consequences of the secularism–postsecular debate are complex, yet philosophers such as Habermas, Dworkin, Taylor and Derrida would agree that neither a secularist model hostile to the manifestation of religion in public sphere nor the majoritarian model are options in pluralist democracies.[22] Their conceptions entail a deepening of the secularization of the state in the West and a search for a viable media to reflect and express the increasing pluralization of our societies (see Requejo, Chapter 11 in this volume). Likewise, various authors in this book look for such an intermediary space between secularism and majoritarianism. From this perspective, taking into account pluralism does not necessarily entail rigid separation between state and religion, but encountering intermediary solutions to contextual problems (Zucca, Chapter 8 in this volume). To illustrate, part of the jurisprudence of the ECtHR could be understood from the contextual perspective that entails the recognition of public manifestations of religion as well as the positive obligation to support democratic pluralism (Martínez-Torrón, Chapter 7; Gamper, Chapter 9; and Iglesias and Ungureanu, Chapter 10 in this volume). Furthermore, beyond the strictly legal logic, co-participatory solutions in the construction of rights may be implemented in specific circumstances. Overall, however, as several chapters of this book argue, state and inter-state practice in Europe has been deeply ambivalent, as it has oscillated between majoritarianism, exclusivist secularism, and the recognition of (non-)religious pluralism.

Notes

1 Two observations should be made here: (1) I do not want to imply that criticizing the reduction of morality and religion to evolutionary mechanisms necessarily entails a positive appreciation of the role of religion (see, for instance, Simon Blackburn's work on ethics); (2) In order to designate what I call the "postsecular" trend, other authors prefer terms such as secularity (Taylor) or open/contextual/inclusive secularism (Bhargava, Modood).

2 One may prefer another term – namely, secularity: open, inclusive, situational or contextual secularism. The term itself is, from my perspective, of minor importance. In this text I will preserve the term "secularism" for a standpoint that is inimical to religion.

3 For the mushrooming literature on Habermas' postsecularism, see www.habermasforum.dk/ (last accessed April 28, 2014).

4 The mutual borrowing, exchange and interaction between modernity and religion does not automatically result in postsecular phenomena (consider fundamentalism). For the emphasis on non-authoritarianism in understanding the postsecular, see especially Maeve Cooke's recent work, e.g., Cooke (2007).

5 In *Philosophical Investigations* (§66), Wittgenstein famously considers the case of games, and asked whether we call something "games" by looking and seeing "whether there is anything common to all…". For Wittgenstein, "the result of this examination is: we see a complicated network of similarities overlapping and criss-crossing: sometimes overall similarities." Wittgenstein famously characterized them as "family resemblances" (§67).

6 Here I follow Wittgenstein (Wittgenstein 2009). In §68, he states:

> I can give the concept "number" rigid limits … that is, use the word "number" for a rigidly limited concept, but I can also use it so that the extension of the concept is not closed by a frontier. And this is how we do use the word "game". For how is the concept of a game bounded? What still counts as a game and what no longer does? Can you give the boundary? No. You can draw one; for none has so far been drawn. (But that never troubled you before when you used the word "game").

The role of the theorist is, from this viewpoint, not that of policing conceptual borders on account of supposedly ultimate definitional criteria.

7 I borrow the term "constellation" from Bernstein (1992). A "constellation" has a certain degree of cohesiveness, yet it does not exclude inner tension and even opposition (e.g., between Habermas and Derrida).

8 It is noteworthy that there has been a rapprochement between the continental and analytical branch of philosophy with respect to religion. An interest in religious issues has been a traditional concern of continental philosophy in its German or French versions from Walter Benjamin to Emmanuel Levinas, in addition to the new wave of thinkers such as Derrida and Vattimo. In analytical philosophy, a postsecular turn has occurred only recently – in particular in the works of Thomas Nagel and Richard Dworkin.

9 For critical perspectives on Habermas' view on values which do not deal with the question of religion, see McCarthy (1995); Putnam (2002); Gorski *et al.* (2012).

10 Like Rawls, Habermas is a monist: he believes that the relationship between religion and democracy should be governed by a master-principle (proviso, translation). However, the complexity of contemporary societies as well as the variety of democracies – from the US, France to India – should be reflected in the political theorizing on the relationship between the two.

11 See also Bell's valuable writings on Confucianism and liberalism, e.g., Bell (2000).

12 Due to limited space, I cannot comment on the current resurgence of interest in political theology from both left-wing and right-wing thinkers. Some radical critics draw on political theology to reject secularism as a local European development. For persuasive criticisms of this view, see Bhargava (2006); and Sen (2005) with reference to Nandy's "An Antisecularist Manifesto" (1985). A more convincing use of political theological reflections from the perspective of comparative political theory is contained in De Roover's and Balagangadhara's recent works (De Roover and Balagangadhara 2011, which contains a useful bibliography). Given the existence of pluralism, the reflection on secularism/postsecularism would need to be shaped by the comparative approach to political theory.

13 There is a significant trend in theology as well. Consider Johann Baptiste Metz' theology of compassion, and his criticism of Habermas (Metz 1995, 1998).

14 For Dworkin, there is a difference between science and morality: "In the special case of value, however, faith means something more, because our convictions about value are emotional commitments as well … they must also feel right in an emotional way" (Dworkin 2013: 19).

15 See the *Buddhist Scriptures*, translated and edited by Edward Conze, Penguin Classics, 1959.

16 *United States v. Seeger*, 380 US 1643 (1965).

17 In the famous case *Employment Division, Department of Human Resources of Oregon v. Smith*, 494 US 872 (1990). The Religious Freedom Restoration Act of 1993 was passed as a reaction to the decision of the Supreme Court that the First Amendment did not require an exemption from the general rule banning the consumption of hallucinogenic drugs. The Religious Freedom Restoration Act reinstated the so-called Sherbert test (1963) that overturned laws that seemed to burden religion (see Laborde, Chapter 2 in this volume).

18 *Torcaso v. Watkins*, 367 US 488 (1961), fn. 11: Among religions in this country which do not teach what would generally be considered a belief in the existence of God are Buddhism, Taoism, Ethical Culture, Secular atheism and others," see Dworkin (2013: 161–162).

19 According to this article, "Everyone has the right to freedom of thought, conscience and religion; this right includes freedom to change his religion or belief and freedom, either alone or in community with others …", at www.echr.coe.int/Documents/Convention_ENG.pdf (last accessed April 28, 2014).

20 In the final analysis, notwithstanding Dworkin's sympathetic treatment of religion, his conclusions at the legal–constitutional level amount to a hostile position with regard to religion that is common to the secularist worldview and ideology.

21 This is a significant difference between my approach and Bhargava's contextualism (Bhargava 2007: 21–22).

22 Postsecular philosophers such as Habermas do not reflect explicitly on the crucial question as to whether religion should enjoy special protection, yet there is there is nothing in his conception that would ground a special moral interest in religion.

Part I

Theoretical approaches

Secularism or post-secularism in Europe?

2 Equal liberty, non-establishment and religious freedom[1]

Cécile Laborde

In South Carolina in the early 1960s, a member of the Seventh-Day Adventist Church, Adell Sherbert, was denied unemployment compensation on the grounds that no 'good cause' justified her unwillingness to comply with her employer's demand that she, like other employees, accept Saturday work. The US Supreme Court reversed the lower court's decision, and found that denying Sherbert's compensation claim violated her rights to religious freedom. *Sherbert v. Verner* (1963) became a landmark case in the constitutionalisation of religious freedom. Consider, however, two different ways in which Sherbert's religious freedom claim could be justified. On the one hand, one could say (as the Court in fact said) that to condition Sherbert's access to benefit on her willingness to violate a cardinal principle of her faith would be unduly to penalise and burden her rights of religious freedom. On this view, Sherbert has a *pro tanto* claim to practice her religion freely (absent a compelling state interest). On the other hand, one could say that denying compensation would entail unjustly discriminating against Sherbert who, *unlike similarly situated workers*, faces an unfair dilemma: either complying with the job's requirements or obeying the demands of her faith (and losing her claim to compensation). On this view, Sherbert has a *comparative* claim to be treated on fair, equal terms with others. This second justification draws on what I propose to call an egalitarian theory of religious freedom. It is the coherence and plausibility of egalitarian theories of religious freedom that this essay puts to the test.

The essay is divided into three sections. The first section lays out the rationale and structure of egalitarian theories of religious freedom, and explains their initial appeal in light of progressive norms of non-discrimination and equality – between majority and minority religions on the one hand, and between religious and non-religious moral commitments on the other. The second section offers a detailed account of the most developed egalitarian theory of religious freedom so far, that proposed by constitutional theorists Christopher Eisgruber and Lawrence Sager in their 2007 book, *Religious Freedom and the Constitution.*[2] Their theory of 'equal liberty' explicitly denies that religion is entitled to special and unique treatment in law, above and beyond that granted to comparable commitments and practices. The third and last section demonstrates that their theory fails on its own terms. It further suggests that this failure is symptomatic, not only of the narrow First Amendment constitutional constraints within which the authors operate but, more widely and more interestingly, of the difficulty encountered by liberal theory in fitting the concept of religious freedom into a broadly egalitarian framework. This essay is part of a larger project which attempts to set out the precise (if limited) sense in which egalitarian political philosophy should treat religion as special, or uniquely special.

Egalitarian theories of religious freedom

Theories of religious freedom ask what the status of religious freedom, *qua* religious, is in the liberal state. Should religious believers be exempted from the application of laws that burden their conscience? Which forms of state support or endorsement of religion, if any, are permissible? Schematically, we might say that the first question relates to the Free Exercise clause of the First Amendment of the US Constitution ('Congress shall make no law … prohibiting the free exercise' of religion) and the second question relates to the Establishment clause ('Congress shall make no law respecting an establishment of religion'). Not surprisingly, doctrinal and political disagreements about these clauses have fuelled a long-standing and vibrant – if somewhat narrowly self-referential – tradition of scholarly commentary about religious freedom among US constitutional theorists. In this piece, I shall liberally draw upon this rich tradition, both in its free exercise and in its non-establishment dimensions, as well as pointing to the broader relevance of the questions it asks. In particular, I shall use the US constitutional debates to distill and explicate a distinctive, new approach, which I call an egalitarian theory of religious freedom.[3] Egalitarian theories of religious freedom describe a family of views that hold that religious freedom is not a distinctive freedom and that it should be treated under a more general equality-based regime. The special and unique place of religion is indefensible in light of the ideal of equality between citizens. Religious beliefs and activities might be *specially* protected, but not *uniquely* so: if and when they are, it is as a sub-set of a broader category of respect-worthy beliefs and activities. Egalitarian theories of religious freedom are based on three main premises. As I shall show, each premise breaks with well-established traditional views about the special and unique nature of religion (either from an 'accommodationist' or from a 'separationist' perspective)[4] and tallies with broader recent developments in egalitarian legal and political theory. I now explicate these points, in relation to each of the three premises.

(1) Religious freedom is a sub-category of a more general set of freedoms, such as freedom of speech, association, and privacy, and does not deserve uniquely special treatment.

Egalitarians deny the basic starting point of accommodationists such as Michael McConnel, for whom religious freedom is basic and distinctive; it is the 'first freedom' in the liberal state.[5] Religious freedom cannot be analogised with, or reduced to, other freedoms, as it serves to protect a uniquely special human good, an autonomous sphere of conscience, ritual and community, from state interference and regulation.[6] Egalitarian theorists of religious freedom concede that religion may be paradigmatic of beliefs, identifications and practices that people have a particular interest in pursuing in their own way, individually or collectively. But they insist that, while religion is a paradigm of those valuable concerns, it does not uniquely capture them. As leading political philosophers have argued, it is the human capacity for moral or spiritual agency, not for leading good lives with a determinate, perhaps religious, content, that should ground the respect that the state owes to persons *qua* persons. John Rawls, for example, treats free religious exercise as part of a broader notion of 'equal liberty of conscience' that extends both to 'moral and religious claims'.[7] More recently, Ronald Dworkin has suggested that religious freedom is not *sui generis* and is only one implication of a right to 'ethical independence in foundational matters'.[8] Nor is ethical independence, or moral agency, the only value that religion can be analogised with, or 'reduced' to. Other such 'reductionist' approaches to religion have shown that, for purposes of constitutional protection, religion is not relevantly different from other categories such as speech and association; or – in equal protection and anti-discrimination cases – race and other 'suspect' classifications.[9]

(2) Religious believers may be exempted from some general laws on the basis of non-discrimination, but not on the grounds that religion must be protected *qua* religion.

Here again, egalitarians challenge a basic accommodationist premise, according to which governments need strong reasons, or 'compelling interests' to justify infringing religious freedom. Failing that, religious believers have a presumptive right to be exempted from the application of general, neutral laws when these unreasonably burden their conscience. Egalitarians deny that religious believers have such a presumptive right. What they are entitled to is a fair scheme of 'equal liberties' guaranteed by the state: they must not be treated differently from similarly situated citizens. They can benefit from specific exemptions from the law when not granting those exemptions would constitute unfair discrimination against them. For example, minority religious citizens might be indirectly discriminated against if, because of a facially neutral regulation, they do not have the same set of opportunities as majority religious citizens. Egalitarian theories, then, invite systemic comparisons between the terms of accommodation of majority and minority religions. This is in line with the rise of norms of equality and non-discrimination as unifying norms in national, international and human rights law. These norms have provided a language to challenge structural patterns of cultural, gender, sexual and racial discrimination in Euro-Atlantic societies, notably by bringing to light the hidden, invidious effects of facially neutral, yet culturally biased, institutions, practices and laws. A range of minority religious claims have been re-described as protests of unfair discrimination against practices which – had they been engaged in by majority groups – would presumptively have been tolerated or accommodated. The Canadian legal norm of 'reasonable accommodation', for example, has allowed special exemptions from workplace regulations (uniform, days of rest) to members of minority religions, often with explicit recognition that members of majority religions already benefit from built-in advantages.[10] The Danish cartoon controversy has brought to light the double standards which permeate free speech doctrine and practice in Europe, with heightened cultural sensitivity towards offence against Christian (and Jewish) feelings unmatched by corresponding empathy towards the harm caused by anti-Muslim speech.[11] And analogies between demands for the recognition of minority faiths in the public sphere and the de facto public role of Christian churches in many European states have been drawn.[12]

(3) The state must guarantee the equal civic status of all citizens, regardless of the particular beliefs and values they endorse and pursue.

In relation to the non-establishment clause of the First Amendment, egalitarian theories endorse a stance of 'neutrality' towards religious and non-religious citizens. This has different implications for state funding and for state speech. Regarding state *funding*, egalitarians argue that religious groups pursuing public-interest activities must not be treated differently from non-religious groups merely because they are religious. Here, egalitarians depart from traditional separationist views which object on principle to any channelling of public money to religious groups. Instead of 'no-funding', egalitarians advocate 'even-handed' funding. This even-handed approach, however, cannot be extended to state *speech.* The state cannot symbolically endorse the symbols and rituals of all religions, but it must decide whether to attach itself to the traditional majority religion – typically Christianity. For egalitarians, the state should generally avoid any endorsement of religion, in order not to convey messages of second-class citizenship or disparagement to minority believers or non-believers.

Against the accommodationist view that the Establishment only prohibits *coercive* entanglement of government with religion, egalitarians point to the unavoidably *expressive* dimension of law and the state – the fact that non-coercive messages and actions can have an impact on the democratic status of citizens.[13] The state should not endorse – even non-coercively or symbolically – the rituals and beliefs of particular religious traditions, so that it can be genuinely be the state of all. Such a perspective has emerged in US jurisprudence with Justice Sandra O'Connor's 'Endorsement Test' (which postulates that the state's symbolic entanglement with religion is wrong insofar as it undermines the equal civic status of citizens);[14] in political philosophy with Martha Nussbaum's civic and egalitarian interpretation of the Establishment Clause;[15] and through growing awareness, within European constitutional and human rights law, that equal citizenship demands greater religious neutrality of traditionally Christian European public spheres.[16]

In sum, egalitarian theories of religious freedom seek to advance equality between minority and majority religions (by challenging the discriminatory prevalence of majority religious norms and symbols within existing states) *and* between religious and non-religious beliefs, practices and identities, be they spiritual, sexual, ethical or racial (by comparing religion with analogous practices and beliefs).[17] In the rest of this chapter, I shall examine in detail how the three premises of the theory are interpreted and combined in an early, groundbreaking work of constitutional jurisprudence, by Christopher Eisgruber and Lawrence Sager.

Eisgruber and Sager's theory of 'equal liberty'

Religious Freedom and the Constitution (2007) is a book-length commentary on recent Religion clause jurisprudence of the US Supreme Court. Eisgruber and Sager's basic intuition is that religious believers should enjoy 'equal not special liberty'. They start from the reductionist premise that religion should not be seen as 'a constitutional anomaly, a category of human experience that demands special benefits and/or necessitates special restrictions'.[18] Instead, religious commitments should be treated as part of a broader class of 'deep' and 'important' commitments and projects that people care about, whether religious or not. Next, Eisgruber and Sager deny that such commitments and projects, however morally weighty and significant, generate *pro tanto* rights against the state. The relevant political question is whether the government, in coordinating different life projects, shares burdens fairly among people.[19] This allows the formulation of a discrimination-centred account of religious freedom: 'persons [should] not be treated unequally on account of the spiritual foundations of their deep commitments'. *Contra* egalitarian critics of exemptions,[20] they argue that exemptions might be demanded by the ideal of equality, insofar as a government enacting generally applicable laws 'may be hostile or insensitive to the needs and interests of minority faiths'.[21] It is as members of discriminated or disparaged groups, not as holders of intrinsically valuable religious beliefs and practices, that minority religious believers deserve special consideration under the theory of equal liberty. This concern for equality, finally, extends to the Establishment question of whether the state can permissibly provide either financial or expressive support to religious groups. Eisgruber and Sager (2007: 52) insist that the clause should be interpreted as prohibiting the 'advantaging or disadvantaging [of] persons or groups because of the spiritual foundations of their deeply held beliefs and commitments'. This entails even-handed financial support to religious and non-religious groups providing comparable services; as well as the strenuous avoidance of expressive endorsement by the state of majoritarian beliefs, rituals or symbols in its own displays, ceremonies and institutions. The theory of equal liberty fits neatly within a broader trend within First Amendment jurisprudence, which tends to de-constitutionalise religion and seek standards of neutrality between religion and non-religion. This trend is exemplified, in the Free Exercise context, by the 1990 *Employment Division v. Smith* decision (which claimed, *contra Sherbert*, that there is no presumptive right of religious exemption from generally applicable laws) and in the Establishment clause context, by the 'equal access to government places and money' principle which motivated the *Zelman v. Simmons-Harris* 2002 decision (authorising the provision of tuition vouchers channelled to religious as well as secular public schools).[22] In the next two sub-sections, I show that equal liberty provides a *prima facie* plausible analysis of recent Free Exercise and Non-Establishment cases, respectively.

Eisgruber and Sager disagree with accommodationists, who hold that religion is a uniquely valuable human good that deserves special protection. To treat religion more favourably than comparably deep secular interests would be to unfairly discriminate against the latter on sectarian grounds. Religious freedom, they claim, will legitimately flourish in a society where all members benefit from general rights of free speech, personal autonomy, associative freedom and private property.[23] To be sure, the freedoms that such rights protect can be regulated by legitimate state legislation, provided its burdens are shared fairly. For example, taxation and zoning regulations are general burdens that should fall on all, including churches.[24] However, Eisgruber and Sager suggest that other, more specific legislation might have been designed with insufficient regard for their unfairly disproportionate impact on religious interests. Such interests should not be *privileged* as religious, but instead *protected* on similar terms as comparably serious non-religious interests.[25]

Three different cases of application of this principle in Eisgruber and Sager's discussion can be distinguished. In the first set of cases, the contested law already provides for exemptions for non-religious interests, to which minority religious interests can easily be analogised. Eisgruber and Sager use the example of Muslim policemen who challenged the Newark police department's requirement that officers be clean-shaven, on the ground that their faith demanded that they wore a beard.[26] Given that the Newark department already exempted officers with skin disorders, such as folliculitis, that made shaving painful or promoted infection, its refusal to accommodate the Muslims' request constitutes a failure of equal regard.[27] In the second set of cases, the contested law does not directly provide exemptions, but is applied against a broader regulatory background, which advantages mainstream or majoritarian interests. The *Sherbert* decision falls into this category. The state of South Carolina had strict Sunday closing laws, which meant that mainstream Christians were not forced to choose between exercising their religious rights and performing the demands of their job. So Adell Sherbert was discriminated against when her claim for compensation was denied.[28] In the third, and most complicated, set of cases, the contested law is facially neutral and generally applicable. Here, Eisgruber and Sager suggest that government may be held to a standard that measures a claim for a religious exemption against *hypothetical* exemptions. For example, in the 1988 *Lyng* case, the Supreme Court considered Native American claims that the construction of a logging road on federal land would disrupt vision quests – sacred rituals that depend on isolation and immersion in wilderness. There were no ready-made comparisons, but Eisgruber and Sager speculate that the Forest Service would not have constructed the road had mainstream religious ('a site sacred to a small but well-acknowledged group of Catholics or Orthodox Jews') or secular ('killing off some of the last great redwood trees') interests been at stake. In light of that hypothetical comparison, they say, the case is revealed as a problem of unjust inequality that should have been decided in favour of the plaintiffs.[29] In sum, through a creative use of analogical and hypothetical reasoning, Eisgruber and Sager suggest that, even though religious interests are not presumptively entitled to unique constitutional immunity from otherwise valid laws, they deserve robust constitutional protection on the basis of equality. It is because minority religious interests are 'vulnerable to hostility and neglect' that they should receive special solicitude.[30] The underlying value of such an anti-discrimination approach is 'parity, not advantage'.[31]

A similar approach, rooted in the value of Equal Protection, is further applied by Eisgruber and Sager to the Establishment clause. They deny that the ban on the establishment of religion should be interpreted as singling out religion for special treatment. Instead, as we saw, they claim that the Establishment is wrong insofar as it means treating people differentially on grounds of their beliefs and commitments.[32] Regarding state funding, Eisgruber and Sager reject both the separationist blanket ban on state support of religious activities and services and the accommodationist partiality towards faith-based, religiously-motivated teaching and charity.[33] They argue that if two organisations, one religious and one non-religious, provide public goods on an equal basis, it would be discriminatory for the state to fund the former and not the latter. For example, they broadly agree with the Court's reasoning in the landmark *Zelman* decision that authorised the Cleveland school authorities to distribute educational vouchers to parents, who can use them either in religious or in public (secular) schools.[34]

Next, the issue of state speech is found to raise 'a different kind of equality-concern: the worry that by sponsoring religious displays or ceremonies, the government affiliates itself with or endorses a particular theological perspective and implicitly disparages other ones'.[35] While the state may fund religious and non-religious organisations on an equal basis, it cannot be similarly even-handed in the choice of the symbols, rituals and ceremonies it promotes in its institutions. Eisgruber and Sager follow O'Connor's Endorsement Test, arguing that governmental expressive action is impermissible if it creates a perception in the mind of a 'reasonable observer' that the government is either endorsing or disapproving of religion.[36] For example, they object to the phrase 'under God' in the Pledge of Allegiance, arguing that non-denominational references to God are alienating not only for agnostics and atheists, but also for polytheists and non-deistic believers.[37]

What, however, is wrong with governmental endorsement of religion, as opposed to other views and symbols with equally controversial expressive content? The state, after all, is not barred from promoting patriotic rituals, teaching Hegel and sexual education in its schools, or sponsoring the causes of anti-racism, anti-socialism, feminism or the death penalty. Eisgruber and Sager recognise that the singling out of religion for non-establishment purposes is a challenge to their egalitarian theory of religious freedom. To address it, they explain that the suspect constitutional status of religious practices and beliefs must be related to their 'social meaning' in American culture, where 'important constituents of identity – most notably, race and religion – ... function as especially significant markers of social division'.[38] It is because of the sociological and cultural features of religions – 'their comprehensiveness; their tendency to treat people as either "in" or "out"; their use of symbol and rituals to signal who is "in"; and, finally, the profound stakes they attach to the status of "in" or "out"'[39] – that they are especially vulnerable to invidious discrimination or neglect by majorities. Specially, but not uniquely so. Consistent with their egalitarian, reductionist approach to religion, Eisgruber and Sager find themselves disposed to extend the ban on state endorsement of religion to patriotic pledges, pro-heterosexual slogans,[40] and more generally to the teaching of controversial partisan 'orthodoxies' in schools, insofar as they might convey a disparaging or exclusionary message to those who do not share them.[41] For them, the Non-Establishment clause should be read in light of the Equal Protection paradigm: just as the officially sanctioned separation between the races carried a message of inferiority and disparagement to Afro-Americans, likewise, the public endorsement of religion carries a special charge or valence given the role of religion in defining civic identity in the US.[42]

This brief synopsis of the main arguments put forward in *Religious Freedom and the Constitution* should suffice to suggest that the text opens up intriguing theoretical avenues of reflection about the normative foundation of religious freedom. Here is a theory that promises non-negligible levels of protection for minority religious interests, while denying the need to grant any special privilege to religion as such. This is an attractive proposition for egalitarians, who worry that formal legal equality leaves minority interests at the mercy of majoritarian preferences; yet see little justification for a McConnell-style privileging of religious interests *qua* religious. Does the theory work, however? In the next section, I show it does not – and I ask what the implications of this failure for the broader ambitions of egalitarian theories of religious freedom are.

Equality of what?

If equality is not to be an empty notion, as Peter Westen and Joseph Raz suspect it is,[43] theories of equality and non-discrimination must specify in respect of what people must be treated equally. Such theories, that is, are not self-standing: they rely on a prior account of which relevant features of existing states of affairs are to be the proper object of comparative evaluations of unfair treatment. For example, it would be implausible to assert that marriage laws unfairly discriminate against business associates or frequent tennis partners, just by virtue of those couples being excluded from its benefits. By contrast, they can be said to discriminate against same-sex couples insofar as the latter exhibit the valued features (intimacy, stability, commitment) that marriage is supposed to protect. Or, alternatively, marriage laws can be said to be indefensible in the first place because they arbitrarily single out, protect and privilege values associated with the traditional family and a conservative social order, and therefore discriminate against non-conventional families and single-person households. In sum, to be able to claim that tennis partners, same-sex couples, or single parents are discriminated against by marriage laws, we need to provide both (1) an account of the features singled out and promoted by those laws and (2) an account of what it means to be 'similarly situated' in relation to these features.

Unfortunately, Eisgruber and Sager fail to appreciate the depth of this problem and this, as I shall show, proves fatal to their theory. It is relatively easy for them to build a formally egalitarian case for the extension of existing benefits of protection from religious majorities to religious minorities. Yet, ultimately, they cannot avoid engaging in a more speculative enquiry: that of specifying the relevant features or criteria that are protection-worthy in the first place. Their valiant reductionist search for non-religious analogies to the treatment of religion ultimately fails, as they end up re-affirming precisely what they seek to deny: namely, the uniquely special nature of religion. This failure should not be surprising, in light of the narrow remit of their constitutional project. For the most part, they are content to analyse and reconstruct the coherence of US First Amendment jurisprudence, which itself assumes (rather than explicates or justifies) the special status of religion. This doctrinal straightjacket limits constitutional lawyers' imagination of what a genuinely egalitarian, 'post-secular'[44] state might look like. In particular, Eisgruber and Sager underestimate the radical implication of their own normative commitment, that no person should be disvalued on account of the spiritual foundations of their important principles.

In what follows, I argue that their analysis either fails to explain, or takes for granted, or implicitly smuggles back in, assumptions about the specialness and uniqueness of religion. And insofar as much liberal political philosophy also implicitly relies on what we could call the 'First Amendment paradigm', it is, similarly, partially defective in articulating the normative grounds of its egalitarian commitments. My detailed engagement with Eisgruber and Sager, therefore, is intended to challenge egalitarian political philosophers (with which I am happy to associate myself) to think harder about the 'equality of what?' problem. While egalitarian critics of marriage have engaged with the prior question of the value of marriage, egalitarian theorists of religious freedom still have work to do to account for what, exactly, is the 'religion' in religious freedom. In what follows, I explicate these points in relation to the two main areas of controversy discussed by Eisgruber and Sager: exemptions from general laws; and the ban on state endorsement of religion.

Free Exercise and accommodation

Eisgruber and Sager's general argumentative strategy is simple. They identify a priori plausible minority religious interests, and then look for reasons to accommodate them. This non-systematic, case-driven strategy partly explains the ad hoc nature of some of their conclusions. Admittedly, when majority interests but not minority interests are exempted by the law, *and* there is a clear analogy between the opportunity set granted or denied their members, the argument for accommodation is relatively straightforward. This is the case when the law specifically makes provisions for members of majorities both to practice their religion and meet professional demands; yet denies minority members the same opportunity set.[45] Thus, it may be defensible to grant Sherbert compensation benefits given that mainstream Christians are advantaged by Sunday trading laws. More complicated, however, are 'flat rule' laws, which do not entail built-in advantages for any particular group, yet substantially burden minority religious practices. Eisgruber and Sager interpret *Lyng*, the logging road case, as a case of discrimination by referring to hypothetical alternative interests ('conservationist' or 'Catholic or Orthodox Jews') that would, they speculate, have been better protected than Native American traditional rituals. One may dispute the pertinence of the proposed hypothetical analogies. But more interesting is the authors' strategy. In all cases, they presumptively analogise minority religious claims with interests which are, or should be, exempted. This means that they assume from the outset that religious practices are worth protecting, and they look for already protected (or hypothetically protection-worthy) comparable interests.[46] But what is the criterion of a comparable, or protection-worthy, interest? Why, for example, are religiously-mandated beards analogised with folliculitis – an exempted medical condition – rather than with a non-exempted aesthetic or merely cultural preference?

Eisgruber and Sager's answer is that, for Free Exercise purposes, religious interests are protected in virtue of being 'deep', 'serious', 'spiritual', 'moral' commitments held by individuals.

Although those terms are nowhere clearly defined, they are pivotal to the theory. They allow the authors to draw a wedge between religious freedom and the protection of 'frivolous' interests, such as fashion or aesthetic preferences.[47] Religious interests are explicitly analogised with disabilities and other 'comparably serious'[48] or 'sufficiently compelling'[49] interests or convictions. Such judgments involve what Charles Taylor called 'strong evaluations' about the central importance and value of certain beliefs, practices and purposes.[50] This strong evaluation is primarily made by the individuals or groups concerned (Eisgruber and Sager explicitly endorse a subjective definition of religion for Free Exercise purposes)[51] but is also checked against wider moral standards (they reject the idea of respect for individual conscience as such, regardless of the content of its injunctions).[52] One virtue of their account of the normative grounds of religious freedom is that it sidesteps the sterile debate about whether religious commitments are to be seen as products of 'chance' or 'choice'.[53] On the strong evaluation view that they favour, religious commitments are neither analogous to unchosen disabilities, nor should they be treated as contingent, negotiable personal preferences. Rather, their normative status merely derives from the fact that individuals closely identify with them and recognise them as theirs, on grounds of their 'deep', 'serious', 'spiritual' nature.[54] Call this, for short, the Depth Criterion. It is because religious commitments are deep that they (sometimes) deserve special protection in law; and this protection extends to non-religious, comparably deep, commitments.[55] The Depth Criterion (DC), therefore, is offered as the standard in relation to which a range of commitments and practices, religious and non-religious, are to be treated equally. Adopting a version of reflective legal interpretation, Eisgruber and Sager's method is to go back and forth between existing case law and the value it is supposed to promote (DC), and to seek coherence between the two.

There are, however, fundamental problems with DC as a coherentist standard of interpretation. To start with, DC does not provide a plausible account of the features in virtue of which religion is protected in existing case law. Many religious practices and rituals are performed out of habitual devotion, customary adherence, fidelity to tradition; and do not necessarily exhibit the 'deep, serious, moral' features characteristic of paradigmatic religious freedom cases, such as conscientious objection to military service. Many important rituals – for example, the consumption of the peyote drug in Native American ceremonies – when they are protected, benefit from categorical, not activity-specific, protection. That is, it is because they are categorically described as religious – required by a comprehensive tradition, set of beliefs and practices presumptively described as such – that they are protected, not because they directly and singly exhibit the features (depth and seriousness of commitment) that make religion itself worthy of protection.[56] Perhaps it can be said that the ritual-based dimensions of religious observance benefit from special protection insofar as they are embedded within significant practices which themselves, *qua* religions, meet DC. If this is correct, however, there appears to be an important asymmetry between religious and non-religious commitments. It is difficult to think of comparable non-religious practices that, while not serious, deep or moral in themselves, would benefit from protection in virtue of their connection to a broader, comprehensive set of beliefs and practices which would itself meet DC.

This suspicion of asymmetry is confirmed when we examine more closely how Eisgruber and Sager deal with the cases of what they call 'secular claimants', who demand exemptions from generally applicable laws on non-religious grounds. The plausibility of the theory of equal liberty crucially depends on demonstrating that exemptions can be applied to deep and serious non-religious claims. Unfortunately, Eisgruber and Sager only provide two examples of such claims, which are very different and importantly limited. The first is that of medical conditions, such as folliculitis in the Newark police case. The example illustrates how, for some purposes, religious claims may be treated by analogy with medical conditions (in some cases, it is useful to analogise burdens on religion with a kind of undue hardship). But it is also meant to illustrate how exemptions on medical grounds can themselves be justified by analogy with existing religious exemptions. To make their case, Eisgruber and Sager are forced to narrow down their original benchmark of comparison – the 'spiritual' foundations of deep 'moral' commitments – into a vaguer and broader benchmark – a 'non-trivial' and 'comparably serious' condition. The upshot is that folliculitis sufferers should be accommodated because their condition is serious and non-trivial.

Here Eisgruber and Sager trade on the ambiguity of their compound definition of DC. This ambiguity – between different senses of 'serious' – allows them to elude the crucial question as to whether it makes a moral difference whether people would (by and large) prefer not to suffer from a disability, whereas they do (by and large) positively endorse and embrace their religious convictions.[57] The former is serious in that it can negatively affect rightful access to opportunity and advantage, but it is not serious in the moralised sense that the multi-criterial definition of DC embraces. The Newark police case, therefore, cannot serve as an illustration of how DC can be extended from religious to non-religious cases. Eisgruber and Sager see the problem, yet do not adequately solve it. Suppose, they say, that the Newark police department had allowed exemptions for religiously motivated but not medically mandated beards, and imagine a police officer – whom they call 'Officer Beard' – who alleges discriminatory treatment. While they concede that Officer Beard's claim would most likely fall under a Disability Act, they still consider the possibility that he might have been discriminated against on religious grounds, because the Newark police department displayed a culpable preference for religiously-motivated obligations.[58] But note how the argument shifts the ground of justification. Instead of showing that both religiously-motivated and medically required beards are relevantly similar in relation to the DC standard, the authors now merely postulate, without argument, that dissimilar treatment is – culpably – discriminatory.

The second, more plausible illustration of a non-religious application of DC concerns cases of conscientious objection to military service on secular pacifist grounds. Here Eisgruber and Sager are on safer ground. In two important Vietnam War decisions, *Seeger* and *Welsh*, the US Supreme Court exempted secular pacifists from military service on the ground that they had 'a sincere and meaningful belief which occupies in the life of its possessor a place parallel to that filled by the God of those admittedly qualifying for the exemption'.[59] Unsurprisingly, the *Seeger* jurisprudence has become a point of reference for egalitarian theories of religious freedom, as a paradigmatic case of conscientious objection extended from religious to non-religious moral commitments by appeal to DC. Unfortunately, the case is exceptional rather than paradigmatic. In *Seeger,* the Court was interpreting the narrow terms of a statute, rather than addressing the constitutional question of what should count as protected belief for purposes of the Free Exercise clause of the First Amendment. As a result, unsurprisingly, the *Seeger* jurisprudence has had few applications outside the exceptional circumstances of war. Free Exercise jurisprudence provides for a 'limited island of exemptions in a world of legal obligations',[60] and judges have been reluctant to extend the constitutional protection of non-religious deep, serious, moral commitments beyond narrowly circumscribed cases of conscientious objection to military service.[61]

Tellingly, Eisgruber and Sager's own attempt to provide a less religion-centred account of DC runs into considerable and ultimately fatal difficulties. In an instructive discussion, they consider the hypothetical case of 'Mother Sherbert', a single mother whose deep commitment to her children prevents her from accepting Saturday work. If she is denied unemployment compensation, is Mother Sherbert been treated unfairly, by comparison to religiously-motivated Adell Sherbert? Eisgruber and Sager answer that there is 'no reason to suppose that the state is rejecting Mother Sherbert's claims because of their relation to religion'.[62] It only makes a judgment about 'childcare needs', without any 'hostility or neglect towards either religion or irreligion'. The state would only treat Mother Sherbert unfairly if it treated her differentially depending on whether she was herself 'thoroughly irreligious' or whether her commitments to her children 'grow out of secular convictions' or 'as part of her duties to God'. In other words, Mother Sherbert is not discriminated against on religious grounds because her religious commitments play no role in the state's decision. But this begs the question. The point of the hypothetical analogy was to enquire whether deep, serious, moral commitments are sufficiently similar to religion (even if not derived from a traditional religious belief) to ground a claim for accommodation. That is, it was to enquire whether Mother Sherbert's commitment to her children is *in itself* sufficiently 'religious-like' to justify that she be treated on a par with Adell Sherbert. Eisgruber and Sager offer no clear answer to this particular question.

Eisgruber and Sager then go on to consider the particular case where Mother Sherbert views her commitment to her children as itself a matter of religious duty.[63] If she is denied compensation, is she not treated less favourably than Adell Sherbert? This is a different kind of enquiry, which leads them to speculation about whether *prima facie* secular duties of care to loved ones can ever be interpreted as 'inflexible religious obligations'. Their answer is that 'the two religiously motivated duties are importantly different'. Sabbatarian convictions yield inflexible obligations not to work on Saturday – while Mother Sherbert could work on Saturday if she could obtain childcare. In the end, then, Mother Sherbert's commitment to her children turns out not to be comparable to Adell Sherbert's religious duties, for two connected reasons. First, the question of discriminatory treatment arises only in the specific case where her commitment to her children itself has a traditionally religious or 'religious-like'[64] cause. So a *prima facie* secular claim is eligible for accommodation only if it is inscribed within a holistic, comprehensive religious worldview, of which traditional religions are the paradigm. Second, even if her commitment to her children is construed as religious in the relevant sense, it does not automatically trigger the same protection as 'inflexible God-given obligations'. This implies that secular claims, even when they meet a cluster of DC criteria, turn out not to meet the specific criteria necessary to ground accommodation – namely, what we may call the *comprehensive worldview* and the *categoricity* criteria, respectively.

While in Officer Beard's case, Eisgruber and Sager narrow DC down to a minimalist criterion of 'seriousness', in Mother Sherbert's case, they expand it to a maximalist criterion of 'categoricity' and 'comprehensiveness'. While this conceptual flexibility allows them to account for existing law, which accommodates disability but not the pursuit of all valuable ethical pursuits, it does not provide a coherent interpretive criterion for it. And it confirms the suspicion that secular claimants, even under their egalitarian theory, face an unreasonably high burden of proof. Secular pacifist Seeger fits the bill because (arguably) his pacifist convictions had the same scope, categoricity and depth as familiar religious convictions. But it is difficult to find similar cases and, tellingly, Eisgruber and Sager have not found any.[65] They conclude their section on hypothetical secular claimants, such as Officer Beard and Mother Sherbert, by conceding that they are hard cases for their theory of equal liberty. Yet as the grounds for accommodation of the former are unclear, and the latter's claim is rejected outright, they might well be fatal cases for the theory. What (*Seeger* aside) Eisgruber and Sager have not demonstrated is that secular claimants have valid claims of exemptions from generally applicable laws on DC grounds. As a baseline for equal treatment, DC works well to extend existing protections from majority to minority religions, but it does not provide a standard with which to analogise religious and non-religious claims. Either non-religious claims are deep but lack scope and categoricity (Mother Sherbert), or they are not deep in the sense singled out by DC, and something else grounds the claim of discrimination (Officer Beard). In the end, Eisgruber and Sager fall back on the First Amendment paradigm, which grants a categorical protection to something called religion – and this categorical protection turns out to encompass more than the reductionist standard DC.

In light of these difficulties, it is not surprising that Eisgruber and Sager struggle to reconcile their theory of equal liberty with another key feature of the First Amendment paradigm: the existence of *sui generis* religious exemptions. *Sui generis* religious exemptions are exorbitant exemptions tailored exclusively for religious organisations. Consider the so-called 'ministerial exception'. It allows religious organisations to be exempted from virtually all regulation of their employment relations (including non-discrimination norms) with clergy. In line with their coherentist project, Eisgruber and Sager endorse what they take to be a 'widely-held view' – but they do so by appeal to generic rights of privacy and associational autonomy. To make their case, they draw on a Supreme Court decision (*Dale*, 2000) which allowed the Boy Scouts of America to be exempt from a New Jersey law that prohibited discrimination against homosexuals.[66] Unfortunately, as legal scholars have commented, this analogy is doctrinally unsound. Boy Scouts and other non-religious organisations have no *pro tanto* right to discriminate in employment: the onus is on them to demonstrate that general anti-discrimination regulation conflicts with their expressive purpose (they rarely succeed, and *Dale* was rightly controversial). No such demand, by contrast, is made to religious organisations, which benefit from a *sui generis*, presumptive right to autonomy in the appointment of their leaders.[67] Try as they might, Eisgruber and Sager struggle to account for this special treatment of religion in US law.[68] Similar difficulties, I shall now show, plague their interpretation of the Non-Establishment clause.

Non-Establishment and the endorsement of religion

We have seen that the benchmark for equal treatment, in Free Exercise cases, were the 'deep commitments', religious or not, held by individuals. This benchmark also does some work in Eisgruber and Sager's interpretation of the Establishment clause, in relation to state funding of different organisations providing equivalent public services. Insofar as associations are free to organise to promote the deep commitments of their members, be they religious or secular in nature, *and* insofar as government is permitted to offer financial support for the provision of public services (education, welfare, etc.) by non-profit associations, it would seem discriminatory to deny funding to a religious organisation providing a public service on the same terms as a non-religious one. Arguably, it is in relation to such cases of fair distribution of public benefits that the theory of equal liberty between 'religion' and 'non-religion' is most plausible.[69] It is in line with recent analyses of the rise of a 'new establishment', characterised by a blurring of the distinction between religious and non-religious services, particularly in the area of the provision of healthcare, which is increasingly construed in spiritual as well as in narrowly medical terms (for example, in US prisons).[70] Moving from funding to speech issues, however, Eisgruber and Sager are faced with a problem. According to standard constitutional doctrine, the state cannot directly endorse religious commitments in its teachings, symbols and rituals, yet it can permissibly take a position on a range of other deep commitments held by individuals. The special treatment granted to religious statements, therefore, cannot be explained by their intrinsically 'deep', 'moral' or 'serious' nature. Something else than DC must be doing the work here.

Indeed, when looking for a standard able to shed light on the constitutional prohibition of state religious speech, Eisgruber and Sager point to a different analogy: racial categories and other 'socially divisive markers of identity'. On their interpretation, the reason why the state should not endorse (or disparage) religion, even symbolically, is because, like race, religion has historically functioned as a social category structurally vulnerable to hostility, discrimination, disparagement and neglect. Call this the Vulnerability Criterion (VC). Even though Eisgruber and Sager do not seem to distinguish between the two, VC and DC are importantly different. We could say that they serve to protect different dimensions of the culturally protean and legally elusive phenomenon of religion. For some purposes, religion is treated like race in law – it is defined in relation to the historically sedimented social meanings associated with certain practices and rituals, whereby dominant groups use state power to affirm and entrench hegemonic identities (Protestant, white, male) as normal, and to construe and disparage minority identities as deviant. Witness the process of the structural racialisation of religious minorities – Jews, Mormons, Catholics, Muslims – in US history. The analogy between race and religion allows Eisgruber and Sager to construe the wrong of state religious endorsement, from an egalitarian standpoint, as an expressive wrong – a wrong connected to the communication of messages of disparagement or exclusion of minorities.

From a VC perspective, religion functions as a third-person, externally defined category of social classification – by contrast to DC, which picks out the first-person, subjective dimensions of religious experience. So, from a VC perspective, a state which proudly proclaims its Christian identity commits an 'expressive wrong', by signifying to minorities that they are outsiders; that they do not belong, on the same terms, to the political community. Regardless of whether members of those minorities themselves see their religion as a source of deep, serious, moral commitments, official endorsement of the majority religion makes their non-Christian identity relevant – negatively – to their civic status. So, it is exclusionary for a state school to adorn classrooms with Christian crucifixes *even if* members of non-Christian groups do not see membership in such groups as a source of deep ethical commitment for them. By analogy, US segregation laws disparaged Afro-Americans, not because they denigrated Afro-American culture and ways of life, but because they construed blackness as a negative ascriptive identity, a marker of subordination and inferiority. So what VC picks out, by contrast to DC, are those dimensions of the socially constructed meanings of religion that structurally resemble other suspect categories of oppression and domination, such as race and gender.

It seems, therefore, that Eisgruber and Sager's theory contains two intriguingly different answers to the 'equality of what?' question. On the one hand, people's ability to act in accordance with their deep beliefs should not be subjected to unequal state burdens (DC) and, on the other hand, the state should not endorse the symbols and rituals of dominant religions for fear of disparaging racial-like minorities (VC). The difference between the two conceptions is obscured by the authors' equal liberty principle: 'no-one should be disparaged on grounds of the spiritual foundations of their deep commitments' (Eisgruber and Sager 2007: 52). Yet DC and VC point to different benchmarks for the fair treatment of religion: for some purposes, religious beliefs, identities and rituals should be treated like racial and gender identities, from a collective, structural, contextual and third-person perspective; while for other purposes, they should be treated like deep moral, comprehensive commitments, from an individualised, case-by-case and first-person perspective. Does this dual-track egalitarian reductionist theory, however, tell the whole story of the constitutional treatment of religion? There are reasons to doubt this is the case: Eisgruber and Sager's coherentist project – to demonstrate that, for legal purposes, religion is not *sui generis* and can be analogised with other social phenomena – is doomed to fail.

Consider the teaching of religion in public schools. On Eisgruber and Sager's interpretation, it is problematic because of the risk of disparagement of non-adherents to the favoured religion, in a context of compulsory and state-funded education. However, many controversial topics are taught in schools, which a range of different groups may find objectionable; yet First Amendment strictures against endorsement only apply to religion.[71] One possible explanation for this is that state schools – and more generally, political authorities – are deemed incompetent judges of truth in religion, in a way in which they are not in relation to other controversial topics.[72] Eisgruber and Sager reject this plausible 'epistemic' explanation of the ban on religious teaching in school. They suggest that there is little reason to suppose that political authorities are better qualified to teach Plato's *Republic* and Hegel's *Phenomenology of Spirit* than they are to teach as gospel the New Testament.[73] The reason they can teach the former, but not the latter, is, in their view, because of the profound equality-based issues – concerns about the disparagement of minorities and the like – raised by sectarian teaching in a public school. What are we to make of this argument? Eisgruber and Sager are right to point out that the question of expertise arises in the same way for (what are standardly considered to be) philosophical as opposed to theological topics. However, what is in question is which experts the state is permitted to entrust with its authority to teach in classrooms. And here it is doubtful that the reason why theological expertise is not on a par with philosophical expertise is because of the exclusionary and disparaging nature of religious teachings. For consider the range of topics that may be normally taught or discussed in schools: anti-racism, sexual education, the legitimacy of foreign wars, environmentalism, the death penalty, the historical treatment of Native Americans, Marxist philosophy and so forth. No doubt many citizens feel excluded and offended by such teachings, and no doubt it would be discriminatory for the state to include or exclude private speakers from a public forum based on their positions about these issues. Yet it is not a priori impermissible for the state to inculcate political 'orthodoxies' (such as gender equality and anti-racism) nor to let teachers debate controversial topics (such as Marxism or the death penalty) with their students. But it is impermissible for state teachers to teach or discuss theological topics. Creedal beliefs, in particular, may not be presented as statements about the truth (religious instruction) nor can they, generally, be subjected to critical discussion (whether secular or theologically based) within schools.[74]

Why not? What the ban on state teaching of religion refers to is a kind of *epistemic integrity* which has (historically) prevented the state from interfering in matters that are not within its remit. This, as Steven Smith has recently reminded us, is the original meaning of the separation between state and Church, which assumed the existence of two separate jurisdictions competing for sovereign power over and across their allocated 'this-worldly' and 'other-worldly' spheres of competence.[75] Such a two-realm conception of religious freedom is precisely what the egalitarian theory of religious freedom seeks to dispense with. But, fascinatingly, Eisgruber and Sager's heroic attempt does not succeed in displacing this older, *sui generis* view of religion in favour of their own reductionist, individualistic and egalitarian approach. Neither the ban on the teaching of religion in US state schools, nor religious exemptions from employment laws (and notably the ministerial exception) can be accounted for by their theory of equal liberty. Religious associations, *qua* religious, suffer burdens (under Non-Establishment) and enjoy benefits (under Free Exercise) which no comparable association has at its disposal (because there is no comparable association). Only they can claim a kind of epistemic integrity which regulates their relationship, *qua* collective agents, with the collective agent of the state. Call this the Integrity Criterion (IC). For some (admittedly limited) purposes, religion seems to be singled out and treated in US law in a *sui generis* way, as an autonomous sphere of human life and action, regulated by specific doctrines and standards.

Note that IC, by contrast to VC and DC, does not provide a benchmark for comparison; rather, it is one criterion which picks out the special and unique – non-reducible – features of the legal treatment of religion. A theory, such as Eisgruber and Sager's, which provides no plausible justification of its own for this singling out, nor considers the possibility that it is irreconcilable with the theory's far-reaching egalitarianism, is at best an incomplete, and at worst a self-contradictory, theory of religious freedom. Eisgruber and Sager simply cannot hold on both to their project of constitutional coherence and to their reductionist interpretation of religion. The US Constitution does give a special place to religion, and this cannot be accounted for by drawing analogies, however creative, between religion and other social beliefs and practices. Neither the Depth Criterion (DC) nor the Vulnerability Criterion (VC) succeed in providing a plausible currency of equality between religious and non-religious claims; and the Integrity Criterion (IC) puts the very possibility of comparability between them into question.

* * *

In this chapter, I have argued that Eisgruber and Sager's theory fails on its own terms. This failure, I have further suggested, is symptomatic of the difficulties encountered by liberal theory in fitting the concept of religious freedom into an egalitarian framework. At this point, a legitimate objection may be formulated. Could a more philosophically ambitious, less narrowly legalist liberal egalitarian theory avoid the pitfalls of Eisgruber and Sager's narrowly coherentist project? After all, why should liberal egalitarian philosophers be constrained by the limitations of US constitutional theory? The answer to this question is that something like the First Amendment paradigm – namely, the view that religion must be uniquely protected and contained – also shapes, albeit in more subtle and discrete ways, much of contemporary liberal egalitarian theory.

There are two desiderata that egalitarian theories of religious freedom must meet if they are not to run into the insuperable problems encountered by Eisgruber and Sager. First, they must *not be doctrinally coherentist*. If religion really is only a sub-set of a broader class of beliefs, identities or practices, which should be treated on a par with them, then large areas of existing law (which carve out special protections or special prohibitions for religion) become normatively indefensible. Fortunately, normative philosophers, by contrast to legal scholars, are not beholden to constitutional coherence. So they can bite the bullet and argue that the special treatment afforded religion *qua* religion in the law has lost any normative purchase in contemporary society. This would allow them to explain away constitutional tenets such as the special ban on state aid to religion and the ministerial exception as archaic remnants of the discredited 'two-realm' theory. Instead, they would start from the idea that the liberal state must be decidedly post-secular and take account of the deep pluralism of values, ideas and identities, both religious and non-religious, in contemporary societies. Second, egalitarian theories of religious freedom must be *more complexly egalitarian*. We saw that Eisgruber and Sager struggled to answer the 'equality of what?' question, and alternated between different standards – depth and vulnerability, for example – in their search for appropriate benchmarks of egalitarian comparison. Ultimately, their theory seemed too ad hoc, because it failed to include factors such as depth and vulnerability into a more complex metric of equality, and into a broader theory of justice.

At least two liberal egalitarian theories, those of Rawls (1971) and Dworkin (2011), *prima facie* meet both desiderata. Although they differ in important ways, they both avoid many of the problems which plagued Eisgruber and Sager's approach. Liberalism, for them, is not a coherentist project and is not textually bound by US First Amendment jurisprudence. The liberal state should be committed to show equal respect to all individuals, regardless of the particular conceptions of the good or ethical views, religious and secular, which they hold dear. Rawls' and Dworkin's liberalism, therefore, is more radically reductionist than Eisgruber and Sager's constitutional theory. It is also more complexly egalitarian: it combines an account of equal basic rights and liberties (including freedom of conscience) with a commitment to socio-economic equality of opportunity. It further asks which 'morally arbitrary features' or instances of 'bad luck' (such as disability, race and other markers of vulnerability) unfairly prevent individuals from accessing equal opportunities. This more complex egalitarianism offers a promising framework for integrating DC and VC, by disaggregating the concept of religion into distinct values within an overarching theory of justice.

Such a complexly egalitarian theory, embedded in a broader theory of liberal justice, is a more cogent way of defending the post-secular state than Eisgruber and Sager's constitutional theory. What remains to be assessed is whether normative post-secular liberalism entirely succeeds in displacing the traditional liberal commitment to a uniquely special separation between state and religion. There is little doubt that something called religion – a complex notion involving faith and belief, conscientious duty, a sense of the sacred, valued communal practices, comprehensive scope, ultimate moral concern, the pursuit of extra-temporal goods, a divine authority, totalising social institutions, historically salient collective identities, divisive and controversial belief systems and so forth[76] – has provided the structural template out of which liberal political philosophers, from John Locke onwards, have conceptualised and justified the liberal state. As a result, the Euro-Atlantic conception of the secular state, as Amy Gutmann has acutely noted, is grounded in an ideal of 'two-way protection' – protection of religion from the state, and protection of the state from religion.[77] Post-secular egalitarian liberalism attempts radically to dispense with two-way protection. But does it succeed in this radical endeavour, and should it? My hunch is that, much like Eisgruber and Sager, normative liberal philosophers yet have to consider the full implications of the (still embryonic) post-secular political theory. In particular, they will need to reflect further on questions such as: is anything of value lost in the reduction of religion to 'conceptions of the good' or 'ethical views'? Can the liberal norm of religious non-establishment be subsumed under a general principle of liberal neutrality? In what sense, if any, is liberal justification, and public reason, secular? In the end, I suspect, political philosophers, not only constitutional lawyers, will have to grapple with the complex epistemological, historical and ethical questions raised by the legal–political construction of religion in the Euro-Atlantic liberal tradition.

Notes

1 This paper has appeared in *Legal Theory* 20:1 (2014).

2 Christopher Eisgruber and Lawrence Sager (2007) *Religious Freedom and the Constitution*, Cambridge Mass.: Harvard University Press.

3 The idea of an egalitarian theory of religious freedom is insightfully adduced (though not fully explicated) in Abner S. Greene (2009) 'Three Theories of Religious Equality ... and of Exemptions', *Texas Law Review*, Vol. 87, No. 963, 963–1007. See also Noah Feldman (2002) 'From Liberty to Equality: The Transformation of the Establishment Clause', *California Law Review,* Vol. 90, No. 3, 673–731.

4 Accommodationists focus on the Free Exercise clause and argue that religious freedom should be specially protected by the state; separationists focus on the Establishment clause and argue that there should be a 'wall of separation' between state and religion. The two positions are neither mutually incompatible nor exclusive of other interpretations of the two clauses, but they provide a useful focus for my discussion here. For comprehensive literature reviews and classifications, see Kent Greenawalt (2008) *Religion and the Constitution*, Princeton: Princeton University Press, 2 Vols. and Micah Schwartzman (2012) 'What if Religion is not Special?', *Virginia Public Law and Legal Theory Research Paper* No. 2012–03.

5 Michael W. McConnell (1985) 'Accommodation of Religion', *Supreme Court Review*, 1–59; Michael W. McConnell (2000) 'The Problem of Singling Out Religion', *DePaul Law Review*. Vol. 1, No. 5, 9–12.

6 For similar views of the special and unique nature of religious freedom, see Douglas Laycock (1996) 'Religious Liberty as Liberty', 7 *Journal of Contemporary Legal Issues* 313; Thomas Berg (2007) 'Can Religious Liberty Be Protected as Equality?', *Texas Law Review*, Vol. 85, No. 5; Andrew Koppelman (2006) 'Is It Fair to Give Religion Special Treatment?', *University of Illinois Law Review* 571; Steven D. Smith (2004) 'Non-Establishment Under God? The Nonsectarian Principle', *University of San Diego Public Law Research Paper* No. 04–08; Abner S. Greene, 'Three Theories of Religious Equality'. More generally, and in a European context, see Rex Ahdar and Ian Leigh (2005) *Religious Freedom in the Liberal State*, Oxford: Oxford University Press.

7 John Rawls (1971) *Theory of Justice*, Cambridge, Mass.: Harvard University Press, p. 206.

8 Ronald Dworkin (2011) *Justice for Hedgehogs*, Cambridge, Mass.: Harvard University Press, p. 376.

9 William Marshall (1983) 'Solving the Free Exercise Dilemma: Free Exercise as Expression', *Minnesota Law Review*, Vol. 67, No. 545; Michael A. Paulsen (1986) 'Religion, Equality, and the Constitution: An Equal Protection Approach to Establishment Clause Adjudication', *Notre Dame Law Review*, Vol. 61, 311, 317.

10 Gérard Bouchard and Charles Taylor (2008) *Fonder l'avenir. Le temps de la conciliation. Commission de consultation sur les pratiques d'accommodements reliées aux différences culturelles*, Archives nationales du Québec; Cécile Laborde (2009) 'Républicanisme critique, républicanisme conservateur: repenser les "accommodements raisonnables" ', *Critique Internationale*, July–September, 19–33.

11 See special issue of *International Migration* (2006) 'The Danish Cartoon Affair: Free Speech Racism, Islamism and Integration', with contributions by Erik Bleich, Tariq Modood, Randall Hansen, Brendan O'Leary and Joseph H. Carens, 44, 5; Robert Post (2007) 'Religion and Freedom of Speech: Portraits of Muhammad', *Constellations*, Vol. 14, No. 1, 72–90; Sune Lægaard (2007) 'The Cartoon Controversy: Offence, Identity, Oppression?', *Political Studies*, Vol. 55, 481–498; Talal Asad, Judith Butler, Wendy Brown and Saba Mahmood (2009) *Is Critique Secular? Blasphemy, Injury, and Free Speech*, Berkeley: University of California Press; Cécile Laborde (2011) 'Rights, Wrongs and the Right to Do Wrong. Jytte Klausen and the Political Theory of the Danish Cartoon Controversy', *Perspectives on Politics*, September, 603–605.

12 Geoffrey Brahm Levey and Tariq Modood (eds) (2009) *Secularism, Religion and Multicultural Citizenship*, Cambridge: Cambridge University Press; Cécile Laborde (2008) *Critical Republicanism. The Hijab Controversy and Political Philosophy*, Oxford: Oxford University Press.

13 Daniel Brudney (2005) 'On Non-Coercive Establishment', *Political Theory*, Vol. 33, No. 6, 812–839; Cécile Laborde (2011) 'Political Liberalism, Religion and the Separation-Establishment Debate', *Journal of Political Philosophy,* Early View, July; Joshua Cohen (forthcoming) 'Establishment, Exclusion, and Democracy's Public Reason', in *Reasons and Recognition*, Oxford: Oxford University Press.

14 Greenawalt, *Religion and the Constitution*, Vol. 2, pp. 182–191; Nussbaum, *Liberty of Conscience*, New York: Basic Books pp. 229, 253, 265–266, 270.

15 Nussbaum, *Liberty of Conscience.*

16 Ian Leigh (forthcoming) 'The European Court of Human Rights and Religious Neutrality', in Gavin D'Costa, Malcolm Evans, Tariq Modood and Julian Rivers (eds) *Religion in a Liberal State: Cross-Disciplinary Reflections*, Cambridge: Cambridge University Press; Peter Danchin (2011) 'Islam in the Secular Nomos of the European Court of Human Rights', *Michigan Journal of International Law*, Vol. 32; Ronan McCrea (2010) *Religion and the Public Order of the European Union*, Oxford: Oxford University Press.

17 More recent egalitarian theories of religious freedom include Charles Taylor and Jocelyn Maclure (2011) *Secularism and Freedom of Conscience*, Cambridge Mass: Harvard University Press; Schwartzman (forthcoming) 'What if Religion is not Special?; Ronald Dworkin (forthcoming) *Religion without God.*

18 Eisgruber and Sager, *Religious Freedom and the Constitution*, p. 6.

19 Ibid., pp. 202–203.

20 See, for example, Brian Barry (2001) *Culture and Equality: An Egalitarian Critique of Multiculturalism*, Cambridge: Polity Press; William Marshall (1989) 'The Case Against the Constitutionally Compelled Free Exercise Exemption', *Journal of Law and Religion*, Vol. 7, No. 2, 363–414.

21 Eisgruber and Sager, *Religious Freedom and the Constitution*, pp. 202–203.

22 On the idea of neutrality between 'religion' and 'non-religion', see William Marshall (2000) 'What Is the Matter With Equality?: An Assessment of the Equal Treatment of Religion and Non-religion in First Amendment Jurisprudence', *Indiana Law Journal*, Vol. 75, 193.

23 Eisgruber and Sager, *Religious Freedom and the Constitution*, p. 4.

24 Ibid., p. 88. This is where their egalitarian theory of religious freedom departs most sharply from accommodationist theories: Eisgruber and Sager have no objection to the even-handed enforcement of such regulatory frameworks, even when they override religious concerns.

25 Ibid., p. 90.

26 *Fraternal Order of Police Newark Lodge v. City of Newark*, 1999.

27 Eisgruber and Sager, *Religious Freedom and the Constitution*, p. 89.

28 Ibid., pp. 14–15.

29 Ibid., p. 92.

30 Ibid., p. 52.
31 Ibid., p. 59.
32 Ibid., p. 70.
33 Ibid., p. 17.
34 Ibid., pp. 212–215. In the particular case of Cleveland, however, they note that the absence of good-quality public schools provided insufficient options for parents, and generated an unfair advantage to the religious schools.
35 Ibid., p. 19.
36 Ibid., p. 122.
37 Ibid., pp. 150–152.
38 Ibid., p. 128.
39 Ibid., p. 164.
40 See Christopher Eisgruber and Lawrence Sager (2007) 'Chips Off Our Block? A Reply to Berg, Greenawalt, Lupu and Tuttle', *Texas Law Review*, Vol. 85, 1273, 1274. They argue that a municipal sign such as 'Finneville – a Town for Straight Folks' would be unconstitutional on this ground: 'race, sex and sexual orientation should all be constitutionally protected against disparagement'.
41 Eisgruber and Sager, *Religious Freedom and the Constitution*, pp. 170, 192.
42 Ibid., p. 126.
43 Peter Westen (1982) 'The Empty Idea of Equality', *Harvard Law Review,* Vol. 95, No. 3, 537–596; Joseph Raz (1986) *The Morality of Freedom*, Oxford: Clarendon Press, p. 240.
44 I use post-secular here in a specific sense, to refer to a state that de-constitutionalises religion and does not apply special and unique legal standards to it.
45 For a similar account of equal opportunities and religious exemptions, see Jonathan Quong (2006) 'Cultural Exemptions, Expensive Tastes, and Equal Opportunities', *Journal of Applied Philosophy*, Vol. 23, No. 1, 53–71.
46 For critiques of Eisgruber and Sager along similar lines, see Jeremy Webber (2008) 'Understanding the Religion in Freedom of Religion', in Peter Cane, Carolyn Evans and Zöe Robinson (eds), *Law and Religion in Theoretical and Historical Context*, Cambridge: Cambridge University Press, pp. 26–43, at p. 35; Thomas Berg (2007) 'Can Religious Liberty Be Protected as Equality?', *Texas Law Review*, Vol. 85, No. 5; McConnell, 'On the Problem of Singling out Religion'; Greene, 'Three Theories of Religious Equality', 1006.
47 Eisgruber and Sager, *Religious Freedom*, p. 101.
48 Ibid., p. 101.
49 Ibid., p. 104.
50 For a thoughtful interpretation of Eisgruber and Sager's theory by appeal to Taylor's notion of 'strong evaluation', see Koppelman, 'Is It Fair to Give Religion Special Treatment?
51 Christopher Eisgruber and Lawrence Sager (2009) 'Does it Matter What Religion Is?' *Notre Dame Law Review*, Vol. 84, 807–836.
52 Christopher Eisgruber and Lawrence Sager (1994) 'The *Vulnerability* of Conscience: The Constitutional Basis for Protecting Religious Conduct' *University of Chicago Law Review*, Vol. 61, 1245.
53 See, for example, the essays in Paul Kelly (ed.) (2002) *Multiculturalism Reconsidered. 'Culture and Equality' and its Critics*, Cambridge: Polity Press. For an attempt to explore the two dimensions of religion as 'ideas' and as 'identity', see William Marshall (1996) 'Religion as Ideas: Religion as Identity', *Journal of Contemporary Legal Issues*, Vol. 7, 385.
54 But one question they do not address is whether, if people identify with their beliefs, they should not take responsibility for them. In other words, this formulation does not quite get to the heart of the luck egalitarian problem, namely, that people must be compensated for things they cannot change or control; but must take responsibility for

their own preferences and beliefs, however these were acquired. The analogy between a medically required and a religious-required beard, therefore, is not as straightforward as Eisgruber and Sager assume.

55 The Depth Criterion is in fact a compound of a number of different features associated with religious beliefs, such as the following: they are particularly weighty and serious; they invoke demanding duties of observance; they are rooted in conscience; they are of 'ultimate concern' to individuals; they address profound moral questions; they are comprehensive and cover the whole of life; they are central to individual identity; they are key to personal integrity. Eisgruber and Sager deny that they need to provide a definition of religion, but their understanding of what it means for a belief to be 'deep', 'serious' or 'moral' appeals to one or more of the features which are traditionally associated with religion, yet are also present in secular worldviews too. Note that the implicit definition of religion used is not, however, uncontroversial. To get off the ground, the reductionist approach needs to deny that whatever it is that makes religious beliefs 'deep' in the relevant sense (the sense that matters to equality) cannot exclusively lie in their appeal to a divine authority or to the prospects of an after-life. But how do reductionist theorists answer the charge that they are able to analogise religious with secular beliefs only at the cost of denying precisely what makes religious beliefs religious? Reductionists have two answers to this challenge: conceptual (the singled out features do not in fact apply to all commonly recognised religions – many religions are this-worldly and/or non-theistic – and therefore assume an unacceptably sectarian view of what a religion is) and substantive (there is no reason to think that belief in God is what gives moral weight to otherwise deep, respectable, foundational ethical views).

56 I have explored a version of this problem in another egalitarian theory of religious freedom, that of Taylor and McLure, in Cécile Laborde (2012) 'Protecting Freedom of Conscience in the Secular Age', *The Immanent Frame* (April). See http://blogs.ssrc.org/tif/2012/04/23/protecting-freedom-of-religion-in-the-secular-age/ (accessed on 1 May 2014).

57 For the view that taking seriously people's beliefs implies asking them to take (at least some) responsibility for them, see Peter Jones (1994) 'Bearing the Consequences of Belief', *Journal of Political Philosophy*, Vol. 2, No. 1, 24–43.

58 Eisgruber and Sager, *Religious Freedom and the Constitution*, pp. 117–118.

59 Ibid., pp. 113–114.

60 Perry Dane (2010) 'Constitutional Law and Religion', in Dennis Patterson (ed.), *Blackwell Companion to Philosophy of Law and Legal Theory*, Oxford: Blackwell.

61 *Smith* – the landmark Supreme Court decision of 1990, which overturned *Sherbert* by positing that there is no constitutional requirement to allow religious exemptions from general laws – did not significantly alter this situation. It was overturned by Congress through the Religious Freedom Restoration Act (RFRA 1993), and only partly reinstated in *Boerne*. The current situation is that RFRA still has constitutional status at the federal level. Furthermore, even when exemptions are not constitutionally required, they often are constitutionally permitted. There are an estimated 2,000 statutory exemptions from general laws in the US (from compulsory vaccinations to prison diets). Out of these, only a few have successfully been extended to non-religious convictions (parents can object to compulsory vaccinations for their children on secular grounds in 20 of the US states, for example). There is, however, an area of potential growth for secular conscientious claims, concerning medical research and controversial medical procedures, such as assisted suicide and stem cell research (where claimants appeal to a secularised view of the inherent dignity of human life). In Canada, where religion has formally no special constitutional status, eco-centric vegetarianism has also been recognised as entitled to 'reasonable accommodation' on the same grounds as religious comprehensive, categorical belief systems (*Maurice v. Canada*, 2002). cf. Taylor and Maclure, *Secularism and Freedom of Conscience*.

62 Eisgruber and Sager, *Religious Freedom and the Constitution,* p. 116.

63 Ibid., p. 116.

64 This is how I interpret Eisgruber and Sager's reference to the possibility that Mother Sherbert has 'secular moral convictions'.

65 They do consider a hypothetical case of unemployment benefit for a pacifist who objects to working in armaments. This is in fact a version of *Seeger,* applied to the workplace (ibid., pp. 114–116). Tellingly, Eisgruber and Sager distinguish this worker from Mother Sherbert by suggesting that his claim, unlike hers, but like Seeger's, bears 'a relation to religion' – which, again, begs the question by re-introducing a maximalist definition of religion. Intriguingly, they do not consider *prima facie* hard cases of real-world, secular conscientious objection, such as possible secular parallels to the *Wisconsin v. Yoder* case (1972). *Yoder* allowed Amish parents to withdraw their children from school aged 14, as an exemption from laws of compulsory education until 16, and did so by appeal to freedom of religion. The Court insisted that such exemptions could only be granted to religious groups – presumably preempting demands for school exemptions from (*inter alia*) radical leftwing libertarians, whose opposition to education was political. It is not clear whether, and on which grounds, Eisgruber and Sager would disagree, and it is unfortunate that they do not discuss *Yoder.*

66 Ibid., pp. 64–65, *Boy Scouts of America v. Dale* (2000).

67 Ira C. Lupu and Robert W. Tuttle (2007) 'The Limits of Equal Liberty as a Theory of Religious Freedom', *Texas Law Review*, April, 1–36, at 29–33. A strong doctrine of ministerial exception was recently asserted by the Supreme Court in *Hosanna-Tabor Lutheran Church and School v. Equal Employment Opportunity Commission* (January 2012).

68 They suggest, however, that there might be a strategic rationale for carving more extensive protections for churches than would be allowed by the strict demands of equal liberty. It is that judges are prone to prejudicial determinations about the risk of discrimination by religious groups, and undue interference with employment relationships that are essential to associational autonomy. Eisgruber and Sager, *Religious Freedom and the Constitution,* 249–252. I am grateful to Chris Eisgruber for directing me to this important passage.

69 Much more remains to be said, however, about what it means for a religious organization to provide a public service 'on the same terms' as a non-religious one. The issue of direct public funding for faith-based initiatives is a complex and controversial one, under-examined by Eisgruber and Sager.

70 Winnifred Sullivan, 'After Secularization: Governing Through Spiritual Care', unpublished manuscript, on file with author.

71 Lupu and Tuttle,' The Limits of Equal Liberty'; Greene, 'Three Theories of Religious Equality'.

72 Greenawalt, *Religion and the Constitution,* Vol. 2, pp. 466–467. For an extended and subtle discussion, see also Kent Greenawalt (2005) *Does God Belong in Public Schools?* Princeton: Princeton University Press.

73 Eisgruber and Sager, 'Chips Off Our Block?', 1273.

74 However, state schools can permissibly teach about religion in two ways: they can present them as historical and sociological objects of study; and they can criticise religiously-inspired commitments when these openly contradict basic rights and democratic principles.

75 Steven D. Smith (2010) *The Disenchantment of Secular Discourse*, Cambridge Mass.: Harvard University Press, Chapter 4.

76 In this paper, I have deliberately avoided providing a precise definition of religion. What should be apparent is that, while many authors work with a common-sense, 'you-know-it-when-you-see-it' understanding of the notion, they select, for the purpose of their analysis, very different features of it. In future work, I aim to

reformulate a viable egalitarian project, which dispenses with the category of religion altogether and instead pursues a strategy of dis-aggregation of the compound concept of religion.

77 Amy Gutmann (2003) *Identity in Democracy*, Princeton, NJ: Princeton University Press, pp. 158–159.

3 Religious pluralism in a deliberative democracy

Cristina Lafont

In all liberal democracies the neutrality of the state is at the core of the debates on religion and politics. However, in the American context, this debate is framed in terms of a broader debate on the ethics of democratic citizenship (i.e., on the question of what kinds of reasons and considerations citizens may use as a basis to justify the coercive power they exercise over one another, so that such coercion can be considered legitimate), whereas this issue is much less prominent in European debates. However, I have the impression that the debate on the ethics of democratic citizenship could actually be very helpful for addressing some of the issues that are peculiar to European debates – e.g., the debates on banning the Islamic headscarf from public places – which have no counterpart in the American context. Thus, I would like to first indicate what motivates the debate on the ethics of democratic citizenship in the American context in particular and then show why, in spite of all differences, this debate is equally needed and relevant in the European context (pp. 46–49). In a second step, I present my specific answer to the question of the obligations of democratic citizenship in a deliberative democracy (pp. 49–54) and then show how it can help illuminate specific European debates on the presence of religion in the public sphere (pp. 55–58). I conclude with some brief remarks on the democratic implications of the concept of public reason and democratic citizenship that I defend (p. 58).

The debate on the ethics of citizenship in the USA and its relevance in Europe

The neutrality of the state is entrenched in the US Constitution as a way of securing equal rights and freedoms for all citizens. This normative goal has two components, which are expressed in the two "religion clauses" found in the First Amendment to the Constitution: the "establishment clause" that prohibits the establishment of a national religion as well as the preferential treatment of any one religion over another by the state and the "free exercise clause" that protects citizen's right to the free exercise of religion. Naturally, these aims oftentimes conflict and this generates hard cases similar to those debated in Europe, such as the provision of public funding for religious activities, the allowance of voluntary prayer in public schools or the display of religious symbols (like the Ten

Commandments) in public places. Despite this similarity, an important difference between the American and European debates arises out of the fact that most American citizens are religious rather than secular. In distinction to Europe, secularism is not part of the majority culture. In fact, nonbelievers are a minority group that is rarely mentioned or represented as part of the official public culture. Now, in the context of a country with a majority of religious citizens, the main problem with the presence of religion in the public sphere is not only that it challenges the neutrality of the state, but also that it influences the outcome of democratic decision-making processes regarding the fundamental rights and freedoms of fellow citizens. What is at stake in debates about same-sex marriage, abortion, euthanasia, stem-cell research, etc. – which are deeply influenced by the religious beliefs of citizens – is the legitimacy of democratic decision-making in light of the possibility that a majority, on the basis of their religious beliefs, may illicitly restrict the rights and freedoms of fellow citizens. This is why in the American context, the debate on the presence of religion in the public sphere has been framed in terms of the ethics of democratic citizenship.

Looking at Europe from this perspective, it seems to me that here we find the opposite situation. Secularism is not merely a reflection of the neutrality of the state, but it is also an important ingredient of the majority culture. In distinction from the American experience, in the context of European countries, the secular state's neutrality is not seen as simply an institutional tool to protect the rights and freedoms of all citizens, but also as an expression of the collective identity of the majority of the population. Against the background of a secular majority culture, it is not surprising that the European debates have focused much less on the issue of what role religious beliefs should play in political deliberation in the public sphere. For, in comparison to the American social milieu, the possibility that a religious majority may curtail the rights and freedoms of fellow citizens on the basis of their religious beliefs seems quite remote in Europe. Nonetheless, as I said before, I have the impression that the American debate on the ethics of democratic citizenship is highly relevant to the European debates on the presence of religion in the public sphere. But before I try to illustrate this claim with some examples, let me try to motivate its relevance by addressing first the most obvious point of overlap between both debates: namely, the question of the neutrality of the state.

Taking the US Constitution as a guide, the principle of neutrality requires that the state finds a balance between two distinct aims: the non-preferential treatment of any religion over another or over no religion, which obviously includes the non-establishment of any particular religion as the national religion, and the protection of the free exercise of all religions. On both counts, European countries are far from doing an ideal job. From the establishment of the Anglican Church as official religion in England and the historical privileges conceded to Christian denominations in most European countries (e.g., public funding provided to Catholic churches and schools in Spain, Italy, France, Poland, etc.) to the official disregard of the obligation to protect in similar ways the right to the free exercise of non-Christian religions, notably Islam. It is not coincidental,

I think, that the wide range of privileges and financial support offered to a variety of Christian denominations by different European states creates a direct problem once non-Christian religions like Islam appear on the scene. The emergence of non-Christian religions puts pressure on the actual lack of neutrality of the state in European countries. As a consequence, these states may be forced to live up to their official secularism and in fact disentangle themselves from the long historical tradition of conceding preferential treatment to those religions practiced by the majority. The popular claim that the presence of Islamic symbols, beliefs and practices in European countries threatens the secular state can hardly be understood without translating it into what seems to be the *real* issue: namely, that the presence of Islam in Europe threatens the possibility of maintaining the pattern of preferential treatment and privileges that different Christian denominations currently enjoy in European states. Without such a translation, inattentive outsiders would have a hard time understanding how the popular debate regarding the presence of Islam in Europe can so easily oscillate between the claim that European countries are secular and the claim that they are Christian. Clearly, Europeans must make up their minds, for they cannot have it both ways. This patent inconsistency in part explains the puzzling fact that such a relatively small presence of citizens of Islamic faith in European countries can produce such agitated reactions. Their presence confronts European countries with a choice they seem equally unwilling to make: either to live up to their official commitment to the neutrality of the secular state as a means to protect the rights and freedoms of all citizens, the Muslim minority included – this would require that these countries dismantle the historical privileges conceded to (mainly) Christian denominations – or to end the current discrimination against Islam and offer Muslims the same kind of support, funding, protections and accommodations that other religions in fact enjoy,[1] in spite of the official doctrine of state neutrality.

Now, regarding the either/or that European countries face, it is hard to take a clear-cut stand between a strictly neutralist and a more accommodative state model. From a purely normative point of view, and assuming all other things to be equal, it seems to me that the more neutral the state, the better it is suited to protect the rights and freedoms of all citizens, most notably those of secular citizens.[2] However, some deviations from strict neutrality may nonetheless be needed to protect the right to free exercise of religion in particular circumstances. For example, if members of some religions are too poor to have effective access to the means or facilities needed for religious practice, then some form of state support may be the best means for the goal of securing effective rights to the free exercise of religion for those citizens. This indicates that the line between a policy of strict neutrality and a policy of positive accommodation is fuzzy and cannot be drawn too sharply in practice.

Moreover, in light of the high diversity of historical circumstances in which different countries find themselves, it seems impossible to extract a "one size fits all" political agenda from the ideal of state neutrality, i.e., an agenda that would be suitable for implementation in all contexts and at all times. This seems true of all political ideals, actually. From a purely normative point of view, it may be plausible to claim that a democratic republic is the ideal form of government, but adopting a political agenda to immediately dismantle all European monarchies on the basis of that ideal may not be an equally plausible claim. Similarly, whether or not the disestablishment of the Anglican Church in England or the removal of public funding for Catholic schools in Spain is the right political goal under current historical circumstances cannot be simply read-off from the normative ideal of state neutrality itself. Sensible political action always involves striking a difficult balance between different goals and risks, opportunities and constraints, short and long-term considerations, etc. Consequently, since there are always alternative ways to strike such a balance, the right political choice in the specific circumstances of each political community ought to be determined by its own citizens through an ongoing democratic process of political opinion- and will-formation.

But, if this is so, we can see why the question of the ethics of democratic citizenship that is at the core of the American debate on the role of religion in the public sphere is equally relevant to the European debate. If in democratic societies it is ultimately up to the citizens to collectively determine the specific ways in which their institutions need to be shaped and transformed in light of their political goals, ideals and historical circumstances, then it is crucial to figure out what kinds of reasons and considerations form an appropriate basis upon which citizens can make those fundamental political decisions so that the coercive power they exercise over one another is legitimate. In what follows, I would like to offer a specific answer to this question and to show, by way of example, how it can be applied to the European debates on the presence of religious symbols in the public sphere.

Mutual accountability: the priority of proper political reasons in public debates

The debate on the kinds of reasons that citizens can use to justify the coercive power they exercise over one another has become very prominent in recent years, due to the increased popularity of the deliberative model of democracy. The ideal of a deliberative democracy contains many attractive features that explain this popularity. Within the context of a discussion on religious pluralism, perhaps the most important feature is that it promises citizens some measure of protection against political domination by majorities. Other models of democracy (notably aggregative models) can only promise citizens the fair treatment involved in the right to vote, that is, in having the equal opportunity to influence the outcome of the democratic decision-making procedures in which they participate. However, it is obvious that the right to vote is compatible with a scenario in which some citizens systematically and repeatedly lose out when decisions are made in a majoritarian fashion. For permanent minorities, this right-to-vote version of equal opportunity can easily amount to the absence of any actual effective opportunity to prevent majoritarian outcomes that are unjust. In contrast, the deliberative model offers citizens some resources that can help them avoid the domination potentially exercised by a consolidated majority. The deliberative model can grant better reasons greater influence over outcomes, while still upholding to equal voting rights by requiring that democratic deliberation takes place before collective decisions are made if the outcomes of such decisions are to be considered legitimate. By adding this requirement, the deliberative model indicates a way in which minorities may be able to prevent political domination by the majority. Instead of resentfully biding their time until they can seize an opportunity for their group's own ascent to dominance, they can try to engage in public deliberation so as to show that their proposals are supported by better reasons and hold out realistic hope that the unforced force of the better argument, to use Habermas's expression, may move the majority to change their initial preferences. The idea that better reasons (and not just a higher numbers of votes) are what lends legitimacy to the outcomes of democratic decisions, is reflected in the criterion of democratic legitimacy that underlies the ideal of a deliberative democracy. According to this criterion, citizens owe one another justifications based on reasons that everyone can reasonably accept for coercive policies with which they all must comply. Only in this way can all citizens see themselves not simply as subject to the law but also as authors of the law, as the democratic ideal of self-government requires.

However, in light of the pluralism characteristic of democratic societies which encompass secular citizens as well as citizens of different faiths, it can hardly be expected that citizens will generally agree on what constitutes "acceptable reasons" for or against specific policies. What is acceptable to a Christian, say, may not be acceptable to a Muslim or to a secular citizen. If this is so, the deliberative ideal is doomed to fail, for it seems to subject citizens to mutually incompatible obligations. Here lies the key difficulty. According to the deliberative ideal, citizens who participate in public deliberation have the cognitive obligation of judging the policies under discussion strictly on their merits (instead of, say, their self-interest). In order to do so, they must examine all the relevant reasons and give priority to those reasons that support the better argument, whichever reasons these may turn out to be. But they also have the democratic obligation of providing reasons that are acceptable to others. And this requires them to give priority to generally acceptable reasons, whether or not they are the most compelling in any given case.

The potential conflict between these obligations poses a serious dilemma for a defense of the ideal of deliberative democracy. It is easy to imagine a scenario in which certain policies (e.g., on abortion or same-sex marriage) are morally objectionable to some citizens for exclusively religious reasons. Since religious reasons are a paradigmatic case of reasons that are not generally acceptable to secular citizens and to citizens of different faiths, the democratic obligation to provide a justification against these policies based on reasons that are generally acceptable to others would force these religious citizens either to be dishonest in their political advocacy (that is, to argue for something other than what they genuinely believe) or to withdraw from participation in political deliberation altogether. If citizens are forced to choose the first horn of the dilemma, public deliberation would not have the requisite cognitive properties. A deliberative practice in which participants cannot assume that all parties are being sincere could not count as a practice of argumentation that tracks the force of the better argument, and therefore such a practice could not lend any special legitimacy to its outcomes. If citizens are forced to choose the second horn of the dilemma, then public deliberation would not meet the criterion of democratic legitimacy, since it would fail to provide justifications based on reasons that the self-excluded citizens could reasonably accept.

Here lies the challenge for defending deliberative democracy. Can public deliberation under conditions of pluralism be structured in such a way that all democratic citizens are able to adopt their own cognitive stances within deliberation, whether these stances be religious or secular, such that they may reach genuine convictions in the deliberative process while nevertheless attempting to fulfill the democratic obligation of providing reasons that are acceptable to everyone, so as to justify coercive policies to which all must comply? In what follows, I would like to offer a proposal to show how an affirmative answer is possible.[3]

An essential element of my proposal is that it does not identify the pool of "generally acceptable reasons" with secular reasons, as authors such as Audi[4] or Habermas[5] do. Although religious reasons may be considered a paradigmatic case of reasons that are not generally acceptable to secular citizens and citizens of different faiths, it does not follow that all nonreligious reasons can be considered generally acceptable just in virtue of being secular. Nonreligious reasons that are based on different and conflicting comprehensive doctrines and conceptions of the good cannot be expected to be generally acceptable to all citizens under conditions of pluralism, regardless of whether or not they are secular. Here, my proposal sides with Rawls in identifying a narrower subset of nonreligious reasons, what he calls "public" or "properly political" reasons, as those that must be endorsed by all democratic citizens.[6] These are reasons based on those political values and ideals that are the very conditions of possibility for a democracy: the ideal of citizens as free and equal, and of society as a fair scheme of cooperation, which find expression in the constitutional principles to which citizens are bound in liberal democracies.[7] To the extent that an overlapping consensus around basic political values of freedom and equality can be expected among democratic citizens, these values provide the needed reservoir of generally acceptable reasons from which all citizens can draw to justify the coercive policies they advocate for their fellow citizens.

However, my proposal does not endorse Rawls's famous proviso, according to which religious reasons can be included in public deliberation but only provided that "in due course" proper political reasons are offered in support of whatever policies the religious reasons are supposed to support.[8] As I mentioned before, the obligation to offer corroborating public reasons leaves citizens two equally unacceptable options whenever the reasons they have in support of the policies they favor are not public reasons: (1) either to be disingenuous in their political advocacy or (2) to withdraw from political participation in the public sphere. In light of this difficulty, critics of the Rawlsian proposal have objected that the obligation to provide nonreligious reasons in support of policy proposals imposes an undue cognitive burden on religious citizens. As Wolterstorff argues:

> it belongs to the religious convictions of many religious people that *they ought to base* their decisions concerning fundamental issues of justice *on* their religious convictions. They do not view it as an option whether or not to do it.[9]

Rawls's proposal may seem plausible if one assumes that citizens will always have at their disposal two parallel pools of reasons to draw from. However, in cases of direct conflict between religious and nonreligious reasons, it seems that being religious consists precisely in giving priority to religious over nonreligious reasons in forming one's own convictions. If this is the case, so the objection goes, Rawls's "duty of civility" threatens the political integration of religious citizens in democratic societies.

However, if, following Wolterstorff's counter proposal, we simply drop the democratic obligation to offer reasons generally acceptable to others, it follows that a majority of religious citizens would be licensed to base their political decisions on their religious convictions and thereby impose coercive policies on other citizens without any obligation to give them reasons that they can reasonably accept.

As a way to avoid this unattractive alternative, Habermas proposes to interpret Rawls's proviso in terms of an "institutional translation proviso." He accepts the Rawlsian proviso regarding political deliberation at the institutional level of parliaments, courts, ministries and administrations, that is, in what he calls the *formal* public sphere. But he proposes to eliminate the requirement of providing corroborating nonreligious reasons in political deliberations in the *informal* public sphere whenever such reasons are not available. Ordinary citizens who participate in political advocacy in the informal public sphere can offer exclusively religious reasons in support of the policies they favor in the hope that they may be successfully translated into nonreligious reasons. But the obligation of translation should not fall exclusively on the shoulders of religious citizens. Instead, all citizens involved in public deliberation, secular citizens included, must share this obligation. This proposal is supposed to yield a more even distribution of cognitive burdens among citizens. On the one hand, religious citizens, like all citizens, must accept the neutrality of the state and therefore must accept that only nonreligious reasons count in determining coercive policies with which all citizens must comply. On the other hand, secular citizens, like all citizens, must share the burden of translating religious into nonreligious reasons. In order to do so, according to Habermas, secular citizens have to take religious reasons seriously and cannot deny their possible truth from the outset. They must open their mind to the possible truth of religious beliefs and reasons as a precondition for finding out whether they can be translated into secular ones.

Now, by shifting the burden of translation from religious to secular citizens, the dilemma facing religious citizens that we saw before comes to face secular citizens as well. For, whenever the reasons that they hold in support for favored policies happen to be of a secularist type that contradicts the possible truth of religious claims, it appears that in order to participate in public deliberation these secular citizens have no alternative but to be disingenuous and come up with alternative reasons that are independent of their authentic beliefs. However, if disallowing citizens to publicly adopt their own cognitive stance is unacceptable, it seems that this would be so whether those citizens have a religious or secularist stance. This problem is also aggravated by what is likely to strike many secular citizens as a disquieting additional obligation: namely, the obligation to open their minds to the possible truth of religious beliefs and reasons as a precondition for finding out whether they can be translated into public ones. Beyond its doubtful feasibility, this obligation seems to deprive secular citizens of the very same right to publicly adopt their own cognitive stance that the proposal aims to recognize for religious citizens. By imposing such additional burdens, Habermas's proposal opens itself to similar objections as those facing Rawls's proposal. Moreover, it is far from clear that his proposal offers religious citizens a way out of their own dilemma. For what is at stake in this debate is not so much whether religious citizens can express their religious convictions in the informal public sphere, but above all whether they can base their political decisions on those religious convictions, as Wolterstorff contends. If the Habermasian proposal allows citizens to vote on the basis of exclusively religious reasons, it collapses into Wolterstorff's proposal against the neutrality of the state. This, however, would directly undermine the criterion of legitimacy contained in the "institutional translation proviso," according to which only secular reasons should count in determining coercive political decisions. But, if it excludes this possibility, then it collapses into the Rawlsian proposal it aims to modify. It lets citizens include religious reasons in political deliberation in the informal public sphere, but when it comes to casting their votes it does not let them base their political decisions on their religious reasons if corroborating secular reasons cannot be found. Thus, these citizens must engage in a way of thinking entirely foreign to their own religious convictions in order to determine how to vote. To the extent that this is so, this proposal does not provide *any* answer to Wolterstorff's objection.

In contradistinction to Rawls's and Habermas's proposals, my proposal interprets the democratic obligation to justify the coercive policies one favors with generally acceptable reasons in such a way that it can be discharged by all democratic citizens, whether religious or secular, without forcing them to abandon their own cognitive stance and disingenuously engage in a foreign way of thinking. To the extent that it does so, it does not impose undue cognitive burdens on any citizens and therefore avoids Wolterstorff's objection without giving up on the ideal of mutual accountability. According to the accountability proviso that I defend, citizens who participate in political advocacy in the informal public sphere can appeal to any reasons they sincerely believe in, which support the coercive policies they favor, provided that they are prepared to show – against any objections to the contrary – that these policies are compatible with the democratic commitment to treat all citizens as free and equal and therefore can be reasonably accepted by everyone.[10] In order to fulfill this democratic obligation, citizens must be willing to engage in an argument on the compatibility of the policies they favor with the protection of the fundamental rights and freedoms of all citizens, and they must be willing to accept the outcome of that argument as decisive in settling the question of the legitimacy of enforcing these policies.

Although the accountability proviso is similar in spirit to the Rawlsian proviso, it is based on an *interpersonal* interpretation of the nature and rationale of the obligation in question. By interpreting accountability in interpersonal instead of intrapersonal terms, it can avoid the objections against the Rawlsian proviso that I mentioned before. Whereas it seems at best unfeasible, and at worst disingenuous, to ask religious citizens who participate in political advocacy to come up with nonreligious reasons in support of the policies they favor, regardless of what their sincere beliefs happen to be in each specific case, it does seem both feasible and legitimate to ask them to address any objections offered by other citizens against such policies, which are based upon basic democratic principles and ideals. Since, according to this proposal religious citizens, just as much as any other citizens, are only obligated to address those objections that are based upon reasons acceptable to all democratic citizens, they are perfectly capable of understanding and engaging them without being cognitively dishonest. But since those who offer the objections drive the challenge, religious citizens do not have to artificially generate a foreign or insincere rationale based on such reasons to support the policies they favor, as Rawls's proposal suggests. Instead, those who oppose such policies fulfill this task on the basis of their sincere beliefs. All that religious (as well as nonreligious) citizens have to do is to come up with compelling reasons to show why these objections are wrong, if they think they are. Their public debate must show that the policies they favor are indeed consistent with treating all citizens as free and equal and therefore can be reasonably accepted by everyone.[11]

It is in virtue of this democratic obligation that public reasons have priority. They are the only reasons towards which no one can remain indifferent in their political advocacy. Whereas public reasons, that is, reasons based on basic democratic principles and ideals, need not be the source from which a rationale in support of each proposed coercive policy must be crafted, they are the kind of reasons that cannot be ignored, disregarded or overridden once citizens bring them into public deliberation. They are the reasons that must be engaged *in their own terms* by all politically active citizens if they are offered as objections to the coercive policies under discussion. Objections to the constitutionality of these policies must be (1) properly addressed in public debate and (2) defeated with compelling arguments[12] before any citizens can legitimately support (or vote for) their enforcement.

A secular bias? Two examples

Let me mention two examples to illustrate the sense in which public reasons have priority over other substantive reasons, as well as the different ways in which this priority may play out in specific public debates on contested policies. The point of discussing these specific examples here is not to contribute to their solution, but to show how my proposal is supposed to work in democratic societies with different dynamics between majority and minority cultures. One is the debate on same-sex marriage as it is currently discussed in the USA, that is, in a country with a majority made up of religious citizens. The other is the debates on banning the Islamic headscarf from public places as they are currently discussed in European countries, that is, in countries with a majority made up of secular citizens. Showing how my proposal operates in these very different contexts will also be helpful in illustrating the issue that I mentioned at the beginning: namely, the way in which, in a deliberative democracy, minorities can be protected from political domination by a consolidated majority.

The same-sex marriage debate in the USA

Let's look first at the debate on same-sex marriage. According to the accountability proviso I propose, citizens may adduce religious reasons against homosexuality and in support of a ban on same-sex marriage, provided that they fulfill the correlative obligation of addressing any objections based on public reasons that other citizens may advance against such policy. Whereas citizens may not feel compelled to address objections based upon, say, the intrinsic value of homosexual lifestyles or the value of cultural diversity – values that they may not share – they must nevertheless feel compelled to address objections based upon the political value of equal treatment that they do share as democratic citizens. Unless next time around they are willing to accept unequal treatment themselves, before their proposal can be legitimately enforced they must present a convincing explanation of how and why is it that "separate but equal" is an acceptable policy with respect to a particular group of citizens yet not towards others. Similarly, secular citizens do not have to address justifications based on religious reasons concerning the sinful nature of homosexuality – reasons that they do not share – in order to meaningfully participate in that debate. A perfectly appropriate way of engaging in that debate is to offer counterarguments in order to show why the proposed policy is wrong, if they think it is. Objecting to the unequal treatment involved in denying the right to marriage to a group of citizens seems a perfectly meaningful way to participate in that debate.

Of course, citizens may disagree about whether or not the reasons offered against the objections are compelling just as much as they may disagree about whether the objections themselves are compelling, and such disagreements will typically be settled (at least temporarily) by majority rule. But, according to this proposal, the cognitive significance of the majority vote should be that it reflects the judgment of the majority regarding whether or not a given policy is consistent with treating all citizens as free and equal, and not simply that it reflects their judgment regarding whether or not the enforcement of that policy accords with what they take to be the right way to act.

This crucial distinction helps to illuminate what is wrong with Wolterstorff's claim that religious citizens ought to base their decisions about justice on their religious convictions. This view implies that religious reasons, whatever they may be, that purport to explain why homosexuality (and thus same-sex marriage) is wrong are at the same time both appropriate and sufficient to justify something totally different: namely, the imposition of coercion on others who have the right to be co-legislators. Once the distinction between these questions is recognized,[13] it becomes clear why reasons geared to prove the compatibility of the proposed policies with the constitutional principles of freedom and equality (i.e., with the equal protection of the fundamental rights and freedoms of all citizens) should have priority in determining the mutual acceptability of coercive policies, even by the citizens's own lights. If this is so, Wolterstorff's claim needs to be qualified accordingly: religious citizens ought to base their decisions concerning fundamental issues of justice on their religious convictions, *provided that those decisions are compatible with treating all citizens as free and equal.*

Now, this claim may suggest that giving priority to proper political reasons stacks the deck in favor of secular and against religious citizens, so that the latter are bound to lose out whenever there is a conflict between religious and secular reasons. To show why the suspicion of a secularist bias in this specific account of public reason is unwarranted, let me introduce the other example I mentioned before to illustrate the correlative claim regarding secular citizens: namely, that these citizens ought to base their decisions concerning fundamental issues of justice on their secular convictions *provided that those decisions are compatible with treating all citizens as free and equal.*

The Islamic headscarf debate in Europe

The current debates in European countries on whether to ban the Islamic headscarf from public places offer a good example. These debates are highly complex. They involve a variety of policy proposals as well as underlying reasons and justifications that I cannot properly address here. But for present purposes, let's (drastically) simplify the example and focus on a single type of reason that each side of the debate may put forward: the appeal made by some secular citizens to considerations of gender equality[14] as the reason that justifies the ban and the insistence on the religious importance (or even obligation) of wearing the headscarf by some of those who oppose the ban. As in the previous example regarding the ban on same-sex marriage, I would argue here that a meaningful political debate among religious and secular citizens about the permissibility of wearing Muslim headscarves in public places is possible and that it would not require citizens to abandon their respective cognitive stance (whether it be secular or religious) and disingenuously engage in a foreign way of thinking. The argument runs as follows: Citizens can adduce secular reasons that appeal to substantive ideals of gender equality in support of banning the Islamic headscarf from public places provided that they fulfill the correlative obligation of addressing any objections based on proper political reasons that other citizens may advance against such policy. Whereas citizens need not feel compelled to address objections based on, say, the religious obligation to wear a headscarf, the intrinsic value of a Muslim lifestyle or of cultural diversity in general – obligations and values which they may not share – they must nevertheless feel compelled to address objections that are based upon the political values that they do share as democratic citizens.

Now, these secular citizens may claim that precisely because their proposal draws on the value of equality, it is already based on properly political reasons and therefore meets the "priority of public reasons" test. But here, like in the prior example, lies an illicit conflation. For such a claim would seem to imply that secular reasons, whatever they may be, that purport to explain why the use of the Islamic scarf by women is wrong are at the same time both appropriate and sufficient for the justification of something entirely different: namely, the imposition of coercion on others who have the right to be co-legislators.[15] Whether or not the Islamic headscarf is a symbol of female oppression and thus undermines gender equality is an interesting and intricate question, but it has no direct bearing on whether citizens have the right to impose coercive measures on other citizens in total disregard of their rights to be treated as equals.[16] Recognizing the right of all citizens to be co-legislators implies recognizing their right *to participate on equal footing within the deliberative process of shaping, contesting and transforming the collective understanding of what is and what is not compatible with gender equality, non-discrimination, freedom of religion, state neutrality, etc.* – in light of the social and historical circumstances specific to a particular political community.

Thus, irrespective of the religious reasons that some citizens may have for wearing the scarf, if these citizens cast their objections to the ban by appealing to the unequal treatment involved in denying a certain group of citizens the right to freely exercise their religion or to freely choose how to dress, or if they appeal to anti-discrimination laws to justify their opposition to the proposed ban, then other citizens have an obligation to address these objections and to offer convincing arguments to defeat them before the enforcement of the ban can be considered legitimate.

The interpretation of the priority of properly political reasons defended here stacks the deck neither in favor of secular citizens nor against religious citizens, but in favor of *political inclusion and against some citizens exercising political domination over others.* This interpretation tells all citizens that they can base their decisions concerning fundamental issues of justice on their substantive views (whether about religion, equality, or anything else), *provided that they can show those decisions are compatible with the democratic commitment to treat all citizens as free and equal.* Consequently, citizens cannot determine in advance of actual public deliberation the substantive reasons upon which their political decisions ought to be based (whether they be secular or religious).

In order to be legitimate, their decisions *ought to be based on those reasons that have survived the scrutiny of political deliberation in a fully inclusive public sphere.*

Conclusion: citizens in robes

As noted at the start, the danger that a majority could, simply on the basis of their *substantive religious* beliefs, illicitly restrict the fundamental rights and freedoms of their fellow citizens provides an essential motivation for the American debate about the kinds of reasons that citizens should use to justify coercive policies. As I hope to have shown, this debate is necessary in Europe because of the very same danger: namely, the possibility that a majority could, simply on the basis of their *substantive secular* beliefs, illicitly restrict the fundamental rights and freedoms of fellow citizens. However, framing the problem in such anti-majoritarian terms may obscure the democratic character of my proposal. So, let me make a brief final clarification.

In *Political Liberalism*, Rawls (2005) famously claims that in constitutional democracies with judicial review, the Supreme Court is the exemplar of public reason. In my view, this claim is trivially true. For supreme constitutional courts are precisely the institutions in charge of ensuring, among other things, that political decisions respect the priority of public reason; that is, that they do not violate the constitutional rights of citizens. However, since this claim immediately raises questions concerning the democratic legitimacy of judicial review, its true significance and implications may be misunderstood. The point of recognizing the Supreme Court as exemplar of public reason can hardly be that citizens should delegate the task of securing the priority of public reason to the court, while allowing themselves to make political decisions without respecting that very same priority. To the contrary, the democratic implication of the Rawlsian claim is that citizens themselves should behave like they expect the court to behave, that is, *they should strive to meet the same standard of public reason that the exemplar they have instituted is supposed to meet.*[17] Indeed, the danger that a majority, simply on the basis of their substantive beliefs, whether religious or secular, may illicitly restrict the fundamental rights and freedoms of fellow citizens can only be averted in a democratic fashion if all citizens respect the priority of public reason while forming their political convictions through deliberation in a fully inclusive public sphere.

Notes

1 For an interesting analysis of this tension in the specific case of France see Laborde (2008). For a defense of the second option out of the dilemma see Modood (2007). His proposals in favor of religious accomodation of Islam are particularly interesting in this context because they are explicitly defended on the basis of their consistency with the moderate secularism actually practiced in most European countries.

2 I do not have the space to offer a detailed defense of this claim here, but as it will become clear later, according to my interpretation of deliberative democracy,

protecting the rights and freedoms of all citizens is not merely a matter of creating formal equality among them, but also of granting their political integration, so that they can see themselves as full members of the political community who have the right to be co-legislators. From that perspective, the less religiously neutral a political community is the harder it will be for secular citizens and citizens of different faiths to see themselves as full and equal members of it. For a defense of a similar view see Laborde (2011).

3 The characterization of my proposal that follows draws on Lafont (2009).

4 See Audi (1993, 1997, 2000 and 2011).

5 See Habermas (2006b).

6 See Rawls (1993: 212–54 and 1997: 573–615). In my opinion, Rawls's interpretation of the content of public reason in terms of basic democratic values offers the most plausible account of the kind of reasons that must have priority in public political deliberation. However, this is all that my proposal borrows from Rawls's account of public reason. In particular, it does not require the endorsment of some stronger (and contentious) assumptions that Rawls includes in his account, such as the completeness of public reason. For a brief discussion of this issue see note 11 below.

7 Rawls's account of public reason also includes trivial elements that belong to common human reason, such as "presently accepted general beliefs and forms of reasoning found in common sense, and the methods and conclusions of science when these are not controversial." (Rawls 1993: 224). For the details of Rawls's account of the content of an overlapping consensus see Rawls (1993: 133–72).

8 See Rawls (1997: 584).

9 Wolterstorff (1997: 105).

10 Cohen (1996: 156) explains the precise content of this democratic commitment as follows:

> To say that citizens are free is to say, inter alia, that no comprehensive moral or religious view provides a defining condition of membership or the foundation of the authorization to exercise political power. To say that they are equal is to say that each is recognized as having the capacities required for participating in discussion aimed at authorizing the exercise of power.

11 As mentioned in note 6, my approach does not share Rawls's assumption of the completeness of public reason. Thus I concede that public reasons alone may be sufficient to rule out some coercive policies in many cases, but may not be sufficient to determine which coercive policy to adopt in cases in which both alternatives either are considered equally compatible with treating all citizens as free and equal, or are equally contested as incompatible. The abortion debate can be seen as an example of the latter case. In my view, both sides to the debate have fulfilled the obligation of articulating their objections to the opposite view in terms of properly political reasons, since both of them appeal to the priority of protecting fundamental rights (in one case of women and in the other of fetuses). They just disagree on their non-political views on what constitutes personhood, whether fetuses are human beings and many such comprehensive issues. So, although the priority of public reasons is indeed reflected in the way the debate has been structured, those reasons alone do not suffice to resolve it. In view of the possibility of a stand-off of these characteristics, the political resolution of those types of cases may just have to be a compromise that both sides can live with (at least for so long as there are basic metaphysical or comprehensive disagreements, which are directly relevant to the issue but irresolvable). Even so, since according to both sides of the debate the protection of fundamental rights is putatively at stake, the priority of public reasons does explain why citizens on both sides may consider accommodation a reasonable (even if temporary) solution in such cases (instead of simply choosing whichever policy happens to be favored by the majority). Thus, as this example shows, accepting the incompleteness of public reason does not require

denial of the normative significance of the priority of public reasons or the practical significance of the accountability proviso. For Rawls's defense of the completeness of public reason based on the example of abortion see Rawls (1993: 243f. and 1996: lvff.). For a similar defense see Freeman (2007: 242–52). For criticisms of the completeness of public reason see Greenawalt (1988: 183–7 and 1995: 106–20), Sandel (2005: 223ff) and Eberle (2002: part III). For an interesting defense of the normative significance of public reasons in spite of its incompleteness see Schwartzman (2004).

12 How high the standard of proof must be in order to count an objection as defeated may vary depending on what is at stake. In some contexts, just showing a preponderance of evidence against the available objections may be sufficient to persuade most people of the constitutionality of a policy proposal, whereas in other cases, it may be needed to show beyond reasonable doubt that the objection is indeed unsound. However, acceptance of a lower standard of proof by the time a decision has to be made only means that if conclusive arguments against the enforced policy are brought to public debate at a later time, the issue will need to be revisited and the policy changed. For an interesting discussion of the appropriate standards of proof in public political debate see Gaus (1996).

13 See Rawls (1999: 148).

14 My focus on this particular reason is not meant to suggest that this is the only or even the main consideration behind the arguments in favor of the ban. Rather, I am focusing on it because it is the kind of reason that may seem most challenging for a defense of the priority of public reasons like the one I am articulating here.

15 As in many other cases (e.g., pornography, hate speech) it is perfectly consistent with democratic principles to be simultaneously against the use of the headscarf and against the ban of the headscarf. For an argument along these lines see Laborde (2012). I agree with much of Laborde's argumentation here. However, in my view she fails to emphasize the different bearing on the democratic legitimacy of coercive legislation that debates based on public and those based on comprehensive reasons (whether religious or secular) have. As a consequence, her defense of the normative significance of non-domination varies from the one I offer here. It does not focus on the *political* domination of Muslim women by a majority willing to impose coercive legislation on the basis of comprehensive (secular) reasons, but only on the putative *social* domination of Muslim women by others (e.g., male family members, religious authorities or oppressive ideologies) and the appropriate legal means for its prevention.

16 From this perspective, one of the main problems with European debates on coercive measures that specifically target citizens who are Muslim is that these citizens are oftentimes not seen as full and equal members of the societies they live in. Their right to be co-legislators, even if it is legally granted in terms of voting rights, is not fully accepted by the population. Indeed, it is quite common in Europe to refer to Muslim citizens as "immigrants," even to those who are native second or third generation co-nationals. As Casanova (2009: 140) points out, "most European countries still have difficulty viewing themselves as permanent immigrant societies, or viewing the foreign-born, and even the native second and third generation, as nationals, irrespective of their legal status."

17 As Rawls (1993: lv) puts it, "public reason sees the office of citizen with its duty of civility as analogous to that of judgeship with its duty of deciding cases."

4 The theological and secular dimensions of the modern state

Historical and contemporary perspectives

John Loughlin[1]

Introduction: the diversity of the modern European nation-state

The modern nation-state is a European invention and is founded on the development of both states and nations throughout European history. While all democratic nation-states share a number of common features, there is also a great diversity in how they express these features. This diversity derives, at least in part, from the religious origins of the modern state especially after the ending of the European Wars of Religion by the Treaty of Westphalia in 1648, that created 'confessional' states. These were initially Catholic and Lutheran states, but they were later joined by Calvinist states in the Netherlands, Scotland and, for a time, England. But the roots of these states go back even further in European history and many of their features derive from theological and philosophical debates that pre-dated the Reformation and the Wars of Religion (Burns 1988). Today, these theological origins are almost entirely forgotten and the nation-state is regarded by most historians and political scientists as the quintessential *secular* state in the sense that it has completely discarded any religious dimension in its practical operations. In this chapter, I wish to explore to what extent the modern nation-state still retains some of these older influences that shaped it and, if it does, to what extent this accounts for its present-day diversity. This, in turn, raises the question of what it means to call the nation-state 'secular' and what the different meanings and uses of this term are.

Today, the nation-state has become the dominant form of political organization and is associated with 'modernity' – with the rise of industrial capitalism and the creation of national markets, with the rise of the industrial bourgeoisie and various forms of liberalism, with liberal representative democracy and Weberian-type systems of public administration, etc. (Smith 1998).[2] It is so familiar that we tend to take it for granted and to assume that it is the 'natural' form of political organization, just as we assume that liberal representative democracy is the natural (and best) form of political practice. However, when looked at from a historical perspective, it is clear that the nation-state is a relative newcomer, historically speaking, and can be dated from about the time of the French Revolution, which began in 1789. Previously, there were types of political and social organization that were called 'nations' and 'states', but these were different in important respects from contemporary nations and states (Spruyt 1994; Larkins 2010). Already, in the eleventh and twelfth centuries, we can see the origins of what would become the modern state in countries such as England, Scotland, France, Spain and Sweden with their centralizing monarchs, while the term 'nation', derived from the Latin 'natus' meaning the place of birth, was used to describe groups of people sharing a similar language or geographic origin in the Crusader armies as well as in the new universities such as Oxford, Paris and Bologna. Furthermore, the Reformation encouraged the growth of a national consciousness with the creation of national churches in those countries, which adopted Protestantism and this was mirrored in Catholic countries such as France and Spain, which adopted Gallican forms of Catholicism (Ozment 1980). This also meant a wedding together of ethnic and national consciousness. We shall return to the problems of religion and secularism in the final part of the chapter.

The religious dimension of political systems in the Middle Ages

It was not inevitable that the modern state would take the form that it eventually did. Hendrik Spruyt, in his book *The sovereign state and its competitors: an analysis of systems change* (1994), identifies six different forms of political organization that were in competition with each other in Europe during the Middle Ages: the Holy Roman Empire, the Papacy, feudal arrangements, territorial states, city-states and city leagues. The older forms were the Papacy, the Empire and feudal arrangements, which developed complex relationships of rivalry as well as collaboration. The principal competitors here were the Empire and the Papacy, who operated within a common understanding of the nature of religion, politics, the economy and society, but who struggled with each other as to which of them was the dominant force within that system. Both accepted the notion of two swords, a spiritual and a temporal, and accepted that the other had the right to exercise one of these swords. At the same time, the Emperor tended to usurp from the Pope the exercise of the spiritual sword, while the Pope tended to usurp the exercise of the temporal sword from the Emperor. But both operated within a system which accepted that legitimation of any human activity derived from the Church and theology. The question was, who sanctioned and decided whether any particular activity was legitimate? At the same time, in most parts Europe, society was dominated by a feudal system of mutual arrangements of protection and service between lords (both temporal and spiritual) and their vassals (Bloch 1989). The feudal system was largely a rural phenomenon and led to the emergence of great aristocratic landowners, who also operated within the imperial/papal system but with greater or lesser degrees of autonomy from the Pope or the Emperor. In some respects, the Holy Roman Empire and the Church reflected this feudal organization of society but, in other respects, they were separate from it.

Three other forms of political organization developed which would eventually challenge the first three. First, centralizing monarchs consolidated territorial states in England, Scotland, France, Sweden and Spain. Second, from around the eleventh century, there was the development of the cities as part of a wider economic, cultural and spiritual renaissance across Europe. In most parts of Europe, cities were thus becoming important political centres. Third, there were city leagues primarily for purposes of trade, but also for mutual protection against rival powers. The best-known example was the Hanseatic League (thirteenth to seventeenth centuries), which had a membership that varied between 70 and 170 cities. Another was the Lombard League of northern Italy.

There was often collaboration between monarchs building territorial states and the cities, as they both opposed the feudal nobility in the countryside. In any case, there was a highly complex system of interrelationships among these competing entities: there were rivalries between Pope and Emperor, between the Empire and the princes and the centralizing monarchies, and with cities competing against each other as well as supporting one or other of their competitors. Besides these complex relationships among the different political actors during the centuries before the Reformation, there were also serious divisions within the Church itself (Burns 1988). Two principal issues were relevant to the later development of both the Reformation and Counter-Reformation, as well as the evolution of the secular modern state. First, there was a conflict between conciliarists and caesaro-papists, that is, between those, such as Marsilius of Padua (*c.*1275 – *c.*1342), who believed that the Church exercised its authority through general councils, which the Pope might call and preside over but to which he was also subordinate, and those who held that it was the Pope who exercised this power and that his authority superseded that of general councils. The views of conciliarists and caesaro-papists became entangled with the struggles among the various political and spiritual powers. Second, Church life went through cycles of corruption and attempted reform. Some reformers such as John Wycliffe (d. 1384) in England and Jan Hus (d. 1415) in Bohemia anticipated the later efforts of Luther, Zwingli and Calvin, who regarded them as proto-Protestants. Although these dissidents were regarded as heretics by almost all the political and religious leaders of the time, they were a sign of what was to come and their protests, although rooted in theological issues such as the nature of the Eucharist, often spilled over into the political domain. As a result, they were severely repressed and Hus himself was burned at the stake (Ozment 1980).

Renaissance humanism

Providing a background to these conflicts was the development of the new learning of Renaissance humanism which was, in part, inspired by a return to the authors of classical antiquity and an interest in the languages of that period, as well as in Hebrew (Skinner 1978: Vol. 1). The older learning of the Fathers of the Church and the great scholastic synthesis of Aristotelian philosophy with Christian revelation by the Dominican St Thomas Aquinas (1225–1274), formed the intellectual context of the debates. From the fourteenth century onwards, much of this learning had degenerated into sterile debates over obscure theological points. Petrarch (1304–1374) has been called the 'Father of humanism' alongside authors such as Giovanni Boccaccio (1313–1375) and Dante Alighieri (1265–1321). Although these authors remained Christian, they wished to go beyond scholasticism and sought inspiration in the classical learning of antiquity found in authors such as Cato and Cicero. In the city-states of Italy, such as Florence and Venice, there was a great flourishing of the arts, especially architecture and painting. But the humanist movement was found right across Europe and some of its leading lights were Sir Thomas More (1478–1535), the Lord Chancellor of England in the reign of Henry VIII and Erasmus of Rotterdam (1466/1469–1536) in the Low Countries. Humanist scholarship affected both religious studies and political thought. The emphasis in religion was a 'return to the sources' of the Bible, that is, to the original languages of Hebrew and Greek rather than the Latin Vulgate edition that had been produced by St Jerome in the fifth century AD. Erasmus produced a translation of the New Testament, which had an enormous impact on theology at the time. Thomas More's *Utopia* (published in 1516) was actually a political critique of European society. Neither More nor Erasmus were revolutionaries, but they and other humanists were aware of scandals and corruption in the Church. This meant also being aware of the difficulties in the political system of which the Church was an essential element. As became clear subsequently, neither man would have dreamt of overthrowing this politico-religious system, but both were equally fervent that it should be reformed. Perhaps, unwittingly, their humanistic learning provided some of the tools that would be used by their contemporary Luther and the younger Calvin precisely to overthrow the older system. The books produced by the printing press invented by Johannes Gutenberg around 1439 facilitated the diffusion of the writings of the humanist thinkers.

The Reformation

Luther, Lutheranism and the modern state

The Reformation was a hiatus in European history and contributed powerfully to what would become the very different political, social and economic systems of modern Europe. However, although it constitutes a break with the older system, it took place within the complex system outlined above and became bound up with the various conflicts described there and, indeed, there are several continuities with the mediaeval period. The key figure who sparked these changes was Martin Luther (1483–1546). Luther had entered an Augustinian friary following a narrow escape from death as a young man. By all accounts, he was a very faithful observer of the Rule of his Order, reached the position of sub-prior (second-in-command in the friary) and even represented the entire Augustinian Order on business in Rome. However, his later writings make clear that, while he observed the Rule externally, it failed to transform him interiorly. This is probably what led to his later fulminations against 'good works' (the ascetical practices of the religious life as well as other practices such as pilgrimages or processions typical of mediaeval Catholicism) and his development of the notion that such 'works' could not bring about salvation but that only God's complete remaking of the soul from the outside could accomplish this. But Luther was also a very learned scholar and, although he would later reject humanism as a philosophical movement just as he rejected Thomistic scholasticism, he was influenced by the humanists' method of 'returning to the sources' and working in the original Biblical languages of Hebrew and Greek. He was also influenced by their critiques of the corruption of the Church and disdain for what they regarded as some of the more superstitious practices of the time. Like them, he did not initially desire the splitting up of Christendom or political revolution, but his own impetuousness and the vehemence of his language would soon have that effect.

From the political perspective, there are three crucial documents penned by Luther that are the first nails in the coffin of the mediaeval political and religious systems, and that contributed to the arrival of the modern nation and the modern state (although not yet the 'nation-state'). The first document, which is generally regarded as the first step of the Reformation was officially known as the *Disputation of Doctor Martin Luther on the Power and Efficacy of Indulgences* or, more commonly, *The 95 theses* (Luther [1517] 1957), which was pinned to the doors of the castle church of Wittemberg in 1517. This document was an indictment of the practice of selling 'indulgences' (remittances for time spent in purgatory after one's death) by the Pope and many other ecclesiastical leaders in the Church at the time. Although this was later seen as a dramatic gesture it was, in fact, quite normal to pin such documents on the door of a church, since most people would then read them on their way in to pray or attend a service (a bit like pasting a message on Facebook today!). The *95 theses* were addressed to Pope Leo X and Luther was convinced that the Pope and other bishops would see the folly of selling indulgences once they read his arguments. In fact, the Pope at first ignored Luther and, later, in 1520, condemned his ideas as heretical in the encyclical *Exurge Domine*.[3] Luther was given 60 days to recant his opinions or risk excommunication, but his response was to issue two further documents that were even more provocative. *To the Christian Nobility of the German Nation* (Porter 1974) was, in fact, addressed to Charles V who, at the age of 19, had just been elected Holy Roman Emperor (the English King Henry VIII was also a candidate) but was not yet crowned. Luther hoped to persuade the young man to take his side against the Pope. The address to the German nobility represents an important moment in the evolution of Luther's ideas on both ecclesiology and on the relations between the Church and the political system. The address contains three basic ideas: first, the notion of the priesthood of all believers and not just of the clergy; second, and related to this, the denial of the Pope's right as the sole interpreter of scripture; and, third, a denial of the Pope's right to call a general council of the Church. Luther clearly hoped that the young Charles V, who as Emperor would be a rival to the Pope as we saw above, might be attracted by this attack on the Pope's legitimacy as spiritual leader of the Church. Charles, however, followed the Pope and placed Luther under the ban of the Empire, thus making him an outlaw.

The political context is crucial for understanding further developments in Luther's theological journey and in how this was 'received' in the Europe of his time. At this time, both the Papacy and the Empire were quite weakened and seeking desperately to maintain their hegemony against each other and against other competitors – territorial monarchs such as France and the restless German princes. Some of the German princes, including the Elector of Saxony, where Wittenberg was situated, were chafing under the yoke of the Emperor and saw this as an opportunity to gain further autonomy from him. Of course, many of the princes were also convinced by Luther's argument for reform, although this became entangled with their political motivations. Each case would need to be examined individually to assess whether the position adopted by a ruler was by conviction or expediency, but certainly there are many cases when rulers switched sides when it suited them.

In 1520, Luther also published his *On the Freedom of a Christian* (Porter 1974) in which he laid out a vision in which Christians were not compelled to obey the law but would live out their lives through love and service of each other. As the Reformation progressed, Luther's writings began to be used, not just by the princes to emancipate themselves from imperial and papal control but also by the lower classes to emancipate themselves from princely control. The best-known example of this was the Peasants' Revolt (1524–1526) led by Thomas Münzer and the Anabaptists. Despite his declarations in favour of Christian 'freedom', Luther was horrified by these developments and condemned Münzer and the peasants in the strongest terms, calling for their torture and execution. In this, he revealed himself to be deeply conservative, both politically and socially, despite his theological radicalism. Luther's ecclesiology also influenced his political ideas. For him, the Church was an invisible society of true believers motivated only by the love of God. As an institution, it should not rival the political powers in the way that the Pope had rivalled the Emperor. In fact, the Church should not even carry out good works, such as caring for the poor or feeding beggars, as the mediaeval Church had done. Luther did not believe that the Church, understood as the society of faithful and loving believers, should exercise temporal power in the way that the Popes had done. Rather, the temporal power – the prince – should exercise this – even over Church affairs such as the punishment of heretics or the excommunication of sinners. The temporal power should provide for the needs of the poor and needy but, more importantly, should suppress their mendicancy and idleness. On the other hand, Luther simply assumed that the temporal power would be a Christian power and would not have been able to conceive of a secular state in the modern sense of the word. The prince was also a member of the Church and his decisions would be taken in the light of the Gospel. Luther, true to his emphasis on looking to the Bible for lessons, saw the Old Testament kingdoms as examples of rulership, while the precepts of the Sermon on the Mount were seen as pertaining to the practice of individual Christians within the 'invisible' Church.

Writing furiously in the throes of the political and religious disputes that he had sparked off, and dealing with new issues that were arising, Luther was not devoid of contradictions as his ideas evolved. These ideas were, in fact, a combination of the political ideas of mediaeval Catholicism and even of the notion of 'Christendom', but reduced to the level of a 'state' such as Saxony rather than spreading across Europe. This notion of scale is important, as it will lead to the distinctive concept of a state church. In fact, Lutheranism was adopted by several German princes, but its most complete expression was eventually that found in the Scandinavian states and especially Sweden. In the German states, there remained Catholic and/or Calvinist minorities (once the latter had also emerged as the other main branch of the Reformation), while Sweden and Norway became purely Lutheran states.

What is interesting for the analysis of this paper are the longer-term consequences of Lutheranism in the development of European states. In fact, there seem to be two principal outcomes. The first is a certain passivity on the part of the Lutheran churches confronted by the state, which derived from Luther's ecclesiological notion of the 'invisible' Church and his handing over of several functions to the civil authorities. In the German states, this has sometimes been thought of as leading to the collapse of the Church when confronted with powerful rulers such as Bismarck and, even more ominously, Hitler. The German state was divinised by Hegel's dialectic and took on a mythical hue in Herder's thought. In the Scandinavian countries, and especially Sweden, the Lutheran state church was also passive when confronted with a powerful centralizing monarchy of which it became a branch of the civil service. Second, Luther had recommended that the temporal power, and not the Church, take responsibility for what we would now call social services; in Scandinavia, this eventually evolved into the famous Swedish model of the welfare state. It is true that this was established by the Swedish Social Democrats in the 1930s, who were not very sympathetic to the Christian Church, but the Social Democrats were undoubtedly practising a secularized version of the Lutheran conception of the state.

Two further comments might be made concerning Luther and Lutheranism's contribution to the evolution of the modern state. The first is that, while Luther accepted the notion of 'Christendom', he now conceived this to be at the level of a medium-sized state such as Saxony, whose Elector provided him with protection and for which he designed a State Church. Saxony was not an independent monarchy such as Sweden, but it is not difficult to see how the notion of a 'State Church' could develop out of this change of scale from the wider European political system, such as we have described in the earlier part of this paper, where the 'Church' covered the entire European territory as it was then defined, to the much smaller territories of Saxony or Sweden. This was the beginning of the notion of 'national' churches, which would receive its final consecration at the Peace of Westphalia, of which more below. The second key notion that Luther encouraged was that of ethnicity. The very title *Address to German Nobility* (Porter 1974) illustrates consciousness of his own 'national' or 'ethnic' identity and the offence he took at the stereotype of the boorish drunken German, which he thought was held by the 'Italians', about whom he, in turn, held the stereotype of being corrupt and decadent. Saxony could not become a 'German' state since Germans were found throughout the Empire, but this was a powerful incentive towards the development of an 'ethnic' conception of nationhood.

Calvin, Calvinism and the modern state

Calvin (1509–1564) was younger than Luther, but his influence on the future direction of the Reformation was as profound and, from the perspective of the evolution of the state, perhaps even more important. While Calvin accepted many of Luther's theological ideas, he also developed lines of his own or interpreted some of Luther's concepts in a different way (Troeltsch 1931).

The key difference between the political ideas of the two reformers is in their conceptions of relations between the civil and the religious authorities. Luther gave the civil authorities much greater power over church matters than Calvin would have allowed. This may be a reflection of the two different sets of circumstances in which the two men worked out their theological ideas. Luther, as already noted, lived in the quite large state of Saxony, while Calvin lived mostly in cities (except for his early years growing up in the Kingdom of France). The more radical versions of the Reformation, which Calvin adopted and carried further, were being worked out by Zwingli in Zurich and Bucer in Strasbourg. Calvin, in fact, was on his way to join Bucer when he was diverted to Geneva, where he would spend most of the rest of his life. The Swiss Reformation of which he became the leading figure was thus fought out at the level of cities and cantons, that is, on a much smaller scale than in Saxony (Close 2009).

Calvin's principal ideas on the relationship between the civil and ecclesiastical authorities are found in Book IV, Chapter XX of the *Institutes* (McNeill 1960). This is a more measured (that is, less violent in its language) document than Luther's writings and is marked more by Calvin's humanistic learning and legal training than by the passion and heat of the battle, which marked Luther's writings. Calvin's theology was dominated less by the notion of human sinfulness than Luther's and more by an awareness of God's glory, which relativizes all human affairs. Nevertheless, he held civil magistracy in high regard and demanded that Christians obey their rulers (as Luther and contemporary Catholics also believed). Calvin's ideas on relations between the Church and the civil authorities were undoubtedly affected by the concrete circumstances in which he formulated them and principally by the fact that his branch of the Reformation was taking place in the imperial cities of the Holy Roman Empire. Calvin's Geneva experience would prove crucial. Even before the Reformation, the civil magistrates of Geneva, an imperial city dominated by a local prince-bishop, had won a certain amount of autonomy from the bishop. When the Calvinist Reformation arrived in the city, the magistrates were determined to keep it under control. Calvin resisted this and, in contrast to Luther, developed the idea that the Church should be responsible for its own affairs rather than have them controlled by the civil authorities. There followed a long struggle between the two groups and at one point Calvin was expelled from the city, but was later allowed to return. Calvin gave more thought than Luther to the form the political system should take; that is, whether it should a monarchy, aristocracy or democracy. Although he would have been happy for any of these systems to become Protestant, he seemed to prefer aristocracy or democracy, or a mixture of the two. Calvin also grudgingly recognized the right of Christians to resist unjust rulers.

Although Calvin saw himself as being in continuity with Luther, and there are important similarities in the two approaches – they shared similar critiques of the mediaeval Church and of scholasticism – both were influenced by humanistic scholarship, especially the return to the original sources of the Bible; they had similar understandings of *sola scriptura* and *sola fide*; and both had an Augustinian pessimism with regard to human nature. But there were also important differences, particularly in their ecclesiologies and sacramental theologies: Luther retained more of the Catholic ecclesiology, particularly of the ministry, and more of the Catholic notion of the real presence of Christ in the Eucharist. However, their understandings of Church–state relations were quite different. While Luther saw the state as exercising both spiritual and temporal swords, Calvin thought the Church should do so especially with regard to its internal affairs. Furthermore, the Presbyterian form of government, with government by elders and 'ministers' being 'called' by the congregation rather than being appointed by bishops from above, was quite different from Luther's acceptance of a more hierarchical system. This is not to say that the early Calvinist congregations were 'democratic' in our sense of the word, but certainly we can see here an important step towards the establishment of democracy. Of course, as both Troeltsch and Max Weber recognized, Calvinism also made possible a move away from the strict control of the market system by the Church characteristic of the mediaeval period, thus taking the first steps towards what Karl Polanyi called 'the great transformation', which was the rise of the market and of industrial capitalism (Troeltsch 1931; Weber 2002 [1905]; Polanyi 2001 [1944]).

Radical Protestantism

As hinted at above, both Luther's (early) writings and those of Calvin seemed to suggest that revolt against the civil and/or religious authorities was permitted if these authorities acted against God's commands and against a godly way of life. These ideas were taken up by various sects in two different ways. One tendency, exemplified by Thomas Münzer, was to resort to violence to overthrow the current rulers and to install a radical version of the Kingdom of God on Earth. Attempts to do so were ruthlessly suppressed by the civil authorities in Lutheran, Calvinist and Catholic countries. The second tendency was to express disapproval of the sinful status quo by withdrawal from the world and the establishment of monastic-style communities living a godly life in a situation of autonomy. This tradition largely derives from Menno Simons, a Dutch Catholic priest who renounced the priesthood and embraced the Reform. Today, this movement is found mostly in North America in the form of the Mennonites, the

Amish, the Hutterites, etc. Some of these groups have been prominent in modern peace movements.

The Reformation in the British Isles: Anglicanism, Scottish Calvinism and Welsh non-conformity

Is there an 'Anglican' perspective on the relations between Church and state? There are, in fact, several different perspectives that derive from the successive stages of the Reformation in England. Although Henry VIII was, in most respects, a faithful Catholic in terms of doctrine, he was also a representative of the Tudor dynasty, which had been engaged in a process of centralization of the state from about the fifteenth century onwards. He should be seen, therefore, as one of the monarchs, alongside the French and the Spanish, who wished to assert the rights of the territorial state against the claims of the Papacy and the Empire. The Tudor monarchs, like their predecessors, had also been concerned to neutralize the claims of the English barons. While Henry was opposed to Lutheran theology, and in particular Luther's doctrine of the Eucharist, he turned the religious turmoil of the early Reformation to his political and personal advantage by setting himself up as the head of the Church of England (and thereby ensuring he could obtain a divorce) but also by seizing the vast holdings of the monasteries and religious houses of England, Wales and Ireland and selling them off, thus replenishing the royal coffers with much needed revenue. However, what is important for the subsequent development of Church–state relations in England was the establishment of an established national Church – the Church of *England* and not of Rome. This gave a powerful impetus to the already existing sense of English nationality (see comments on the nation on p. 72), which could only grow with the advent of Henry's successors to the throne (with the exceptions of the Catholic monarchs Mary Tudor and James II). Whatever the regime – monarchy, Cromwellian dictatorship or parliamentary constitutional monarchy – the Church now 'belonged' to the nation and came to be seen as an essential element of *Englishness.* This persists even to the present day (for the moment) as the Church of England is still the established church and Anglican bishops sit in the House of Lords, the upper house of the legislature.

As a result of the spread of the British Empire, Anglicanism became an international religious movement, with a world-wide Anglican 'communion'. In some cases, the Anglican Church became the established church of the territory or colony. The key issue was whether subjects would pay tithes to the established church as they did in Ireland and Wales, where the Church of *England* was established. In these two countries, there were movements for disestablishment closely connected to Irish and Welsh nationalism, which eventually succeeded (in Ireland in 1869 and in Wales in 1920). The Anglican Church survived in Ireland (as the Church of Ireland) and Wales (as the Church *in* Wales) and also existed in Scotland, where it is known as the Scottish Episcopal Church. The Anglican Church was also established in several colonies or parts of colonies in the United States: in Virginia in 1609, in the lower part of New York in 1693, in Maryland in 1702, in South Carolina in 1706, in North Carolina in 1730 and in Georgia in 1758. This meant that all the inhabitants of these states had to pay church taxes. These arrangements came to an end with the setting up of the Confederation and then the Federation. One of the aims of the Federal Constitution was to prevent an established church in the Federation, although the American separation of Church and state has a different meaning from the French approach adopted in 1905. In Canada, the Church of England was established by law in Nova Scotia, New Brunswick and Prince Edward Island.

However, my concern in this section is to explore the connection between changing ecclesiological conceptions of Anglicanism and their impact on church-state relations. Although, as we have noted, the Church of England passed through different phases, the overall position has been the Erastian one that the state should have supremacy over the Church. Constitutionally, the Prime Minister (even if he were an atheist like Lloyd George) must approve the appointment of Anglican bishops, although Gordon Brown promised reforms in this area when he became Prime Minister. At the same time, the Church of England could not achieve hegemony in the same way that the Church of Sweden did, where the latter eliminated all rivals. First, in England – but also in Scotland, Wales and Ireland – there was much greater religious heterogeneity: the Church of Scotland was Calvinist but co-existed alongside the Anglican Episcopal Church, the Roman Catholic Church and various smaller Protestant sects, such as the Free Presbyterians (the 'Wee Frees'); in Wales, non-conformists (Methodists, Evangelicals, Quakers, etc.) were stronger than the established Church of England; in Ireland, the majority of the population remained Catholic, with an Anglican Anglo-Irish aristocracy spread out through the entire island and a strong Presbyterian minority in Ulster, alongside a variety of Protestant sects. All of this meant that, although the state (the monarch and the organs of government) remained in Anglican hands, it had to come to terms with the great variety of other Christian faiths. This may be one of the factors that led to what political scientists call Anglo-Saxon pluralism. Interestingly, in (Protestant) anglophone Canada this notion of political pluralism, expressed through 'multiculturalism', contrasts strongly with (Catholic) Québec, where there is a more statist notion of politics and where 'interculturalism', rather than 'multiculturalism', is the dominant approach.

Roman Catholic perspectives

As with the other theological traditions, there is no one Catholic position with regard to Church-state relations. We need to distinguish between the Papacy, which, as noted above, was a temporal as well as a spiritual power in the Middle Ages, and the different ecclesiastical situations in different parts of Europe. First, even before the Reformation, there were tensions between advocates of conciliarism, such as Marsilius of Padua who held that the supreme spiritual authority of the Church lies with councils of bishops, and the advocates of papal monarchy, who saw the Pope as the supreme authority. Temporal rulers chose from these positions, less from theological conviction than from political expediency, and there were even cases of advocates switching position depending on which ruler was supporting them (Ozment 1980).

With the Reformation, the political situation changed dramatically alongside the rise of political nationalism and the first signs of the modern state, particularly in Protestant Europe as outlined above. The Papacy looked on these developments with disfavour and this eventually became a systematic opposition to modernity, which reached its culmination in Pius IX's notorious *Syllabus of Errors* (1864).[4] Catholic ecclesiology in the nineteenth century saw the Catholic Church as an embattled fortress besieged by the forces of Protestantism and Enlightenment modernity – nationalism, liberalism, freemasonry, socialism and revolution. The *Syllabus* was a panic reaction to these threats from without. This began to change when Leo XIII was elected Pope in 1878 and moderated the extreme stance of Pius IX by beginning to come to terms with modernity at least to some extent in, for example, his encyclical *Rerum Novarum* (1891). But it was not until the Second Vatican Council (1962–1965) that the Church finally came to accept modernity and a new eccesiology can be found in its basic documents – the *Dogmatic Constitution on the Church* (*Lumen Gentium,* 1964) and the *Pastoral Constitution on the Church in the Modern World* (*Gaudium et Spes,* 1965).[5]

The papal position on Church-state relations rejected the Lutheran and Erastian positions that the state should have supremacy over the Church, seeing itself as exercising the spiritual sword, which was superior to the temporal sword. However, it is also necessary to consider the positions of different national hierarchies. Although the Papacy looked askance at the growth of nationalism, several Catholic countries in practice became Catholic nations: Gallican France, Spain, Ireland and Poland. There were also Catholic thinkers and movements, such as Lammenais and Lacordaire who published the journal *L'Avenir*, which was sympathetic to the ideals of liberalism and democracy. However, such figures tended to incur condemnation from Rome and sometimes ended by leaving the Church.

The Reformation and the modern nation

We now turn to the impact of religion on the evolution of the notion of the modern nation. Liah Greenfeld, in her book *Nationalism: Five Roads to Modernity* (1992), argues that the *modern* nation began with the Protestant Reformation, particularly that which happened in England. She argues that England led the way by defining itself as a *Protestant* nation in contrast to *Catholic* France, which was the second modern nation. Germany, Russia and the United States followed their distinctive 'roads' to modernity. In each case, religion played an important role. It should also be noted that the Reformation, by introducing the principle of 'national' churches – the Church of Sweden, of England, of France, etc. – consolidated the notion of a nation being identified with a particular confession and with a particular state. The 1648 Treaty of Westphalia ended the

Wars of Religion through the application of the principle of *cuius regio, eius religio*, 'the religion of the ruler will be the religion of the state and people', which had been in existence since the 1555 Peace of Augsburg. Westphalia implied two features of importance for the subsequent development of nation and state: first, it consolidated the existence of state churches; second, it introduced the principle of non-intervention by one state into another, thus clarifying the notion of 'sovereignty'. Modern international relations is a secularized version of this principle.

My argument is that these different ways of organizing the state according to specific concepts of nation and state derive, at least in part, from the different and competing theologies of the Church, of Church and state, and Church and politics more generally outlined above, that were present in the most crucial period of nation and state building in the sixteenth century. We might argue that Lutheranism developed a concept of society and nationhood based on honesty, sincerity and brotherliness, but also uniformity and homogeneity and under the control of an overarching state, at least in the Scandinavian countries. Calvinism led to a much greater assertive individualism, such as is found in Scotland and the Netherlands. English Protestantism, in its various manifestations from High Church Anglicanism to Low Church Methodism and Quakerism, created a sense of nationhood that has a much greater acceptance of diversity and pluralism. But my interest here lies in what were the consequences of these positions for subsequent political organization and the development of political theory, even in its most secularized expressions.

The contemporary situation: religions, secularization and 'post-secularism'

Do these historical and theological considerations have any relevance to the contemporary state? Surely, thanks to the secularization processes initially identified by Peter Berger (1967) and today held by Steve Bruce (2002), whose work was inspired by sociologists such as Weber and Durkheim, religion has been consigned to the purely private sphere and is no longer relevant to contemporary politics except in the negative sense of having to be excluded from it. The sociological version of the secularization thesis was a rather crude reading of modern European history, which thought that with increasing 'modernization' and the emphasis on scientific explanations of the world and more 'rational' forms of social organization, then 'religion' would eventually disappear or at the most be confined to the sphere of private individual beliefs and activities. This became a dominant paradigm in the social sciences, including not just sociology but other disciplines such as political science, international relations, and economics.

It would appear that secularization in the sense mentioned above did occur in Western European countries but, in recent years, there has been a vigorous debate about the original thesis. Die-hards such as Steve Bruce have dug in their heels and refused to abandon the 'thesis'. Other sociologists, political theorists, theologians and historians have adopted more nuanced positions. Berger (1999) now admits that the original thesis was wrong in the sense that religion has not disappeared but, on the contrary, seems to be alive and well even in the United States, the world's most 'modern' state, although he does think that it may be true in Europe (Berger *et al.* 2008).

This change of position is based on empirical realities. Religion simply has not disappeared, but seems to thriving in most parts of the world (Micklethwait and Woolridge 2009). The secularization thesis largely holds in Western Europe and some countries similar to Europe, such as Canada, Australia and New Zealand, but not in other parts of the world such as the United States, Latin America, Africa and Asia. Even China is experiencing a revival of religious faith and practice and, given the huge size of the population there, absolute numbers of religious believers and practitioners will outnumber their equivalents in Europe (e.g. the number of Chinese Christians attending church services on Sunday may be greater than European Christian church-goers). Furthermore, the liberation of the former Communist states of East and Central Europe and the Soviet Union has also led to a revival of religion in several countries of that region. This is admittedly uneven and ranges from the strong Catholic presence in Poland to the majority atheism in the Czech Republic (Slovakia by contrast is also strongly Catholic). The 2004 EU enlargement meant that large numbers of Poles, Lithuanians and other East and Central Europeans who were practising Catholics arrived in Britain and Ireland and helped to reanimate declining Catholic parishes in those countries. Finally, the presence of large Muslim immigrant populations in several European countries, and the rise of militant Islamism, has placed the question of religion on public and political agendas through issues such the status of women, Muslim attitudes to homosexuality, sharia law, etc. There has been a resultant questioning of multiculturalism and attitudes of tolerance in the UK, the Netherlands and Germany, while the French have resorted to the traditional notion of *laïcité* on issues of dress codes in schools and public places (the *burqa*). Besides these recent manifestations of the presence of religion in European states, there is also the fact that churches and other religious organizations have never completely gone away, even if religious practice has declined. Churches are constitutionally and legally recognized in all European states and by the European Union. Furthermore, they are responsible for the delivery of a range of public services. The key question is how this recognition and involvement in public service delivery relate to liberal representative democracy. We will examine these three aspects of the religious question in turn.

Nevertheless, even if there are empirical manifestations of religion at the level of society, is it not true that *states* are becoming more secular. John Milbank (1990), founder of the theological school known as 'radical orthodoxy', claims that, in reality, what we think of as 'secular' institutions and the social theories that try to describe and explain them, have in fact a religious foundation. In other words, they are not fully 'secular' in the sense that they have completely escaped from their religious or even theological roots. This is close to what we are arguing in this paper, although I think one can also speak of the 'secularization' of concepts and phenomena that may have their origins in theological constructs. This is what we have been arguing above with regard to the development of European states such as Sweden and the Netherlands, where the original theological concepts have been all but forgotten but where the content of those concepts still plays a role in shaping the form of the state and the political, policy and administrative culture of that state. David Martin, writing as a sociologist, has long been a critic of the cruder versions of the secularization thesis and he argues that religion and society have always existed in a dialectical relationship with each other, and that this is true in the modern period as well as in previous periods (Martin 1978). Charles Taylor (2007a) argues something similar in his massive volume, when he states that it was the reforming efforts of the Christian Church – even before the Reformation itself – which laid the foundation of the modern secular state. So how secular is the contemporary state? We now turn to this question.

Constitutional and legal recognition of religious groups

The Treaty of Westphalia was originally established to end the Wars of Religion, which had followed the Reformation and which had principally divided the Holy Roman Empire, although religious conflict broke out in other parts of Europe as well. Although the Westphalian state is today taken to mean a state that does not intervene in the affairs of other states, its original meaning was to recognize the confessional state. One consequence of this was the phenomenon of 'established' churches in Protestant Europe and a special recognition of the Catholic Church in Catholic Europe. This arrangement still largely holds today in several European states. Church–state relations in Europe could be described as a spectrum with, at one end, established churches as in England, Norway, Denmark and (until 2000) Sweden. At the other end of the spectrum is France where, since 1905, there has been complete separation of Church and state and a distinctive concept of *laïcité.* In between, there are various arrangements which regulate Church–state relations, such as concordats between the Holy See and the state, as is the case in Italy and in some of the former Communist states. Ireland's 1935 Constitution gave 'special recognition' to the Catholic Church, although this has since been removed as part of the reconciliation process between the two parts of Ireland (there is a large Protestant population in the North). Even if the Constitution does not explicitly mention religious groups, many countries have passed legislation to regulate religious activities and, in practice, many public services – such as education and health care – are delivered by religious organizations. In the United States, there was also the separation of Church and state following the establishment of the Federation and the first Amendment to the Constitution (1791) forbids both the establishment of religion but also guarantees its free exercise. Unlike in France, this was not designed to stifle religious expression in the public sphere, but rather to ensure that no one church dominated over others as had been the case in Europe. The result has been a lively presence of Christian groups in American civil society and even an assumption that all political leaders will have a religious faith. That is, it is highly unlikely that an atheist would be elected to high public office, whereas in some European countries candidates tend to play down any religious affiliation of beliefs. The most notorious of this is, perhaps, Prime Minister Tony Blair, who wished to become a Catholic but waited until he left office before doing so. Alistair Campbell, his 'spin doctor', notoriously said: 'We don't do God!'

The question of the place of religion in European integration was debated during the Convention on the Future of Europe, presided over by Valéry Giscard d'Estaing. This attempted to devise a Constitutional Treaty for Europe, with a preamble laying out some of the values and principles of the European Union. The question was whether Christianity or, more simply, 'religion' should be explicitly mentioned in this preamble. The Member States were divided on the question, with countries such as the UK, the Scandinavian countries and France being opposed and others, such as Poland (then a candidate member), Spain (before Zapatero), Italy and Malta (also a candidate) being in favour. Interestingly, this was a division between northern (Protestant) Europe and southern (Catholic) Europe. France, although originally Catholic, opposed the reference on the grounds that it would interfere with its tradition of *laïcité.* In the end, the reference to Christianity or even 'religion' was dropped in favour of a vaguer reference to 'spiritual' traditions. Nevertheless, the Constitutional Treaty (and the subsequent Lisbon Treaty) gave constitutional recognition for the first time to churches and religious groups as organizations of European civil society.

Religious groups and the delivery of public services

Religious organizations, mainly Christian churches but also other groups such as Muslims, Jews and Sikhs, are involved in the delivery of a wide range of public services, many of which are delivered on behalf of the state. The largest sector here is education where, despite the efforts of secular liberals to remove the Church from this sphere, many schools are run by the churches. This is the case in the UK, Ireland, the Netherlands (where about 70 per cent of the schools are church schools), Italy, Spain, Germany and even France (*l'école privée*). There is also a growing number of Muslim, Jewish and Sikh schools. Other services are health, social services, care for the elderly, orphanages and care of immigrants, refugees and asylum seekers. Many of these services are, at least in part, funded by the state but also partly by the religious organizations themselves, through donations from their members.

Of course, the mere fact that religious organizations deliver these services does not mean that all those involved in delivering the services and all those who benefit from them are religious believers. For example, many of those who teach in Catholic schools may not be practising their faith or even be convinced believers. Many pupils in these schools may come from homes which are highly secularized and only nominally Catholics. Nevertheless, the delivery still ensures that religious organizations do in practice occupy a place in the public sphere. A basic issue that has arisen in contemporary Western societies is to what extent these organizations remain free to practise their own beliefs and whether there may be limits to this. We now turn to the question of religious freedom in political theory.

Contemporary approaches to religious freedom in political theory

Rawlsian secularism

Political theory in the Anglo-Saxon world has been dominated by the work of John Rawls, the American political scientist whose books *A Theory of Justice* (1971) and *Political Liberalism* (1993) provided a philosophical underpinning to the kind of secularist liberal democracy described above. In fact, this is the form of liberal democracy as practised in the United States, although other forms of democracy exist elsewhere. Rawls was concerned with how to reconcile the principles of equality and freedom in a society marked by inequality and unfairness. He developed two principles of justice: the *Liberty Principle*, establishing equal basic liberties for all citizens; and the *Equality Principle*, which would guarantee liberties that represent meaningful options for all in society and ensure distributive justice. Catholics, drawing on the principle of Catholic Social Teaching of the 'preferential option for the poor', would agree with Rawls's insistence that the application of these principles is just if they benefit the worst-off members of society. However, in order for members of society to agree to these principles, Rawls introduces a mind-game in which he argues that they start from an 'original position': from behind a 'veil of ignorance' they should agree on certain basic rights and the redistribution of benefits. This is based on the idea that they set aside knowledge of their own personal characteristics and their own place in society (their social class, religion, economic situation, etc.) as well as what he called 'comprehensive doctrines' (doctrines which make negotiation difficult and of which religion is the most striking example), using 'public reason' in order to arrive at a consensus on what are the basic rules of co-existence. It is here that Catholics, and other religious believers, part company with Rawls as he assumes that religious beliefs are inherently incompatible with 'public reason'. However, the intellectual and cultural elites who have come to dominate Western institutions and the academy since the 1960s tend to agree with Rawls. As Thomas Farr has argued, 'Rawlsian assumptions about the inherently anti-liberal and anti-rational characteristics of religion are widely shared among intellectuals in the West and the United States, including both secularists and many Protestants and Catholics' (Farr 2008: 49).

Rawls's work has provoked a vast debate, with critiques from scholars from a wide variety of intellectual traditions such as Michael Walzer (communitarian), Robert Nozick (libertarian), Amartya Sen (capabilities research), etc. But probably most of these scholars would agree with Rawls's position on the negative consequences of religion for liberal democracy and would agree with restricting religious belief and practice to the private sphere. Others, however, see a more positive role at least for certain religious traditions and, in fact, believe that these traditions may even be necessary to support democracy and that, far from suppressing them in the name of democracy, they should be actively encouraged. In fact, Rawls himself later adopted such a position; but it is the early Rawls that has been most influential. Before examining this latter position, however, it is useful to examine another secularist position that is different from the Rawlsian approach: 'value pluralism'.

Value pluralism

This approach derives from the thought of Isaiah Berlin and has been developed by Joseph Raz (1986), John Gray (1995) and, more recently, by Peter G. Danchin, who has applied it to the application of the principle of religious freedom in international and domestic law (see Danchin 2008a, 2008b). Value pluralism rejects the Rawlsian idea that there is something called 'public reason', which can supply a 'meta' liberal legal framework that takes precedence over any particular value system, including a set of religious beliefs. Berlin argues, in his *Four Essays on Liberty* (1969) that:

> If the claims of two (or more than two) types of liberty prove incompatible in a particular case, and if this is an instance of the clash of values at once absolute and incommensurable, it is better to face this intellectually uncomfortable fact than to ignore it, or automatically attribute it to some deficiency on our part which could be eliminated by an increase in skill or knowledge; or, what is worse still, suppress one of the competing values altogether by pretending that it is identical with its rival – and so end by distorting both.
>
> (quoted in Danchin 2008b)

Berlin, in *The Crooked Timber of Humanity,* suggested that value systems may be ultimately 'incommensurable', that is, no one value system may be placed in a hierarchy of more or less true beliefs (Berlin 1998). They are different sets of beliefs that are simply different interpretations of the good life, which are valid within their own communities. Gray accepts this position but argues (unconvincingly in my opinion) that this is not the same as moral relativism. The political consequences of such an approach are very different from those of Rawls's legal liberalism and, in fact, value pluralists argue that difficulties are resolved not through law but through politics and debate, although Peter Danchin has developed this perspective from the point of view of international and domestic law.

What is positive about this approach from the perspective of religious freedom is that it takes seriously the substantive content of religious beliefs and practices and argues that these should be respected as different accounts of what their adherents perceive to be the good life. It also seems to imply that the Rawlsian meta-legal framework for managing plurality based on the 'original position' and the 'veil of ignorance', is itself an account of what is the good life that has no inherent superiority over any other account, but which it claims to have. However, there is also something inherently relativistic about the 'value pluralism' approach in that it seems to deny that there is the possibility of developing an approach that derives from our common humanity, which could form the basis of relationships among different groups and between these groups and the state itself. It is difficult to see how 'value pluralism' is different from the Western 'multiculturalist' approach, which it criticizes, except that, unlike the latter, it does not denigrate Western Christian culture or see this as inferior to other cultures (Bloom 1987).

The Twin Toleration Thesis – Alfred Stepan

The underlying assumption of the Rawlsian approach is that 'religion', as a comprehensive doctrine which is alien to 'public reason', is difficult to reconcile with liberal democracy and should therefore be confined to the private sphere. Challenging this idea is a third approach, which has been developed in recent years by Alfred Stepan of Columbia University (Stepan 2005). Stepan and the Spanish political scientist Juan Linz, conducted an extensive empirical research survey in different parts of the world on the relationship between religion and democracy. They were concerned with answering the question of whether religion and democracy are compatible. They found that democracy is indeed possible, although not inevitable, in countries with majorities of believers, including Islamic countries. In his article summarizing the findings of this research project, Stepan argues that religions such as Islam and Christianity are actually quite complex and may contain different currents of thought – what he calls 'multivocality' – some of which may be congenial to democracy. In actual practice, there are a number of democratic states where religion is fully recognized and accepted by the state – Hindu-dominated India, with its Muslim, Buddhist, Jainist and Christian minorities and Muslim Indonesia. Other democracies include the Orthodox countries of Romania, Bulgaria and Greece (although this country only recognizes the Orthodox Church). Several countries of Western Europe are democracies with established churches, or where religious groups are present in the public sphere through their provision of public services such as education and health care. Furthermore, the Catholic Church, following the Second Vatican Council has been one of the prime movers in the third wave of democracy in Latin America and Africa. However, Stepan also recognizes that some strands within religious groups, including both Islam and some strands of Catholicism, are not congenial to liberal democracy. Some Muslim groups reject democracy, which is based on the notion of 'sovereignty of the people', since only Allah is sovereign. In Catholicism, we have seen that historically the Church refused to recognize the legitimacy of liberal democracy and accepted this fully only after the Second Vatican Council. Furthermore, there is a strand of 'intégriste' Catholicism, which clings nostalgically to old conceptions of 'Church' and 'throne' or, even more sinisterly, to extreme right ideas as represented by movements such as Jean-Marie Le Pen's *Front National.*

It is with this background in mind that Stepan has proposed what he calls the 'Twin Toleration Thesis'.[6] He argues that the Rawlsian approach of secularism cannot succeed in societies with significant religious communities and, in fact, is likely to be counter-productive, by alienating such communities from the common life of society. In fact, almost no liberal democracy has actually followed the Rawlsian approach, nor is any likely to do so. This is because democracy 'is a system of conflict regulation that allows open competition over the values and goals that citizens want to advance', but there are democratic boundaries within which such competition takes place. This requires the negotiation of a democratic covenant between civil and religious authorities (the 'twin toleration' of one by the other). Government permits both private and public religious activity, including activity designed to influence public policy, within very broad, equally applied limits. Religious individuals and communities agree to avoid actions which 'impinge negatively on the liberties of other citizens or violate democracy and the law'. The Stepanian approach could have a number of positive effects, both for the practice of democracy and for the religious organizations that are present in pluralistic societies.

First, it would enrich democracy itself as it would allow religious groups, with all their rich experience of humanity and of delivering a wide range of services that benefit the common good. Robert Putnam has spoken of 'social capital' as essential for the functioning of a democratic society and religious groups make an important contribution to this. In the United Kingdom, the current coalition government's 'Big Society' programme has strong affinities with Catholic Social Teaching and the involvement of the churches and other religious communities in this programme could be a factor of enhancement of social capital (Loughlin *et al.* 2012). Furthermore, some of the underlying principles of liberal democracy and human rights have their origins in religious concepts: the intrinsic dignity of the human person, the equality of all human beings by virtue of their common Creator and heavenly Father, the imperative to love one's neighbour as oneself, etc. Contemporary human rights lists are often secularized versions of these principles but, by themselves, have little intrinsic justification. Without this philosophical and ethical underpinning and without a truly humanistic (that is an integral humanism) understanding of them, they may become manipulated by powerful lobbies and groups which may, in fact, promote something that is less than human.

Second, the twin toleration approach would assist religious organizations to adapt themselves to democracy. As mentioned above, no major religious group – Christianity, Islam, Hinduism or Judaism – is 'univocal', but is made up of different tendencies, some of which are more compatible with democracy than others. Stepan's approach would encourage these latter tendencies to come to the fore, and this may help the group as a whole to become more successfully integrated into a pluralist, democratic society. In fact, this approach may be important in developing democratic theory and practice and it may be that new forms of democratic expression will develop. Secular Rawlsianism, multiculturalism, and value pluralism all tend, on the contrary, to reinforce the more anti-democratic tendencies within religious groups and either force them into, or encourage them to maintain, their position in a ghetto. Encouraging them to participate fully in the public sphere is thus good for democracy itself in whatever form this takes.

It is obvious that the Stepanian approach can only work if the principle of religious freedom, understood in both its individual and collective senses, is fully respected.

The implementation of the principle of religious freedom in domestic politics and in international affairs

There exists today a somewhat paradoxical situation. On the one hand, many authors have acknowledged that the 1960s 'secularization thesis' has failed to materialize and, to the contrary, religion is still alive and kicking in almost all parts of the world. Peter Berger, one of the original proponents of the thesis, has now declared that he and other sociologists of the 1960s were mistaken, at least with regard to countries outside of a few countries in Western Europe and Canada (Berger 1999) although Bruce (2002) is still holding fast to the old secularization idea. Two journalists from *The Economist*: John Micklethwait and Adrian Woolridge, published a book in 2009 with the title: *God is back: how the global rise of faith is changing the world.* Monica Duffy Toft and her colleagues confirm this on the level of global politics (Toft *et al.* 2011). On the other hand, in recent years there has been a rise in the denial of religious freedom in all parts of the world, both in the form of attacks by aggressive secularism in Western countries and in the remaining Communist regimes and in the denial of religious freedom to religious minorities in countries with a hegemonic religious majority. The latter is the case mostly in Muslim countries, but it may also occur in countries where other faiths are dominant (e.g. in Russia and Greece, where Christian Orthodoxy is the dominant religion). Undoubtedly, the two phenomena are closely related. It is intolerable to some secularists that religion should leave the private sphere and, indeed, feel threatened by the more extreme tendencies within religious groups, such as radical Islamism or the Evangelical Christian Right. Nevertheless, the principle of religious freedom is itself a fundamental freedom, and some today see it as the guarantor of all other basic rights – thus, it is important to resist secularist attempts to undermine it. We may examine its implementation from the perspectives of both domestic and international politics.

Freedom of religion in domestic politics

Article 18 of the Universal Declaration of Human Rights [7] states that:

> Everyone has the right to freedom of thought, conscience and religion; this right includes freedom to change his religion or belief, and freedom, either alone or in community with others and in public or private, to manifest his religion or belief in teaching, practice, worship and observance.

The European Convention on Human Rights has a similar article (Article 9),[8] which seeks to protect freedom of thought, conscience and religion. This states that:

> 1 Everyone has the right to freedom of thought, conscience and religion; this right includes freedom to change his religion or belief and freedom, either alone or in community with others and in public or private, and to manifest his religion or belief, in worship, teaching, practice and observance.
> 2 Freedom to manifest one's religion or beliefs shall be subject only to such limitations as are prescribed by law and are necessary in a democratic society in the interests of public safety, for the protection of public order, health or morals, or for the protection of the rights and freedoms of others.

Recent developments in Western states and elsewhere indicate that the full provisions of these articles are not being respected. A valuable source of information is the International Religious Freedom Report, which is drawn up each year by the US State Deparment. The Report for 2011[9] stated: 'Governments restricted religious freedom in a variety of ways, including registration laws that favored state-sanctioned groups, blasphemy laws, and treatment of religious groups as security threats.' The Report identifies what it calls 'chronic and systemic violators of religious freedom': China, North Korea, Iran, Saudi Arabia, Eritrea, and other countries with authoritarian governments. However, the Report chronicles violations of religious freedom right across the world, including in Western developed countries. Although not mentioned in the US State Department's Report, these infringements range from the closing down of Catholic adoption agencies in the UK, because of their refusal to allow homosexuals to adopt children, to the attempt in Italy by a Finnish atheist to remove crucifixes from school classrooms. There have also been a series of controversies over the wearing of religious symbols or clothing (in France, Belgium, and the UK) and whether Christians may refuse to participate in abortions, or civil partnership ceremonies for homosexuals. With the recent legislation of homosexual 'marriage' being proposed in France and the UK (in England and Scotland), these tensions will become more pronounced. Although we should not compare the position of European Christians with the violent persecution of Christians taking place in other parts of the world, nevertheless, there seems little doubt that the human right of religious freedom of these Christians is being denied in some instances.[10]

One of the problems has been in the way that Article 9 of the European Convention and Article 18 of the Universal Declaration are interpreted. Courts and administrations in some countries (including the USA and the UK) and in the Council of Europe, have interpreted these as meaning that individuals are exercising their freedom by being allowed to 'worship' or pray as individuals. The individualist interpretation in fact seems to derive from the secularist Rawlsian version of liberal democracy, which argues that religious groups have no right of voice or presence in the public sphere. The articles, however, can also be interpreted as meaning that religious groups have the right to express and practise their beliefs also as organized communities. These are group rights rather than the rights of simple individuals. The notion of group rights has been developed by Kymlicka with regard to linguistic and cultural minorities, but it could also be applied to religious minorities (Kymlicka 1995). Furthermore, such organized religious communities have as much right to participate in the public sphere as any other groups and have an equal right to try to influence public policy. The Rawlsian approach leads to a situation where a secularist approach is regarded as somehow being superior to a religious freedom and where it alone has a right to voice.

This leads to a secularist interpretation of the law, and this seems to underlie some recent legal judgments in the United Kingdom and the European Court of Human Rights. In the UK, in cases of a conflict between Christians, for whom sexual activity outside of heterosexual marriage (including homosexuality) is morally unacceptable, and homosexuals who argue that, on the basis of equality, diversity and non-discrimination, they should not be refused bed and breakfast in a B&B (bed and breakfast) run by Christians, judges have rather arbitrarily come down on the side of the homosexuals. They have argued that in cases of conflict between two sets of rights, each held equally fervently, then the secularist interpretation trumps the religious. Despite much evidence to the contrary, some English judges have argued, also rather arbitrarily, that the Judaeo–Christian tradition has played no role in the formation of English law. In the case of the display of Italian crucifixes in Italian public schools, the lower instance of the European Court of Human Rights in Strasbourg upheld the complainant's arguments that this was an infringement of her human rights. The Italian government appealed this judgment and the higher instance of the Court upheld the appeal, but only if the display of the crucifix is regarded as a 'cultural' rather than a 'religious' phenomenon. In other words, even a country such as Italy, profoundly influenced by Catholicism and where culture and religion are closely intertwined, cannot express this religious dimension in the public sphere.

Freedom of religion in international affairs

It is interesting that the academic discipline of international relations (IR) has traditionally paid little attention to the phenomenon of religion. This is undoubtedly because the dominant approaches in IR, known as realism, neo-realism, or liberal institutionalism, all accept the secular nation-state as the key actor in international affairs (Farr 2008). International affairs are conceived as a system of 'anarchy' (in the literal sense of there being no world government and not in the popular sense of 'chaos'), in which national self-interest is the dominant driving force that motivates states in the international arena. States are regarded as unitary actors driven by self-interest and power in the same way that individuals in society are so driven. IR theorists have tended to share the Enlightenment and Rawlsian secularist idea that 'religion' is inherently irrational and should not enter into relationships between states. This secularist mentality, dominant in many departments of foreign affairs in Western states, is also often shared in international organizations such as the United Nations (UN) or the World Health Organization (WHO). 'Religion' is at best seen as irrelevant and, at worst, as an obstacle to development programmes. This is despite the fact that the majority of the world's population is religious in some sense and very often religious organizations and non-governmental organizations (NGOs) are at the coal-face of development programmes.

One of the first breaches in this secularist understanding of international relations came with the passage in the United States of the International Religious Freedom Act (IRFA) in 1998 by the US Congress, and the establishment of a special unit within the State Department at Foggy Bottom to implement the Act and to monitor religious freedom internationally. The background to the passage of this Act and the difficulties of its implementation have been described by Thomas Farr (2008). The Act committed the US administration to take action in cases of infringements of religious freedom in other countries. The Act made provision for the establishment of a 'Roving Ambassador' of religious freedom as well as the preparation of a yearly report on religious freedom in the world, which remains a valuable survey. Farr, who was a member of the unit at Foggy Bottom that implemented this, is highly critical of its operation and blames the 'secularist' training (in America's elite Ivy League universities) and mentality of US diplomats and foreign affairs experts for not taking it seriously. He also criticizes the Obama administration for taking a year- and-a-half to appoint the Roving Ambassador in Religious Freedom, while it appointed a Roving Ambassador in LGBT rights almost immediately.

Peter Danchin criticizes the Act for promoting a unilateralist approach to religious freedom rather than a multilateralist approach (Danchin 2008a). According to him, the unilateralist approach was developed under the influence of the American evangelical Right, who had a strong distrust of international organizations and especially of the United Nations. Danchin, however, suggests that the Act would be more effective if the US were to cooperate with the existing bodies for the protection of human rights. Drawing both on the experiences of Thomas Farr and on the analyses of Peter Danchin, it does seem to be the case that the IRFA is something of a damp squib at present. There does not seem to be much appetite in the US administration (whether under Bush or under Obama) to pay its reports more than lip service and to engage in finger-wagging. It is, however, important that those with a concern for religious freedom in international organizations – such as the UN – in different parts of the world, continue to press for the full application of the provisions of Article 18, understood both as individual rights and as a collective right of religious organizations.

Conclusions

A number of points emerge from these reflections. First, religion and even theology have been crucial in the development of the modern Western nation and state, and the different theological traditions following the Reformation led to the diversity of understandings of nation and state in Europe and elsewhere. Second, despite the efforts of secularism to remove religion from the public sphere, religion and religious organizations remain important both constitutionally and legally, and in the delivery of a range of public services that are delegated to them by the state in many countries. Third, there are different understandings of the way in which religion affects democratic practice. Most Christian churches would accept that we have in the West a secular state, but insist that a healthy democracy demands they be recognized as actors in the public sphere and should not be confined to the private sphere. Secularists, to the contrary, would try to remove religion entirely from the public sphere and even from the delivery of public services. In theoretical terms, this might be seen as a conflict between the versions of democracy of Alfred Stepan and John Rawls respectively. One general conclusion that may be reached is: religion has definitely not disappeared, nor has it become irrelevant.

Notes

1 Fellow of St Edmund's College, Cambridge, Director of the Von Hügel Institute, Cambridge (www.vhi.st-edmunds.cam.ac.uk/) and Senior Fellow in the Department of Politics and International Studies, University of Cambridge.

2 However, the nation-state has also been associated with non- and even anti-democratic political regimes such as Nazi Germany, Fascist Italy, China, Albania and the former Communist states of East and Central Europe. Japan is another example, being the first Asian nation-state.

3 The full text of *Exurge Domine* is available at: Papal Encyclicals Online: www.papalencyclicals.net/Leo10/l10exdom.htm (accessed 12 May 2014).

4 Available at: www.papalencyclicals.net/Pius09/p9syll.htm (accessed 12 May 2014).

5 Both documents are available at: www.cin.org/v2church.html (accessed 12 May 2014).

6 In this section I am following the excellent summary of Stepan's thesis provided by Thomas Farr (2008: 95).

7 Available at the UN website: www.un.org/en/documents/udhr/ (accessed 12 May 2014).

8 Available at the Council of Europe website: www.echr.coe.int/Documents/Convention_ENG.pdf (accessed 12 May 2014).

9 Available at US State Department online: www.state.gov/j/drl/rls/irf/2011religiousfreedom/index.htm#wrapper (accessed 12 May 2014).

10 The Observatory on Intolerance and Discrimination against Christians (Dokumentationsarchiv der Intoleranz gegen Christen) is a non-governmental and not-for-profit organization registered under Austrian law and headed by Dr Gudrun Kugler, which has produced extensive documentation of cases of discrimination against Christians in Europe. See, www.intoleranceagainstchristians.eu/index.php?id=818 (accessed 8 November 2012).

5 Postsecular awareness and the depth of pluralism

Paolo Monti

Introduction: the burdens of religious pluralism

In contemporary democratic societies, conditions of significant cultural, moral and political pluralism are often celebrated as a resource and a value in themselves. However, while religious pluralism is often considered an integral part of this diversity, the role of religion in public discourse is surrounded by doubts and concerns, and the place of religious arguments in political deliberation is questioned and limited. It has been widely argued that religious citizens should join political discussion on secular terms, find secular reasons and motivations to support their positions, or express in secular terms the moral insights behind their religious convictions. Whether this is simply accepted as a feature of liberal democracy or straightforwardly refused as a form of discrimination against religious people, it is reasonable to question what is so special about religion to the point that, in an age of flourishing diversity, it is still set apart in different ways. This is especially problematic if we focus on the deliberative aspect of democratic life and we consider the different kinds of burdens that religious and secular citizens are expected to bear in order to engage in political conversations.

Any inquiry concerned with this restless and unsettling status of religion in the public sphere includes, more or less overtly, some kind of understanding of secularization. My aim here, in particular, is to discuss the postsecular outlook as an account of the features of religious pluralism, which offers relevant conceptual resources to normatively frame the process of democratic deliberation within a more egalitarian distribution of the burdens required from secular and religious citizens to join the conversation. To this purpose, we need both to clear the field of some reductive interpretations of the postsecular and to overcome some of its internal limitations.

The notion of postsecularism (Calhoun *et al.* 2011; Gorski *et al.* 2012; Nynäs *et al.* 2012), which owes much to Habermas' later writings and the reactions they provoked, has often been discussed along two lines: inclusion versus exclusion of religious utterances in public discourse; resurgence versus decline of religions in the public sphere. The first line is based on the argument about the universalistic claims of political liberalism and their conflictive relationship with communitarian commitments of various kinds, which have certainly contributed several important conceptual premises to the discussion of postsecularism. The second line has revolved mainly around the philosophical and historical assessment of the role of religion in contemporary societies and has sometimes led to polarizing outcomes within the democratic debate. The logic of inclusion and exclusion, though, is premised on the notion of a sharply defined and shared political perimeter, which, in time, has been rather obfuscated by several factors, including strong processes of migration, the weakening of political powers in globalized settings and significant trends of disaffection for political participation (Crouch 2004). On the other hand, the decline or resurgence of religions seems too narrow an interpretive scheme to capture the complexity of a situation where religious and secular beliefs are increasingly detached from fixed memberships of institutional groups, are often distributed along diverse, nuanced and personal arrangements (Davie 2000; Beck 2010: 47–92) and show a significant diversity in weakness or strength within different regions of the world (Norris and Inglehart 2004).

By drawing mainly, but not only, on the work of Jürgen Habermas and Charles Taylor, I am going to suggest that the postsecular turn provides a more substantial and insightful contribution to the understanding of religious pluralism in contexts of late secularization,[1] thanks to its focus on how the self-understanding of religious and secular actors is affected by their co-implication within the same discursive space. The ensuing attention to the processes of self-critique and reciprocal learning allows for a fairer distribution of the burdens of participation, consistently with standards of parity which can be properly, but not exclusively, understood within an egalitarian liberal outlook. The participation in a shared conversation about the primary goods is seen, here, as a primary good in itself.[2] Equal opportunities of participation require more than just accessibility, but also a fairly equal effort to be considered as legitimate, active members within that conversation. In this sense, the accessibility issue cannot be properly addressed by the definition of some epistemic boundaries of public reason, but rather needs to take into account the overall effort which is expected from each interlocutor, particularly when it comes to the impact that entering the public conversation demands on his or her own self-understanding as an individual, a believer and a member of society. The postsecular literature is, in general, widely aware of this problem of the distribution of burdens and it often directly engages with its implications, but it is also still entangled in an indecisive characterization of the differences between religions and secular worldviews, to the point that it seems unable to appropriately justify the egalitarian distribution it generally advocates.

I argue that it is possible to move away from this problem while still retaining the distinct awareness that the postsecular stance articulates about the role played by self-critical understandings of religious and secular views when it comes to the cooperative effort necessary to realize conditions of genuine epistemic parity and equal access to public discourse. To this end, I suggest that three further steps should be taken: the boundary between the religious and the secular should be more decisively conceived as a shifting and porous border; the resources of public discourse should not be too rigidly divided between the argumentative and the non-argumentative; and the presence of stoppers and enablers of public conversation should be acknowledged both in the religious and in the secular domains. The resulting kind of postsecular perspective will be relevant at two levels: that of the relationships between individuals who actively engage in public discourse and that of the relationships between religious and secular institutions.

Religious pluralism and the problem of deep politics

The problem of the inequality of burdens between religious and secular citizens is heavily influenced by the dispute over the relationship between the two defining domains. It is not surprising, then, that this problem has become increasingly apparent as the idea of secularization has increasingly come under scrutiny. The traditional theory of secularization, which foresaw the substantial disappearance of religious belief and the strict privatization of religious commitment, has been challenged by views which underline the transformation of religious experience and the persisting public weight of religious groups (Berger 1999). The process of secularization has changed the conditions of belief and has transformed religious commitment into one option among others (Taylor 2007a: 539–44), but religions are still far from being socially irrelevant or publicly absent. Secularization has also changed the conditions of political cooperation, by separating and diversifying the spheres of social agency, but those spheres, including the religious one, have kept a significant level of permeability and interconnection (Casanova 1994).

It seems, then, that the increasing pluralism of ideas, practices and identities has transformed the religious and the secular domains, equalizing the respective conditions of commitment and increasing their level of interaction. On the other hand, although they have been changed, their features and differences have not been dissolved in the process. In other words, we could say that with the decline of the secularization narrative, the border between the secular and the religious has become more porous, but has not vanished.

Within this kind of scenario, when religious commitment is at stake, public disagreement cannot be framed merely as a conflict about specific normative contents. More profoundly, it is a conflict about the self-understanding that individuals hold of the relationship between their fundamental values and their public identity. What I am suggesting here can be grounded in a hermeneutical framework similar to that which Taylor articulated around the idea of self-interpretation:

> We have to think of man as a self-interpreting animal. He is necessarily so, for there is no such thing as the structure of meanings for him independently of his interpretation of them; for one is woven into the other. But then the text of our interpretation is not that heterogeneous from what is interpreted;

> for what is interpreted is itself an interpretation; a self-interpretation which is embedded in a stream of action. It is an interpretation of experiential meaning which contributes to the constitution of this meaning.
>
> (Taylor 1985: 26)

My focus here is especially on the implications of this self-interpretive structure of the practices of public discussion and deliberation. Again, as Taylor points out, the way the individual actors are involved within these practices is related to their implicit understanding:

> That some practice is voting or negotiating has to do in part with the vocabulary established in a society as appropriate for engaging in it or describing it. Hence implicit in these practices is a certain vision of the agent and his society, which is that of the society or community.
>
> (Taylor 1985: 35)

Most notably, though, under conditions of strong pluralism, there is not a simple shared understanding attached to these practices and there is not even a composition of several specific communitarian understandings of these practices, which is what Taylor used to suggest in his works on multiculturalism.

In this scenario, characterized by the increasing individualization of belief and by the crisis of institutionalized religions, it seems that the implications of religious pluralism can be better described as a problem of 'deep politics' (Talisse 2009: 35–8):[3] the democratic system, which creates and nurtures the conditions for this kind of pluralism, is challenged by the need to integrate the diversity of self-understandings that its citizens express and to provide them with fair and effective conditions of access into the space of public deliberation. As Robert Talisse noted, any notion of pluralism that construes the phenomenon of disagreement as a difference negotiable within the framework of democratic procedures misses how this negotiability may be exactly what is at stake and needs constantly to be discursively arranged:

> There is a good reason to think that citizens cannot adopt such a self-understanding without transforming and thus violating the values they hold most dear; for, according to many citizens, their moral commitments – along with their particular understandings of justice, liberty, dignity, equality, and the right and the good – are prior to their democratic commitments.
>
> (Talisse 2009: 35)

The conditions and features of those conflicting self-understandings, and the scope of their possible transformations, are thus crucial to any serious attempt to deal with the problem of deep politics. It is at this level that the issue of the inequality of burdens has to be addressed: the heaviest burdens do not come from the exercise of negotiation, but from the efforts required to shift one's own self-understanding in relation with the condition of being discursively co-implicated with others.

The Habermasian stance and the asymmetric effort

Postsecular views are built upon the acknowledgement of the limits of the standard theory of secularization (Martin 2005: 123–40) and focus on the relevance and possible transformation of the religious and secular self-understandings in public discourse. In particular, they suggest a new kind of epistemic and practical attitude whose expected outcome is a reciprocal, self-reflective learning process between the actors involved which assumes the transformative consequences that pluralism and secularization are historically having on their identity. This is particularly relevant within Habermas' influential work on the topic, where he embarks on a revision of the understandings that draw the line between some basic correlate notions such as the rational and the irrational or the religious and the secular, and consequently suggests the need for a reconsideration of their normative applications. In particular, Habermas argues that the liberal tradition is biased regarding the definition of the boundaries of the deliberative public sphere, which is often designed from distinctively abstract and secular premises and unfairly imposed upon religious citizens, to the detriment of the vitality and diversity of public discourse. From this concern stems his idea of the postsecular as a social and historical awareness, which allows for a self-critical re-assessment of the epistemic borders of religious and secular views and for a cooperative effort of translation of religious resources, which can serve as a necessary support to the disaffected political life of the Western democracies. While this is clearly a burdening process for the religious citizen, it is also quite engaging for the secular one, as Habermas underlines:

> Historically speaking, religious citizens had to learn to adopt epistemic attitudes toward their secular environment, attitudes that enlightened secular citizens enjoy anyway, since they are not exposed to similar cognitive dissonances in the first place. However, secular citizens are likewise not spared a cognitive burden, because a secularist attitude does not suffice for the expected cooperation with fellow citizens who are religious. This cognitive act of adaptation needs to be distinguished from the political virtue of mere tolerance. What is at stake is not some respectful feel for the possible existential significance of religion for some other person. What we must also expect of the secular citizens is moreover a self-reflective transcending of a secularist self-understanding of Modernity.
>
> (Habermas 2006b: 14–15)

A significant premise of this process of self-reflective adaptation is the influence of the postmetaphysical perspective on both religious and secular views. Roughly, within this perspective, both secular and religious views are subject to pressure to carry out a revision of their epistemic attitudes in a self-critical manner – if nothing else, to admit a certain significant degree of cognitive value to the inputs that come from different outlooks. This allows for a relatively porous border between the secular and the religious domains, and sets the stage for the subsequent transformation and diversification of the self-understanding that each view holds.

The Habermasian stance addresses the transformative effects of the contemporary condition of cultural and political pluralism over the secular and religious traditions, and favours an enhanced awareness of the increasing internal pluralism within secular and religious identities (Calhoun *et al.* 2011: 114–44). Moreover, it not only captures some deep features of contemporary religious pluralism, but also expresses a distinct normative stance when it points to the necessity of renewed terms of cooperation and aims for a more equal distribution of the burdens implied by political coexistence. It should also be noted, though, that to some extent the requirement of translation of religious contents into a non-religious, widely accessible language, even if meant as a cooperative effort, still characterizes his view of the public sphere, particularly in its strong sense (Fraser 1992), as fairly prioritizing a secular, liberal paradigm of discourse. Around the normative implications of the requirement of translation, though, his view is especially questionable, since on the inequality of burdens over secular and religious citizens it does not seem to go as far as the postsecular premises themselves would allow.

In Habermas' understanding, the burden of translation is equal because some of the effort is to be shared by everyone, religious and secular, but it is still not exactly the same kind of burden for everyone. Within the Habermasian framework, then, a status of substantial parity of the epistemic conditions of participation in public discourse does not seem to be undermined by the radically different weight of burdens as much as it is by a significant asymmetry in the nature of the expected effort. While it cannot be denied that in Habermas's view every citizen is expected to take a step forward to bring about a condition of communicative equality and to avoid the imposition of any worldview as the main public representation of the world, the required translation effort is still strictly a one-way process, from a religious language to a secular one. Therefore, the postsecular stance prescribes a process of cooperative translation and reciprocal learning, but this does not entail a strictly symmetrical effort for the religious and the secular citizen. Habermas is aware of the issue, and accounts for it as follows:

> That the expectation of tolerance does not have a neutral effect on believers and unbelievers is not surprising but as yet does not reflect an injustice per se. For the burden is not one-sided. A price is also demanded from religiously tone-deaf citizens. The understanding of tolerance in liberal pluralistic societies requires not only believers to recognize that they must *reasonably* reckon with the persistent disagreement in their dealings with adherents of other faiths. The same recognition is also required of unbelievers in dealing with believers. For the secular consciousness, this implies the nontrivial requirement to determine the relation between faith and knowledge *self-critically* from the perspective of secular knowledge.
>
> (Habermas 2008a: 309–10)

The burden is thus shared, but not in the same way and to the same effect. In Habermas view the expectation is nonetheless acceptable, since it finds on the other side a corresponding, but not mirroring, expectation from secular citizens to accept to some extent an informal use of religious language and to join the translation efforts of their counterparts. It is probably in this sense that Habermas elsewhere speaks of a complementary effort, a term which suggests a cooperative engagement, but not of the same kind for each interlocutor.

The uncertain specificity of religion

The premise behind this still 'unbalanced' burden is that the line between accessibility and inaccessibility, or at least between narrow and wide accessibility, is still essentially identified with the distinction between the secular and the religious. If we look at the dialogue between Habermas and Taylor, we can see how it exemplifies this kind of contrast between different views on the status of religions and their relationship with the status of other cultural and ideological actors. Taylor is concerned that the separate status that liberal views, including the Habermasian one, acknowledge to religion could be connected with a condition of radical epistemic imparity between secular and religious beliefs. His own conception of the immanent frame, as the distinct setting of late secularization, where the religious sphere is defined as optional but the struggle between openness and closure is still very much vibrant, shares some of the features of the Habermasian conception of the postsecular, but is less committed to the priority of secular language and to the Kantian heritage of a comprehensive postmetaphysical perspective (Taylor 2007a: 539–617). Nonetheless, Taylor agrees on the primacy of non-religious language, at least when it comes to the 'strong publics', the sphere of institutional powers.

These different takes on the status of religion compared to that of other kinds of worldviews, or ideological frameworks, bring us back to the underlying question that the postsecular outlooks inherit from the traditional liberal debate on the role of religion in the public sphere: what is so special about religion to the point that it must be subject to distinct constraints? If religion is different from other worldviews and, due to that difference, it brings to the table some unique cognitive and motivational resources that the tradition of the Enlightenment seems unable to express, as Habermas suggests,[4] how does the translation into a secular form preserve that uniqueness? On the other hand, if religion is not different, why is it so problematic in a way that other worldviews are not, to the point that religious language should be excluded from the institutional sphere in a way which is not generally expected from, say, Marxist, Kantian or utilitarian conceptions?

Admittedly, Habermas and Taylor, and the postsecular stances in general, bring to the table a significant awareness concerning the historically mutual influence of secular and religious perspectives and the internal role that self-critical understandings have on the epistemic attitudes of both sides. This does offer some resources to articulate the conundrum. Habermas himself seems aware that translation may fall short of its purpose if in transferring religious insights, they get lost in the process. As he asserts:

> the purely procedural definition of the act of translation with a view to an 'unrestricted reciprocal justification' does not do justice to the semantic problem of transposing the contents of religious speech into a post-religious and post-metaphysical form of representation. As a result, the difference between ethical and religious discourse gets lost.
>
> (Habermas 2006b: 23)

Habermas suggests that a cooperative form of translation should overcome this difficulty, but it does not seem clear how. The examples of translation he mentions, like the idea of individual fundamental rights being derived from Christians' insights into the dignity of human beings as children of God, are not very helpful, since they seem to go directly towards a substantial 'moralization' of theological views. The specific way in which meanings are articulated within the original religious language seems essentially absent within the traditional juridical and political discourse on human rights and Habermas does not show how a cooperative effort could offer a different outcome.

Taylor, on the other hand, acknowledges that if there is no profound distinction between religious and non-religious worldviews, then there is not even much room to express a strong preference to one or the other's language. He thus argues that:

> If you want an emphasis on negotiation, where we put together our charter of rights from different people, it can't be in Benthamite language, it can't be simply in Kantian language, it can't be in Christian language. What Jürgen calls 'secular' I'll call 'neutral.' That's how I see it. I see it as absolutely indispensable.
>
> (Habermas and Taylor 2011: 66–7)

It is to be noted, though, that an extensive 'neutralization' of language, even if just within the boundaries of institutional discourse, while it is more equal in the treatment of participants, seems to make public discourse in some way even less hospitable to the cognitive and motivational resources of different traditions, both religious and secular. If the principle of translation fails to be hospitable to the diversity of religious and secular contributions, though, it also loses much of its appeal. Moreover, if the destination of the cooperative effort is a neutral one, it can be fairer in the treatment of different contents, religious and secular alike, but it is still not *fair* towards the diversity of self-understandings. Some people may be differently affected by the estrangement of a normative outcome, which is intentionally neutral towards their linguistic horizon if, say, their deepest personal motivations have always been articulated exclusively within that horizon or if they are less committed to a comprehensive perspective.

More traditionally, liberal views have often justified the special status of religion by reference to its peculiar traits of epistemic and practical authority and to its essential role within the identity of religious people. It is the kind of stance that has been taken, among others, by Audi (2011: 70–2). His work on the topic of religious commitments in the public sphere is, in general, an example of a liberal view that is practically quite inclusive of religious reasons and motivations in public debate, but which maintains a strong division between secular and religious discourse and does not embrace postsecular views on the translation of religious contents and the self-critical understandings of the secular. It is in this sense that, in his reply to some remarks made by Habermas about the unequal burden that his 'principle of secular rationale' imposes, he argues how the requirement of translation could actually impose a greater burden as it seems to imply that religious citizens should be able not only to understand secular discourse, but also to find a significant level of correspondence between the two (Audi 2011: 88–9). On the other hand, though, by focusing generically on authority and identity to define the specificity of religion, this kind of perspective falls somewhat short of accounting for the diversity of religious groups and for the remarkable similarities that non-religious factions can have when it comes to their internal profile of leadership and authority.

Moving beyond the entanglement of the inconclusive alternative about the, supposedly special, status of religions may thus prove useful to the advancement of the inquiry into the normative boundaries of religious discourse in the public sphere and, especially, into the issue of the unequal burdens they may impose. This kind of move may be performed in various ways. One of Dworkin's last contributions to the debate has been precisely an account of religion that vastly extends the application of the term and redesigns its boundaries by drawing the line between naturalistic views and views hospitable to the intrinsic value of human life and nature, regardless of their stance, say, on the existence of God (Dworkin 2013: 1–21). While this kind of perspective is certainly stimulating, insofar as it pushes for a strong reconsideration of established borders between the religious and the secular, my claim here is smaller. The matter at stake is limited to public conversation and to how religious and secular actors can fruitfully interact within it on equal terms. The postsecular weakening of the separation between secular and religious discourses, is, I argue, a decisive factor to redefine the terms of that conversation in a fairer way and, I argue, it should be stressed further. However, this kind of stance does not strictly imply, or deny, anything about the nature of secular and religious views per se. More modestly, it makes two points: that there is no obvious priority between the religious and the secular in the ability to contribute to the shared conversation, and that it is necessary to acknowledge the role of a plurality of self-understandings, religious and secular alike, over the conditions of a shared conversation.

Acknowledging the plurality of discourses

Drawing the line of universal accessibility to public discourse in a way which does not immediately prioritize the secular over the religious, or vice versa, means that we may not need to rely decisively on the kind of content and not even on the genre of discourse, whether it is mainly argumentative, narrative or expressive. It is in this sense that Jean-Marc Ferry has argued for a 'consensus through confrontation', which conceives public discourse as a process of open and practical discussion that takes seriously the deep moral resources of each citizen, regardless of their religious or secular character, along with their normative self-understanding, which may not be compatible with the privatization and negotiability of some personal values and beliefs (Ferry 2005: 81–6).[5] From this perspective, the process of self-reflective understanding that religious views undertake when entering the public square does not necessarily imply, at least prima facie, a substantial translation into non-religious, argumentative terms, where the symbolic and mythical elements are removed along with the specific resources of meaning they express. The process is rather seen as a softer kind of elaboration, which aims to preserve the original moral grammars embedded in religious languages and leads to an internal re-framing of the narratives and imaginaries of the religious actors in new terms, which may still be of a religious character and non-strictly argumentative when it comes to their genre, but which are epistemically characterized by the acknowledgement of their fallibility, in a non-dogmatic fashion (Ferry 2010a; Lingua 2012: 257–311). Certainly, this kind of shift within the epistemic claims connected with religious contents and narratives may still be seen to be as demanding, say, as the Habermasian process of translation. Nonetheless, Ferry's view suggests that, within a postsecular outlook, which accounts for the intertwined processes of self-understanding of religious and secular actors, the decisive alternative to the participation in public discourse may not lie in the religious or secular, narrative or argumentative nature of the utterances, but rather in the interlocutory or dogmatic character of the contribution they bring to the table. Certainly, Ferry also argues that within the political and judicial institutions, the priority of non-religious language is still necessarily normative (Ferry 2010b: 54–6), but it is interesting enough that, when it comes to public discourse in general, the focus here shifts from a requirement of translation to a requirement of internal reformulation of the epistemic claims while staying within the linguistic resources that forge the self-understanding of religious citizens, without having to be transferred to the area of arguments.

It seems, indeed, that sometimes religious participation in public discourse may not be an argument at all. Consider the protest of the monks who led the Saffron Revolution in 2010 by chanting Buddha's words and benedictions in the streets of Burma. The case may be extreme and it does not represent an instance of participation in formal democratic deliberation within specific institutional procedures. Nonetheless, it is a reminder of the fact that, when some basic rights and some foundations of political coexistence are at stake, a social movement may make a strong and widely accessible political case precisely by acting outside the argumentative and secular terms of liberal public discourse. While this may be considered in some way as an exception under extraordinary circumstances, it can also be seen as a significant expression of the fundamental openness of the public sphere to a wide array of content and forms of social communication. Also, it may call for a deep institutional renewal in circumstances when the ordinary political procedures are stuck or even detrimental to the cohesion of the social fabric. In this sense, categorizing this case by underlining its non-institutional nature is descriptively correct, but misses how it was precisely the set of religious meanings accompanying their persons, their role within that society and the strength of their religious testimony, which made their discourse so eloquent to the point of questioning the institutional sphere. The distinctly religious identity and words of the monks started a discursive process and it is not obvious that the process could have been more effective or accessible to their interlocutors if it had been developed in non-religious terms.

Both the genealogies and the genres of public discourse are more pluralistic, and above all more religiously pluralistic, than the views centred around the model of secular argumentation seem prepared to admit. This can be properly appraised by weighting the structural influence exercised over political discourse by the narrative and theatrical qualities of the public sphere (Szakolczai 2013), and by looking at the historical role that religious traditions had in the pre-modern era, when they helped in shaping the basic premises of a rational conception of the public sphere (Salvatore 2010).

Conversation stoppers and conversational requirements

Accommodating a wide plurality of forms of discourse and criticising the exclusivity of a secular and argumentative model may be essential for a more symmetrical and equal distribution of the consequent epistemic burdens, but it still leaves largely unattended the question about the normative boundaries that should nurture an accessible and tolerant conversation and ease the risks of degeneration and conflict. To be able to establish an order between the different kinds of discourse and to identify some distinctions between institutional levels of public debate, we need to take a step further towards the criteria of access and cooperation.

To avoid the pitfalls of the controversy about the 'special status' of religions if compared to that of other kinds of worldviews, we can pursue a shift of the normative burden from a set of constraints which revolve around the religious or secular nature of the public arguments, to a set of less religious-specific communicative and conversational requirements. This should guarantee a more egalitarian distribution of burdens and, at the same time, preserve the principle of universal accessibility to public discourse and political deliberation.

The postsecular perspectives we have considered share the idea that a successful public conversation between religious and secular citizens is the result of a cooperative effort and that this effort is possible, at least partially, because of a process of self-critical re-assessment of one's own epistemic attitudes undertaken by every actor involved. The expected outcome of such a process is, ideally, the mutual acknowledgment of the interlocutor as an epistemic peer, i.e. the acknowledgement of the interlocutor as a rational and competent subject on the matters at stake.[6] Now, this kind of framing can be maintained without implying that the cooperative effort should always consist of a translation into a secular language. The requirement can be more widely conceived as a commitment to reformulate a religious or secular stance into terms that are compatible with the continuing development of the conversation with all the given interlocutors. In this perspective, every understanding of the relationship between personal commitments – religious and secular alike – and public identity, is acceptable insofar as it does not imply a halt to the conversation. A deep pluralism is a radical obstacle to public discourse once it becomes a conversation stopper, but that does not necessarily imply that the self-understanding that characterizes each participant should be translated into a radically different linguistic arrangement to become 'conversational', i.e. loyal and supportive to the ongoing conversation.

The issue of conversation stoppers has been widely debated by several neopragmatic authors. A significant point of arrival of several authors has been the recognition that the status of stopper is not exclusive to religious beliefs, which in some circumstances may actually even enhance the chances of a shared dialogue, but can be entertained also by secular stances (Stout 2003: 86–90; Clanton 2008: 46–7; Rorty 2003: 141–9). As Jeffrey Stout argued against the positions articulated by Rorty on the subject, and which was later reformulated:

> The same sort of difficulty arises for all of us, not only for the religious believers, when we are asked to defend our most deeply ingrained commitments, especially those that we acquired through accumulation instead of through reasoning. We are normally entitled to hold onto commitments of this kind unless they prove problematical in some way – for example by turning out to be either internally incoherent or too hard to square with newly acquired commitments that strike us as highly credible. If the reason for excluding the expression of religious commitments is that they create this kind of discursive impasse, then the only fair way to proceed is to exclude the expression of many nonreligious commitments, as well. But if we go in this direction, Rorty's view will require silence on many of the most important issues of the political agenda.
>
> (Stout 2003: 87–8)

If the property of being a conversation stopper is not essentially bound to the religious or secular nature of content and it does not follow necessarily from its non-argumentative form, it is probably to be found more in general within the epistemic attitudes of the interlocutors, more precisely in the character of the self-understanding of the relationship between personal commitments and public identity, which is at the basis of the problem of 'deep politics'. Talisse has argued that the epistemic conditions of every kind of belief implicitly entail a certain level of endorsement of the democratic principle, understood through a basic 'folk epistemology', which includes some form of intersubjective dialogue and discursive confrontation as indispensable for holding any belief: since holding our beliefs entails some social processes of reason exchange, proper epistemic agency can be exercised only under the implicit acceptance of the conditions of discursive pluralism (Talisse 2009: 121–7). This insight proves useful to our considerations insofar as it suggests that everyone, as a bearer of beliefs, is always within an epistemic condition that allows for the acknowledgement of the justificatory value of cooperative and pluralistic conversations just by relying on premises which are internal to one's own holding of a certain belief. For this epistemic condition to be the basis of a genuine normative requirement upon the self-understanding of one's own role in the public sphere, though, it is necessary to achieve a reflective awareness of one's own practical co-implication, even with all those interlocutors who hold different beliefs and who entertain different kinds of religious or secular self-understandings. The postsecular emphasis on the intertwined articulation of the epistemic practices of the secular and of the religious within the same historical frame of late secularization pushes decisively towards this kind of self-reflective awareness.

Religious and secular citizens should also enter into a shared conversation with their own beliefs and with their own self-understandings, provided that in time they become reflectively aware of the fact that, by doing so, they expose their reasons to the cooperative nature of the shared conversation and are thus expected to cooperatively join the process of reformulation, enrichment and even falsification of their own views. The self-reflective awareness of this essential co-implication of one's own personal commitments with those of others who share the same public sphere is what establishes the minimal conditions of a genuine cooperative effort and reciprocal learning. In this perspective, the effort is not necessarily a one-way translation and the burden it imposes on the participants is variable, depending on the level of cultural and historical understanding that is shared by the different actors, and it is symmetrical, since everyone is involved in the process with the same kind of epistemic status and is potentially required to engage in the same kind of reformulation and revision. In this sense, what acts as a conversation stopper here is neither the religious or secular nature of the arguments nor the narrative or metaphorical nature of the symbolical resources in themselves, but the lack of a cognitive and practical disposition to cooperatively re-arrange and re-formulate those arguments and those resources, which comes from a lack of self-reflective awareness about the co-implication of one's own belief with the beliefs of others within the same public space. To inhabit a certain public space – with its own historical, cultural and social characters – while holding certain beliefs, religious and secular alike, is indeed to be already implicated with others and their beliefs. One's own epistemic practices are to some extent shaped by the presence of different beliefs, under conditions of pluralism, since these beliefs are held by people who are constantly, directly or indirectly, one's co-practitioners at various levels of social life. One's own cooperative practices are to some extent shaped by the presence of different beliefs, since one's co-practitioners, more or less directly so, are believers on their own, with a certain self-understanding about the relationship between their belief and their public identity. Self-understanding and other-understanding are correlated and their interaction shapes the understanding of the social relationship.

It should be noted that I am here pointing to a co-implication that is distinctively both epistemic and practical, in a wide sense. Talisse's own solution to the problem of deep politics is, instead, all on the epistemic side of agreement and disagreement. He asserts that:

> We experience disagreement over fundamental matters of religion and morality as conflicts because we are implicitly committed to the idea that our own commitments are true. [...] The problem of deep politics arises precisely because we are deeply committed not simply to our moral and religious doctrines, but to their truth. I have argued that the commitment to the truth of a belief compels us to engage in certain epistemic activities that can exist and thrive only within a democratic political context.
>
> (Talisse 2009: 149)

Here I am trying to suggest that our commitment is not only to the truth of our beliefs, but also to their goodness, particularly when it comes to religious beliefs, which are always to some extent embedded in some view about salvation, but also when it comes to secular beliefs, which in some way are connected with a sense of value of the exercise of critical thinking against myths and superstitions. Our beliefs in the public sphere are co-implicated with those of others relative to the practical realization of their goodness as much as relative to the epistemic pursuit of their truth.

Troubled conversations

All the actors, individuals or groups can react with hostility to this condition of co-implication and their own epistemic and social practices may consequently take the form of refusal, defence and isolation. Persistent disagreement over the most relevant issues is extremely common and there is no kind of reflexive awareness that could, or maybe even should, get rid of it. The point is, rather, how to define boundaries that can at least keep that kind of disagreement within a conversational horizon and minimize the chances of degeneration into open conflict or radical estrangement. The egalitarian nature of these boundaries is functional to this purpose, insofar as the burdens that come with it do not create or exacerbate a condition of imparity between the interlocutors. Differences and contrasts are not going to disappear, but they can be clarified, adapted and reshaped to be meaningful within the interlocution.

Beyond ordinary disagreement, fully fledged positions of estrangement and conflict still remain a very real possibility. The actors, though, by taking that kind of stance, implicitly reveal how deeply the form of their own belief is intertwined with 'foreign' beliefs and those who hold them. It is in this sense that a reflective awareness of one's own conditions of belief within a pluralistic public sphere may lead, in postsecular terms, to a self-critical re-assessment and, consequently, may enable an enduring conversation: insofar as it grasps how the conversation with others is already in some way internal to one's own beliefs. The social effect of this emerging awareness about a shift in the conditions of belief within pluralistic contexts is captured in these terms by Berger:

> Pluralism also has profound consequences for individual life. [...] Indeed, modernization can be described as a gigantic shift in the human condition from one of fate to one of choice. [...] This means that even if the same traditional beliefs and values continue to be affirmed, the manner of affirmation has changed. Put simply, the what of belief may not change, but the how does.
>
> (Berger 2010: 6)

If denied, this structural co-implication with the beliefs of others implies a contradiction within the grounds of one's own self-understanding as a believer who inhabits a public sphere. It is a co-implication that, reflectively, cannot be entirely denied, even if its normative bearing over one's own self-understanding can be voluntarily ignored or refused.

In dealing with the issue of persisting disagreements, it is also important to distinguish between absolute conversation stops and relative conversation halts. Violence and suppression of the interlocutors can be seen as the most obvious cases of absolute conversation stops, but strong insulation and indifference may count as well. Established disagreements on normative issues, electoral outcomes or the promulgation of a certain piece of legislation are typical instances of relative conversation halts (Wolterstorff 2012: 47–9). The latter category of halts still falls within the conversational requirements, since it may be seen as a form of punctuation that articulates the conversation but does not bring it to an end. Within a situation of relative halt, we are unable to keep the conversation going. We are still in a conversational relationship, even if we might have to readjust somewhat the terms of the discursive process from that point on. A controversial political decision on ethically sensitive issues like, say, stem cell research or assisted suicide, may come to determine a situation in between a relative halt and a full stop to the conversation. Within these troubled times for public discourse, a more egalitarian framework may once again prove relevant to keep the conversation going, insofar as it does not expect the interlocutors to drop their religious or secular standpoint about matters of deepest concern, but rather pushes them to re-articulate it in a way open to the discursive evolution of the state of affairs.

Truly un-conversational is thus only any self-understanding of the relationship between personal commitments and public identity that actively rejects any structural co-implication with the self-understandings of others. The social expressions of those deeply un-conversational self-understandings cannot be easily integrated within the realm of public discourse – and even less political deliberation – since they are indifferent to the cooperative pre-conditions of an enduring conversation. As we noted, though, this kind of un-conversational trait is not religious or secular per se. Let us consider the famous example of Martin Luther King's religious discourse within the history of the Civil Rights Movement. It has been seen by several authors as an interesting case of how a non-secular kind of discourse had a major impact on the effect of expanding civil rights and enhancing the democratic character of a whole nation. In many ways, though, it has been to some extent regarded as a marginal case, if not an outright exception to the basic normative boundaries of political discourse, justified by special circumstances and special goals, or at least as a less problematic instance of religious speech in public debate, since it did not express an argument for coercion, but for increased liberty (Audi 2011: 47–9). In our account, it is rather to be seen as an exemplary case: secular citizens could understand and join that cause, because it was a public act which performatively enlarged the scope of public discourse and political participation, and by doing so it was widening the boundaries of a conversation they were already practically engaged with. By cooperatively joining that effort, they could also understand how those religious words were positively modifying and expanding the semantics of their own discourse. It is in this sense that conversational and un-conversational traits are not tied to pre-defined, confessional identities and conceptual areas: they are rather shifting, sometimes uncertain, attributes whose boundaries are set by the successes and failures of a cooperative effort of constant interpretation and re-assessment of one's own position in the public sphere in relation to that of others.

Postsecular walls of separation

The debate over the secular nature of political institutions and the concerns about the relationship between churches and states is directly affected by this kind of view. In a deliberative perspective, the fundamental political institutions should act as conversation-enablers, and their relationship with individuals and groups should be shaped by this purpose.

We could ask ourselves if a secular state acts as a conversation stopper for its sincerely religious citizens, or if it is rather an antidote to the constant obstacles to public conversations that may result from a direct political involvement of religious organizations. Such a question, though, cannot receive a simple and straightforward answer, since it seems that in appropriate circumstances, both scenarios may be plausible.

We should probably rather look first at the traditional principle of the separation between church and state and re-assess its relevance within the view on public conversation we have sketched. In this perspective, a certain degree of respect and protection for the peculiarity and the autonomy of each interlocutor appears to be a condition for any proper conversation to happen and endure. As we mentioned, the democratic state lives upon the practice of a vital public conversation and it is thus internally bound to the purpose of preserving and enhancing the conditions of that conversation;[7] therefore, should it be identified with one of the participants of the conversation or subject to its unilateral influence, it would in the end undermine the possibility of a genuinely conversational self-understanding of the actors, since they would not be co-implicated within the same discursive space in an equal manner. A requirement of distinction between the institutional actors is thus needed to avoid the fusion, and confusion, of the several kinds of participants which articulate the conversation of a democratic society. Such a requirement of distinction is to be translated into a normative principle of separation between churches and states, but also between secular groups and states and, in general, we could say, between the actors of civil society and political institutions. This kind of articulation of the principle of separation can certainly still allow for a distinctively secular state, insofar as, under certain historical and social conditions, a strongly secular characterization of the political authority, say within the French republican tradition, may prove necessary to counter the long-standing political influence of some religious subjects over the order of political power. In this sense, Casanova has argued that the strength of the secularization process in Europe has been the consequence of a local history characterized by long-standing connections between religious and political powers, where the churches were late in understanding the need to re-articulate the distinction between the spheres (Casanova 2006: 65–92). However, the enforcement of a principle of separation does not necessarily entail that kind of secular model either. Under different historical conditions it is at least possible to admit that the active enforcement of a strong non-religious character of public institutions, say by requiring state schools and hospitals to be free from any kind of religious reference, may prove to be more of a conversation stopper than a conversation enhancer, because of the sense of detachment and distrust it would create in the self-understanding of religious people as citizens of that state. It is useful to keep as a reference a model of citizenship not just as a juridical status but as a condition of full membership within a given society (Weithman 2001). In this perspective, citizenship is a multi-layered condition, and access to public conversation is but one component of that membership. Economic and social factors also play a distinct role: the issue of power and recognition is always crucial when it comes to the exercise of democratic conversation. The separation of church and state and the equality of burdens, which are here the object of our direct concern, are just two elements within the overall problem of the material conditions of a genuinely open and accessible public conversation.

It should be noted that a similar line of reasoning may be followed regarding the specific issue of the acceptability of religious language in institutional contexts. The language of parliaments and courts should generally reflect the conversation-enabler role of the institutions, thus clearly keeping on average a considerable distance from any typical and clearly confessional religious language. At the same time, the sites of formal deliberation are also meant to reflect the plural nature of the ongoing public conversation, thus being hospitable to possible references to some specific religious or secular resources, as long as these are articulated within the awareness of their structural discursive co-implication with other resources. Again, this approach will not necessarily lead to a single kind of arrangement. The differences between American and

European political rhetoric when it comes to references to God or to some form of civil religion are notorious, and at the same do not necessarily imply that one of the two is less capable, per se, of enabling participation relative to the conversation between religious and secular actors. The conversation will always live upon cooperative arrangements made from the linguistic and symbolic resources available within those discursive contexts at any given time.

In the end, just as the self-understandings of secular and religious citizens are at stake within a postsecular framework, so it is for the self-understanding of political and religious institutions. This point is often less emphasized, mainly because the linguistic requirements of the institutional public sphere and of the deliberative procedures are meant to be stronger, if nothing else for cautionary reasons. Still, some more work certainly needs to be done to investigate the possible consequences of the postsecular stances over the institutional order, as some of its transformations are already in their early stages.

Conclusions: living in conditions of deep pluralism

Is the postsecular picture really viable? And is it able to distribute the burdens of a plural and accessible public discourse more equally? The perspective I have offered here, while arguing substantially in favour of the notion of postsecularity, takes different stances over different aspects of it. Some have raised much more radical concerns, though, as sharply exemplified by the positions that Veit Bader has articulated against both the Habermasian framework and the ensuing popularity of the postsecular perspective (Bader 2012).

Bader is persuaded that both secularism and post-secularism should be left out of our constitutional and legal language as a fundamentally flawed conceptual strategy that perpetuates and reinforces the influence of a set of inaccurate generalizations about the religious and the secular. The dualism between secular and postsecular perspectives should then be replaced with a new overall view centred on liberal-democratic constitutionalism (LDC) as the main normative reference for the languages and contents of public discourse. Interestingly enough, my view is compatible with Bader's claims about the 'postsecular exclusivism' represented by the Habermasian translation requirement and it could easily welcome the conviction that, when it comes to the freedoms of political communication, 'at stake is not the secular or the religious character of speech, but whether or not it presents a clear and present danger or seriously discriminates' (Bader 2012: 24). The roads diverge about the fundamental issue of the role of the historical evolution of secular and religious self-understandings. Setting aside Bader's debatable critique about the absence of solid empirical research to support the postsecular picture, if nothing else because Bader seems to offer nothing more than Habermas in this regard, the main point is how feasible and fruitful the option of dropping the category of secularization and its subsequent postsecular evolution could really be. Bader argues that 'replacing secularism with LDC should not be misunderstood as a replacement of one ideology (secularism) with another equally cacophonous or ambiguous one (liberalism). LDC is not a foundational ideology or philosophy, but a meta-constitutional and meta-legal ideal' (Bader 2012: 26). One of the most valuable features of the postsecular perspective is the ability to grasp the importance of secular and religious self-understandings in dealing with the problem of deep pluralism. While Bader is correct in pointing out that the individualization and de-institutionalization of belief renders implausible most essentialisms and generalizations about religion, he seems to entirely miss the point of the postsecular turn when he advocates, as a remedy, for the normativity of a liberal scheme that appears considerably abstract and de-historicized. A deep pluralism of religious and secular self-understandings needs to be integrated within a common conversational framework rather than measured by a supposedly neutral constitutional perspective, which will hardly be capable of resonating in any way with their internal normative resources.

The kind of postsecular framework we have presented here rather aims to offer a normative formulation to the increasing awareness of the resilience of secular and religious traditions within the postmodern horizon. Those traditions were not dissolved by the crisis of grand narratives, but they were internally unsettled when it comes to their epistemic and practical claims. The consequences of late secularization generated conservative reactions, religious and secular alike, but also fostered unexpected transformative processes of self-critique, translation, and cooperation. Thus, the specific contribution of postsecularism to the understanding of pluralism lies in the awareness that the pluralistic nature of contemporary societies is not just a condition, the so-called 'fact of pluralism', but also a complex process of shifting interpretations and self-re-assessments, where religious and secular identities are deeply co-implicated. In this context, it is less and less obvious how a single position could claim a regulative role over others and it seems that the mutual relationship should rather be regulated through a cooperative epistemic process of reciprocal learning and eventual adaptation. As has been soundly noted by Habermas himself:

> Rawls developed his 'Theory of Justice' into 'Political Liberalism' because he increasingly recognized the immeasurable relevance of the 'fact of pluralism'. He did posterity a great service in thinking at an early date about the political role of religion. Yet precisely these phenomena should have made a supposedly 'freestanding' political theory aware of the limits of normative arguments. After all, whether the liberal response to religious pluralism can be accepted by the citizens themselves as the single right answer depends not least on whether secular and religious citizens, each from their own respective angle, are prepared to embark on an interpretation of the relationship of faith and knowledge that first enables them to behave in a self-reflexive manner toward each other in the political public sphere.[8]
>
> (Habermas 2006b: 20)

The definition of secular perspectives is internally and dialectically indebted to the ongoing transformation of religious worldviews and vice versa. Such a process mutually binds the self-understandings that the social actors bring into the public sphere and a self-critical reflection on this peculiar co-implication, which defines the identity of secular and religious citizens alike. Within this perspective, the boundaries of public discourse are, to some extent, always the outcome of a cooperative process. Even controversies, as open as they can be, are grounded in a situation of co-implication where each side defines its own stances while exposed to those of others within the same public arena. Everyone is dependent on social cooperation but, at the same time, nobody owns it: the reflective assumption of this co-implication with the interlocutors should lead to the development of a consequent kind of language, a way of joining the conversation, which reflects the ability to distinguish between personal and public narratives, individual commitments and public bonds, but is also able to cooperatively build new forms of shared conversation and mutual understanding of the secular and of the religious alike.

Notes

1 It should be noted that in Habermas' original analysis, this kind of postsecular context is first and foremost the European one, given the still strong and widespread religious character of American society. This view, though, is not necessarily present within every interpretation of the postsecular.

2 If nothing else, because it is directly related to access to all other primary goods. A similar case could be made by considering capabilities instead of primary goods as the equalisandum.

3 While Talisse offers a more general take on the problem of moral conflict, he acknowledges religious self-understandings to be at the basis of the deepest forms of disagreement, as in major controversies over abortion, stem cell research or same-sex marriage.

4 Among others, it is useful to recall this passage:

> However, this same strict rational morality explains why enlightened reason unavoidably loses its grip on the images, preserved by religion, of the moral whole – of the Kingdom of God on earth – as collectively binding ideals. At the same time, practical reason fails to fulfill its own vocation when it no longer has sufficient strength to awaken, and to keep awake, in the minds of secular subjects, an awareness of what is missing, of what cries out to heaven.
>
> (Habermas *et al.* 2010: 19)

5 It is remarkable how the concern displayed in Ferry's work about the different understandings of normativity which come with the deepest moral and religious convictions of citizens mirrors the similar concern articulated by Talisse, from very different philosophical premises, with the concept of 'deep politics'.

6 We cannot pursue here the multiple ramifications of the topic of epistemic parity within the debate about the role of religious reasons in public debate. An interesting view is articulated in Audi (2008: 225–47, 2011: 117–20).

7 This is especially true under deliberative models of democracy. The whole debate about secular and religious reasons in the public sphere, after all, is largely indebted to the focus that deliberative and participatory approaches brought on the discursive dimensions of fundamental democratic institutions.

8 Habermas (2006b: 20).

6 Reconciling diversity and solidarity?

A critical look at Charles Taylor's conception of secularism

Bernard Gagnon

Whose secularism? Which solidarity? These are key questions in the recent works of Charles Taylor. Indeed, what happens to collective solidarity when the "Big Bang" in the universe of human beliefs and convictions is taken into account? After all, secularity – to which Taylor has devoted most of his writings since the publication of *Sources of the Self* (1989a) – has not only resulted in offering a purely human alternative to belief in God, but also has exploded the options to the point of producing a "supernova" in ontological positioning. If, to be viable, democratic societies must be based not only on rules of law and a few shared political principles, but also a set of "common meanings and sensibilities," (Taylor 1991, 1992a) must we not conclude that modern diversity brings with it major constraints to the expression of collective solidarity?

According to Taylor, the problem is not with diversity, which expresses the wealth of human possibilities, both religious and secular, vis-à-vis fundamental questions about the meaning of life. The problem instead lies with democracy, in that it requires a strong collective identity to guarantee the solidarity needed for stable and meaningful collective life. A patriotism strong enough, as he wrote in the mid 1980s, to make acceptable the constraints and sacrifices resulting from collective life, and to make the state something more than an agent for protecting individual rights – namely a space for expressing a common good (Taylor 1988, 1989b). But as his writings have stressed in recent years, the collective identity that underpins democracy has been a source of exclusion and alienation in its quest for unity to the detriment of diversity. Moreover, this exclusion becomes increasingly intolerable with the growth of diversity stemming from within or without society (Taylor 2002a, 2007b). The observation may seem basic, but the problem is complex. "We face a challenge that is unprecedented in human history: creation of a powerful political ethic of solidarity self-consciously grounded on the presence and acceptance of very different views" (Taylor 2010b). This is what Taylor expresses, with certain Aristotelian undertones, by the search for unity "in" and "through" difference.

For Taylor, part of the answer can be found in the model of secularism he advances. This model must be able to reaffirm an ideal of community and sharing, not by transcending differences but, rather, by using them as a springboard. More than just a political model, secularism is then the public spirit that should guide public debates and political institutions in a context of profound diversity. Yet from my perspective, Taylor's model poses a conceptual problem when it comes to reconciling *diversity* and *solidarity*. While I agree with him that both, today, must find new anchors, in my view the model of secularism he puts forward remains too vague about the theoretical basis for their reconciliation.

To illustrate this point, I will begin by briefly discussing links between Taylor's model of secularism and the way he conceives of modern secularity, since only a clear understanding of the latter will reveal the specificity of the former (pp. 107–109). I will then discuss, on the one hand, the inclusivism of Taylor's conception of secularism with respect to the two most influential models: namely, those set forth by Habermas and Rawls (pp. 109–116). But, on the other hand, I will discuss difficulties arising from Taylor's more inclusive perspective and his endeavor to reconcile diversity and solidarity (pp. 116–120). Taylor's perspective also proves demanding in terms of the civic virtues expected of citizens, but unlike with Habermas and Rawls, the origin of this demand can be entirely attributed to the value systems of individuals, whether religious or non-religious. This makes solidarity reliant upon citizens' subjective values in the context of a model of secularism that is aimed at promoting diversity. Indeed, it seems to me that the inclusivism of Taylor's model is "overly optimistic" in the capacity of diversity to produce harmony and underestimates the role of civic integration in consolidating the social and political bond, and hence solidarity. To conclude, I will nevertheless tease out what appear (to me) to be Charles Taylor's answers to this criticism.

Secularism in the wake of secularity

The model of secularism advanced by Taylor must be placed in the context of his writings on the subject of secularity and the conditions for belief in modern Western societies. Secularity refers to the long historical and cultural process that profoundly changed relationships to belief in Western societies and introduced a diversity of ontological options, both religious and non-religious, in the public sphere. Secularism (*laïcité*) is therefore the political response to secularity. The two concepts are closely related, since one of the problems with secularism today is, for Taylor, that we base ourselves on false premises about secularity. We see it as a model that aims to preserve common institutions from any religious influence, "whereas in fact it has to do with the response of the democratic state to diversity" (Taylor 2011a: 19).

The chief aim of secularity for Taylor is to allow for a *diversity* of beliefs and philosophical views. And this diversity, far from being foreign to the culture of modernity, is intrinsic to it. The real issue in this context is not to adapt the standards of modern political principles to a new social reality marked by the phenomenon of pluralism. Instead, it is to understand how modernity brings about a process that creates an ever-growing breach in the domain of belief. Secularity is "... a move from a society where belief in God is unchallenged and indeed, unproblematic, to one in which it is understood to be one option among others, and frequently not the easiest to embrace" (Taylor 2007a: 3).

This original reading of secularity, which is contrasted with a subtractive understanding that sees modern secularity as a withdrawal of the religious from the social sphere or a retreat of belief and religious practices, also leads to the thesis that the substratum of modernity is not based on any set religious or philosophical view. Instead, this bedrock can be asserted and articulated by a plurality of views. Diverse spiritual and philosophical options are indeed possible, and each individual must find an answer that best corresponds to his or her aspirations and expectations. In other words, secularity is not specifically about religion, even if its marked consequence has been the appearance of a humanist and immanent alternative, along with the establishment of religion as one option among others in the field of ontological answers about the order of things. This diversification of beliefs and convictions, which has taken root in modernity, has progressively gained ground and then skyrocketed with the cultural and expressive revolution of the 1960s in the West – which Taylor calls the Age of Authenticity (2007a). So much so, in fact, that a "nova effect" is unfolding today, with the multiplication of moral and spiritual options across society at large. Modern secularity therefore must be understood as this field of increasingly multiform contestation, in which every position is rendered uneasy and questionable because it can be challenged from many angles (Taylor 2010c: 306).

This ontological diversification is not without social or political consequences; the issue cannot merely be relegated to the sphere of private beliefs and personal convictions, without regard for the repercussions on the political order. The expression of a democratic community critically requires that a strong bond be preserved between the ethical and the political, over and beyond the ontological indeterminacy introduced by the secularization process. Outside these singular ethics, no collective agent is conceivable. "Democratic societies, in their tremendous diversity, are powered by many different engines of commitment to a common ethic. They cannot afford to switch off any of these engines and hope to maintain a political community" (Taylor 2010b). Ontological answers, both religious and philosophical, are guideposts that not only orient our individual lives and interactions with others, but also offer ethical foundations that compensate for the ontological indeterminacy of the political order. However, it is clear that this substantive ethic can no longer take the form of a single ethic shared by all, or replace the void on a supra-individual level. It must take the path of diversity. There is no turning back: the diversity of perspectives is here to stay.

In reference to Claude Lefort, Taylor (2010a) notes that modern secularity ends up leaving a "void" – in the sense of indeterminacy – in place of what should be the ethical foundations of the modern political order. But, on the other hand, the political requires a substantive ethical complement, not only for ontological orientation, but as a driving force for the collective belonging of individuals and common identity. We need a basic political ethic that must be agreed upon by distinct substantive views – religious and non-religious – but each according to its own beliefs. Taylor accordingly points out that "Religion provides a profound and powerful base of solidarity, and to marginalize it would be a big mistake, just as marginalizing atheistic philosophies would be a mistake" (Taylor 2010b). Yet, while the state in a diversified society may no longer be able to dictate the (substantive) good, it is not morally and spiritually indifferent. "… the state must seek to become politically secular but without promoting social secularization" (Maclure and Taylor 2011: 16). Far from aiming for a public space "free" of religious influence, the secular state should strive for the unbounded fulfillment of ontological views.

These recent considerations suggested by Taylor regarding diversity and the political ethic contrast with his past views on the common good and the state. Indeed, *Multiculturalism. Examining the Politics of Recognition* (1992b) sets out that a state, while remaining liberal, could enforce the primacy of the common good based on the principle of equal consideration of citizens' views, as long as it respected the fundamental rights and liberties of each individual. Yet the account of secularization he offers in *A Secular Age* (2007a) renders this avenue obsolete. Although his model of secularism is certainly more inclusive than the politics of recognition that he proposed in the past, in my view, his notion of solidarity is today more ambiguous and largely indeterminate, as the idea of unity or harmony is still fully dependent on adhesion by comprehensive doctrines and various beliefs. Does Taylor then still see a "strong collective identity," a "We," as being essential to liberal democracy? Or has he ultimately agreed, without openly admitting it, that civic integration centered on a few fundamental principles – liberty, equality, the rule of law – today constitutes the main basis – and perhaps the only basis – for social and political cohesion in a context of substantial diversity? The question arises of whether the model's inclusiveness may be at the expense of a spirit of civic humanism or the idea of a strong conception of a politically, historically and socially determined ethic.

The Taylorian critique of the Habermas proviso

The Taylorian model of secularism appears more inclusive than the competing models – notably those of Habermas and Rawls – and better able to avoid the differentiated treatment that they introduce in terms of the respective place of secular and religious discourse in the political spheres. Taylor approaches religion in terms of a transcendent experience that can take multiple and varied expressions (2002c, 2007a). Accordingly, even if in democratic and secular societies religion conserves traditional, hierarchical and institutionalized expressions, a diversity of religious experiences exist. New relationships to transcendence take a radically internal path and stem no longer from the recognition of external authority, but rather from the individual discovery of moral and spiritual sources within oneself. The religious/secular (heteronomy/autonomy) opposition which largely characterizes the structural approach to the question of religion, as found in the works of Habermas (2006a), therefore has no equivalent in the thought of Taylor, for whom religion – the experience of a transcendent truth that extends beyond human life – is not de facto bound to the historical, traditional or authoritarian forms it may have assumed within institutionalized religions (2007a, 2011b).

Habermas, like Taylor, acknowledges that religious views contain recognizable content from a plurality of religious and non-religious viewpoints: they express deeply held or under-valued moral intuitions that would not otherwise be voiced (Habermas 2006a, 2008b). But if he considers that religious discourses have their place in the informal public sphere, they nevertheless must translate their discourse into secular terms, accessible to all, in the formal public sphere if they desire to change laws and policies (Habermas 2008a, 2011; Habermas and Taylor 2011). Conversely, Taylor states that religious discourses and justifications have their place not only in the informal public sphere but also in the formal public sphere (legislative assemblies and government decision-making bodies) except for the specific language of the law. To ask believers to speak the language of secularists in order to be effective in the political sphere is to ask them to renounce their deep convictions about fundamental questions of society without receiving anything in return from secularists, and to make them second-class citizens (Habermas and Taylor 2011). It also goes against the principle of neutrality, which suggests that no ontological perspective, religious or otherwise, should be given privileged status and become the official doctrine of the state. These are hardly the foundations for authentic dialogue:

> [A] political system that replaces religion with a comprehensive secular philosophy as the foundation of its actions makes all the faithful members of a religion into second-class citizens, since these citizens do not embrace the reasons and evaluations enshrined in the officially recognized philosophy.
>
> (Maclure and Taylor 2011: 13–14)

Yet the translation proviso, in Taylor's view, reproduces an inclusive/exclusive dynamic that hinders contemporary democracies' openness to cultural and religious diversity, "Its problem is that it too demands not only the sharing of the political ethic but also of its foundation – in this case, one supposedly independent of religion" (Taylor 1998: 37–38). Reason alone is thought to be inclusive in the abstract – in that it transcends all differences – but in practice it excludes (or treats differently depending on the translational conditions) those who may have reason not to see themselves as coming under the umbrella of reason alone, but who may fully acknowledge the principles of the modern democratic order based on other justifications. Significantly, democratic principles in no way exclude the coexistence of these multiple justifications, even in the accepted language of the law and collective decisions. For Taylor, human-centered political thought is not a more reliable guide than theories informed by political theology:

> If we take key statements of our contemporary political morality, such as those attributing such rights to human beings as, say, the right to life, I cannot see how the fact that we are desiring/enjoying/suffering beings, or the perception that we are rational agents, should provide any surer basis for this right than the fact that we are made in the image of God.
>
> (Taylor 2011a: 21)

The secularist intransigence of Habermas, from this perspective, merely exacerbates the current malaise of democratic societies vis-à-vis diversity instead of responding to it (Taylor 2011c). In a context of diversity, the state cannot in itself produce an independent and ontologically self-sufficient political ethic; this can only lead to marginalizing religious discourse, and in a context of growing diversity, to promoting exclusion (Taylor 2010a).

Taylor's conception of secularism is more inclusive and less constraining, since, to be accessible to all, it is enough that the law be ontologically neutral; it does not require translation into the terms of secular reason, and it is up to each citizen to find reasons to justify his or her belonging to the democratic constitutional order. The Taylorian position is in fact even more inclusive than that of Maeve Cooke (2006), who, in her critical re-reading of Habermas, suggests an improvement to his proviso by differentiating between authoritarian and non-authoritarian epistemological approaches rather than religious and secular ones. But this perspective reproduces the same difficulties as those perceived with Habermas, in that it judges individuals not based on their contribution to the public and political debate, but rather on their beliefs. Moreover, even if Taylor may concede that from a strictly legal standpoint, the position of Habermas introduces no distinction between believers and non-believers, from the standpoint of the equal dignity of citizens, it does since it brings into question the moral equality of individuals. The translation proviso –from religious to secular or from authoritarian to non-authoritarian, according to Cooke – requires that a religious believer renounce deep convictions in a domain – the political sphere – that plays a primary and central role in defining what we are, collectively and individually. It compels the believer to accept that what he or she believes on a deep level can be put on hold when it comes to shaping a collective destiny.

This critique underlines some difficulties with the translation proviso. If one recognizes the semantic and cognitive virtues of religious discourses – a recognition that precedes any translation – why compel those who bear such views to translate them into the terms of secular reason? If non-religious citizens can see some truths in religious discourses, without adhering to religious doctrines, why do they need to translate it into secular reason to be truth for all? The translation proviso appears unnecessary for mutual understanding and results in imposing a constraint on religious believers based solely on their psychological background (Habermas and Taylor 2011). In addition, the Taylorian conception of neutrality offers an amendment to the translation proviso by making it a condition for institutions instead of individuals. For Taylor, the language of the law and political institutions – not the language of citizens – must be neutral and accessible to all, meaning that it uses neither the discourse of religious reason, nor that of secular reason. Dialogue between religious and non-religious citizens, as posited by Habermas, cannot be symmetrical if the results need to be translated into the language of secular reason. According to the Taylorian conception of secularity this would be just as unfair as requiring non-religious citizens to adopt the language of religious reason. Owing to the non-neutral, ontological commitment that is the supremacy of secular reason, this kind of proviso inevitably leads to the infringment of the freedom of conscience and religion of religious persons in the political sphere, and – when this condition of translation applies to one specific group – to the compromising of the moral equality of individuals.

Moreover, regarding Habermas' model, from a Taylorian perspective, religious citizens' belonging to the democratic order and their acknowledgment of the primacy of secular reason in the political sphere is ultimately not based on anything other than a modus vivendi. Indeed, for Habermas, "religious citizens who regard themselves as loyal members of a constitutional democracy must accept the translation proviso as the price to be paid for the neutrality of the state authority toward competing worldviews" (Habermas 2011: 26). Religious citizens' belonging to the democratic order is therefore not a rational recognition of its normative superiority. From the believer's point of view, the proviso is justified by the advantages procured by rights and liberties and not, as Habermas would have it, owing to the primacy of secular reason. Therefore, even if the democratic constitutional state is justified based on autonomous criteria originating from reason alone, this does not, from a practical standpoint, constitute an autonomous and sufficient basis for solidarity in a diversified society. Since Habermas *et al.* (2010) recognizes that religion is here to stay for a substantial portion of populations in democratic societies who do not identify themselves as coming under the aegis of reason alone, we are indeed dealing with a modus vivendi.

The Taylorian re-reading of Rawls' overlapping consensus

Taylor's critique of liberalism maintains that if liberal principles offer the necessary and minimal conditions for a peaceful society in a context of diversity, they remain incomplete to ensure a common identity. Also needed is a sense of sharing that is strong enough to replace the previous substantive ethic that gave body to the political community: the importance of "maintaining harmony and comity among the supporters of different religions and views" (Taylor 2011a: 18). The viability of democratic societies is based on solidarity and this solidarity depends upon the existence of an identity shared by the members of these societies (Taylor 2007c, 2010b; Smith and Laitinen 2009). A common identity is built around a political community and can be conceived as the "sharing" of a collective experience strong enough to give substance and life to a collective agent, a "We":

> ... for a democratic project to succeed, for people to commit themselves to it and accept the discipline and the sacrifices which they often must undergo, they will have to feel linked to a common project which involves some degree of solidarity between certain people and not others.
>
> (Taylor 1992a: 60)

The current problem facing democratic societies today is therefore how to renew this solidarity in a context in which greater diversity renders unacceptable the older forms of assimilation or integration to a homogenous identity. Traditional forms of common identity are contested: both from within by the requirements of recognizing differences; and from without by the arrival of new cultures and new religions. The main difficulty resides in that previous common identities rested on a singular moral and spiritual foundation. In the case of United States, this identity maintained common belonging to a people united by their shared belief in God, and in the case of France, it manifested as an antithesis to religion, as a civil religion (Taylor 2010a). The rub is that, if the heritage of Christianity is here to stay in the culture of modernity, this heritage can no longer serve, whether by synthesis or lack of antithesis, as the foundation for a common identity. Nor can it be replaced by a similar foundation. Taylor does not renounce the "We," the "patriotism" or the "civic humanism" that animated his earlier writings (Taylor 1989b). However, he does observe that the foundation on which they have developed in the past is fading: "Solidarity ... is an indispensable imperative in our democratic times, and at the same time, it is a calling which we cannot answer unconditionally. This is the tragedy of our current position" (Taylor 2007c: 77).

Taylor recently argued for the idea of an overlapping consensus, which he has borrowed from Rawls and adopted as a leitmotiv in his political thought over the past dozen years (Taylor 1998, 2007b; Mendieta and Van Antwerpen 2011):

> The whole point of the overlapping consensus – better put, its superiority as a basis for society over the old post-Enlightenment independent ethic – was just that it doesn't prescribe any underlying justification. These are left to the different spiritual families whose members make up the society.
>
> (Taylor 1998: 51–52)

The consensus is built around a few political principles – individual rights and liberties, democratic rules – to which Taylor has added a few considerations (language, memory, symbols) specific to each national community; for example, in the case of Quebec, preserving the French language comes under the national consensus. These principles constitute shared values that are essential for maintaining a society's democratic life and political cohesion. Overlapping consensus means that individuals will have not only different motives, but also different underlying justifications – some religious, others not – for adhering to these principles.

Taylor considers it undesirable to differentiate religious and secular reason for the purposes of justification, because he rejects the possibility of both an autonomous political ethic and a political reason independent from comprehensive doctrines. In a context of great diversity, the issue of justification, like that of motivations, must then remain an open one in which various sources, sometimes conflicting among themselves, serve as ethical grounds for the democratic constitutional order. The Rawlsian separation between political reason and doctrinal reason (Rawls 2005) is too strong a concession to secularist ontology and to the primacy of the moral value of autonomy; the distinction is too restrictive for those according to whom religion is not a matter of choice, but of faith, deep conviction, or impregnation. Hence, Taylor (2011a) is opposed to Rawls' proviso, according to which, when discussing fundamental issues of justice and politics relating to the basic structure of society, only "proper political reasons," and not reasons originating from comprehensive doctrines, can be taken into account. For citizens, this comes down to finding a way to transpose their doctrinal reasons, whether religious or secular, into political ones that will be accessible to all (Rawls 2005: 462). Taylor's opposition to this proviso, as in the case of the Habermasian proviso, is that it limits the expression of religious views in the political sphere.

But the interest of the contrasting views between Taylor and Rawls mainly resides in the question of political cohesion and the stability of the democratic order. Both draw on an overlapping consensus, but with major differences as to the modes of this consensus. For Taylor, overlapping consensus is based on various belief and value systems – comprehensive doctrines – and is underpinned by different motivations and justifications for adhering to the democratic order:

> A Kantian will justify the rights to life and freedom by pointing to the dignity of rational agency; a utilitarian will speak of the necessity to treat beings who can experience joy and suffering in such a way as to maximize the first and minimize the second. A Christian will speak of humans as made in the image of God. They concur on the principles, but differ on the deeper reasons for holding them. The state must uphold the ethic, but must refrain from favoring any of the deeper reasons.
>
> (Taylor 2011a: 19)

In Rawls' view, at best, this can only produce a "constitutional consensus" in which each individual conserves his or her own reasons for adhering or not to the democratic constitutional order (Rawls 2005: 158–164). While some political principles will be agreed upon (fundamental rights and freedoms), in such a constitutional consensus there can be no agreement on the basic structure of society or on a conception of justice. The democratic constitutional order remains fragile, as citizens adhere to it not on the basis of an autonomous political ethic, but on the basis of doctrinal reasons in which democratic foundations are ordered into different hierarchies depending on each individual's beliefs and philosophies. Both harmony between citizens and civic friendship are also compromised, since the very idea of a public good – grounded in the basic structure of society – is not the chief goal of the consensus. Indeed, this consensus rests only on a few liberal and democratic values whose content is necessarily limited by the requirement of consensus between a plurality of comprehensive doctrines that agree on neither the reasons, nor on the motivations, for adhering to it. Taylor's consensus – more constitutional than overlapping – is an agreement on a few common values (political values and values specific to national particularities), but with no fundamental agreement as to the justifications for these values. Solidarity or civic friendship depends on an agreement upon the political ethic, but not an agreement upon the reasons for adhering to it, which would only lead to one or another form of exclusion in terms of beliefs or philosophical convictions. As a result, it would ultimately be based on a modus vivendi according to Rawls' definition (Rawls 2005: 146–150).

To those – myself included – who may be skeptical about the overlapping consensus' ability to address the requirements for democratic solidarity, Taylor simply answers, without further arguments, "Let people subscribe for whatever reasons they find compelling, only let them subscribe" (Taylor 1998: 52). In some of Taylor's writings, the consensus appears to be taken for granted, the result of an inclusive perspective in which various beliefs and convictions are spontaneously attuned to the ambient liberal political ethic. "If Christians see it as central to their Christianity, if Muslims see it as central to their Islam, and if the various kinds of lay philosophies see it as central to their philosophies" (Taylor 2010b). In other writings, the consensus appears to be a challenging task, or an unresolved and fundamental problem for the political cohesion of democratic societies (Taylor 2002a, 2007c):

> The basic fact underlying this diversity is that a political ethic doesn't interpret itself, any more that a charter of right does. As it extends to further cases, it will be interpreted in the light of the entire background of justification from which it springs. When there are several such backgrounds, the interpretations are going to diverge, often seriously.
>
> (Taylor 1998: 51)

This ontological indeterminacy also demands great civic virtues of citizens in a democratic and pluralistic society. It requires that many citizens find in their own beliefs the reasons and motivations to adhere to the democratic constitutional order. But going even further, in order to avoid a merely "constitutional" consensus, it also requires that they share a common civic philosophy of openness to fellow citizens that encompasses their singular beliefs or philosophies, without which the political order would boil down to a modus vivendi around a few liberal principles. This civic ideal is that each singular view can elevate itself to a higher stage and experience a form of sharing in complementarity with other ontological views, without needing to renounce its own metaphysical or religious convictions. Such complementarity provides a way not only to escape the narrow-mindedness of our own views, but also to be enriched by the views of others and to form a unity with them, while respecting differences. Belonging to a political order is not here merely instrumental – the best society for one's individual fulfillment – but also enables the development of a friendship, an impulse of solidarity, between different ontological views. The inclusivist position of Taylor therefore still remains demanding in terms of the civic virtues expected of citizens.

The agonistic diversity

From my point of view, the Taylorian position on secularity and secularism creates difficulties for the possibility of forming a political community in and through differences. The reasons have to do with the relationships between the civic virtues and various ontological options, the cross pressures exerted on individuals, and the common ethic needed for democratic life.

First, a striking contrast stands between the civic virtues required of citizens and the promises of fulfillment and beatitude conveyed by various religious and non-religious ontological options (Bernstein 2008). The experience of political modernity and ontological diversity requires disciplined work on the self (self-control) and respect for civic rules in relationships with fellow citizens, in addition to the requirements of participating in social and political life. A neutral political ethic, non-autonomous and incomplete, must be completed by ontological options, some of which are expressed as promises of eternal life or transformation – in the case of religion – or fulfillment – in the case of humanist views. Yet this relationship is more complex than might appear at first glance, and it is not without frictions. Taylor (2005) acknowledges that certain ontological options are borderline cases or rejections of democratic order. Religious anti-modernism (Taylor 2006) and Neo-Nietzschean anti-humanism (Taylor 2005) could be cited in this regard, to name only two. A generalized pacification of options could only lead to an unbearable intensification of the disciplinary order far beyond tolerable bounds for a democratic society. But what Taylor fears above all is a form of materialism, that consists in rejecting the relevance of ontological questions altogether and proposing a world closed in on itself: a closed-world structure. The ethics of diversity and the wealth of ontological options must not make us forget the existence of ontological conflicts about not only the best way to articulate the democratic order, but also its very relevance, as well as its possible negations. Indeed, these conflicts suggest a tragic history of violent and sweeping failures resulting from attempts to realize or deny the promises of political modernity (Taylor 2004). The problem here is that the civic virtues expected of citizens remain entirely dependent on their adoption by the belief systems of individuals.

Second, Taylor examines the cross pressures exerted on individuals today. These pressures come from different sources, religious and non-religious, and many are new requirements put on people in their moral and spiritual quests. One example can be found in the pressure between meeting the needs of everyday and immanent life and seeking out, in the transcendent beyond, the sources of true fulfillment. In *A Secular Age* (2007a), Taylor also maintains that, in an age of authenticity, individuals do not so much strive to fit into a determined ontological tradition as to forge an original path while drawing from different beliefs or philosophical views. These individuals are more susceptible to cross pressures and do not necessarily seek refuge in a particular tradition. However, singular ethics also constitute resources for strongly affirming a collective identity, that is, unity in and through difference. From this standpoint, modern democracies offer a social space where individual and subjective approaches that no longer fall under particular traditions are nevertheless called to search, within themselves, for ethical foundations for living together. Taylor himself expressed uncertainties on this subject when stating that previous solidarities – those of strong national identities – could be threatened by the refusal of "age of authenticity" generations to commit in the long term to an association or to a specific project. Two difficulties arise. First, it is quite possible that the effects of secularity will produce more subjective ontological views that are experienced without, in return, leading to a substantive ethical substratum or a sense of common allegiance by overlapping consensus toward the political community. And second, the ontological indeterminacy of the political ethics might only end up leading to more indeterminate answers. In this case, will allegiance to a democratic society become more random and less certain? Or will these societies require an even stronger political belonging than the one suggested by a plurality of substantive ethics?

Third, according to Taylor, individuals are not alone in needing to find spiritual and moral answers as beings capable of strong evaluation; societies, too, must find answers. The democratic ideals may be shared by a very large number of people, but, in his communitarian perspective, this is not enough, ontologically speaking, and requires more substantive ethical contributions. Yet the path to an external order is no longer an option, and the diversity of options is here to stay. Taylor will find a way to address this difficulty in an "overlapping consensus." But is this enough to form a "We," a "people," a community that shares common meanings and sensibilities? Such a community becomes possible only when overlapping consensus paves the way for authentic dialogue between different views. There is therefore a need for meta-ethical presupposition behind the conception of secularity: an ongoing and open dialogue that brings differences together under a principle of harmonization – in and through differences – as the only principle truly able to meet the requirements of modern democratic societies for solidarity and community. But this very meta-ethical presupposition in itself contradicts the principles imposed by secularity, according to which the political ethic cannot be based on any meta-ethical guarantee, whether secular or religious, but rather essentially on a diversity of ontological conceptions.

Agonistic diversity and civic friendship: a response from Taylor

The problem is not "diversity" but that of renewing with 'solidarity.' Democracies don't work well without some kind of strong cohesion, which is usually some kind of cocktail of ideas around certain powerful democratic principles, as well as some sense that we the people are attempting to realize a particular historical project (Taylor 2008). We need a sense of sharing that is strong enough to replace the previous substantive ethic that gave body to the political community. This last goal remains dependent on establishing open dialogue that strives for a "fusion of horizons." The idea is that each singular view can elevate itself to a higher stage and experience a form of sharing in complementarity with other ontological views, without needing to renounce its own metaphysical or religious convictions. While solidarity finds a political model in the overlapping consensus, it still remains dependent on dialogue, which alone remains the true bridge to a meaningful experience of sharing, "The challenge is to be able to acknowledge the humanity of their way, while still being able to live ours" (Taylor 2002b: 142).

This last point brings us to a difficulty inherent to any attempt to substantially reshape a common identity: Is it possible to state the foundations of solidarity in an ontologically neutral way? Taylor's answer is clearly negative. As he stresses himself in several places, the idea of harmony – and sometimes communion – falls, for him, under an ontological perspective that sees ontological views as different sources of fulfillment which complete one another. "I'm a hopeless German romantic of the 1790s. I resonate with Herder's idea of humanity as the orchestra, in which all the differences between human beings could ultimately sound together in harmony" (Taylor 2010c: 320). This complementarity provides a way not only to escape the narrow-mindedness of our own views, but also to be enriched by the views of others and to form a unity with them while respecting differences: "This the oneness of diverse beings who come to see that they cannot attain wholeness alone, that their complementary is essential, rather than of beings who come to accept that they are ultimately identical" (Taylor 1999a: 14). Belonging to a political community is not here merely instrumental – the best society for one's individual fulfillment – since it also enables the development of a friendship, an impulse of solidarity, between different ontological views:

> We're in the business of friendship, which incorporates the kind of understanding where each can come to be moved by what moves the other.
>
> Now, what has that got to do with Christianity? Everything, to me: that is what it's all about. It's all about reconciliation. It's all about reconciliation between human beings, and it doesn't simply mean within the Church, and it doesn't mean that it's conditioned or being within the Church.
>
> (Taylor 2010c: 320)

Taylor's political ethic is embedded in a "metaphysical" ideal of unity that is opposed to other perspectives that take otherness as a point of departure and arrival (Butler *et al.* 2011). Yet from a Taylorian perspective, this in itself is not a problem. It is true that anti-religious, fundamentalist and anti-humanist perspectives are part of the conversation, so that the possibility of a fusion of horizons between religious views and views of exclusive humanism remains a wish – an ideal ethics (Taylor 2002b) – whose outcome in anything but certain. Open and respectful dialogue does not necessarily lead to harmony, and, in fact, the conversation is more hodgepodge and heterogeneous. Seen from this angle, the search for harmony is one ontological vision among others. To want to impose it would go against the diversity of metaphysical and philosophical views, and would radically reshape the political ethic based on a singular metaphysical perspective; this would generate new forms of exclusion. The ideal of a common identity, in the sense of a sharing process, has fallen by the wayside with the impossibility of reshaping a substantive political ethic. Even so, this observation is nothing other than an account of a modernity that finds itself tugged between the affirmation of differences and the desire for unity: "Solidarity [...] is an indispensable imperative in our democratic times, and at the same time, it is a calling which we cannot answer unconditionally. This is the tragedy of our current position" (Taylor 2007c: 77).

The political ethic needs to be grounded in a more substantial ethic of the good; however, unlike the ethic supposed by the collective identities of the past, it must be constructed based on a plurality of religious and philosophical perspectives in a context of profound diversity. The problem of contemporary democracies is then neither an absence of substantive ethics capable of supporting them, nor an absence of collective identities, but rather the profusion of such ethics and identities. In the words of Taylor, "let people subscribe." A skeptic might reply, "What if they don't?" Although secularism allows a diversity of access points to political society, it is harder to see how it permits the expression of a strong collective identity. In other words, while Taylor's position may account for the way democratic institutions can find sources of allegiance in the diversity of metaphysical options, it does not explain how individuals who identify with these options share a "special" solidarity or ties of civic friendship. A Muslim, Christian, Kantian or utilitarian can, each from a different standpoint, share substantive reasons for supporting a political ethic – and be ready to make great sacrifices to defend it – yet does this mean that they form an instance of "sharing" that is, according to Taylor, the very essence of the political community? We may be nostalgic about lost solidarity, but, even if it is with regret, perhaps we must simply recognize that it is no longer a possibility for us.

Taylor provides two answers to this objection. First, such sharing exists in the practices of democratic societies. Some examples, such as those in the sphere of humanitarian work, could be cited in which individuals with diverse convictions unite their efforts for a common cause, even while expressing their differences

> They are in a sense actuated by the same impulse, but some very different ethics lie behind the common dedication in each case: different views of human life, of the possibilities of transformation, of the modes of spiritual or mental discipline that are to be engaged in, and so on.
>
> (Taylor 2011d: 69–70)

Otherwise put, from the standpoint of human possibilities, while one could always object that our world is composed of crises, conflicts and misunderstandings rooted in culture and religion, some counter-examples exist, like the new ecumenism (Taylor 2009) or the relative success of multiculturalism and interculturalism (Taylor 2012). Second, collective experiences of diversity are richer than the vocabulary at our disposal to describe them, and this very fact may serve as a starting point for the renewal of our democratic practices. Collective identity, in a strong sense, is a reality that can be unveiled and made manifest through different symbolic or linguistic expressions – "We," the People – but without needing to assert anything about the generic or specific nature of this identity. If we take as an example the idea of communion or harmony, we know that something happens which binds us together in a common enterprise, but a reality created in this way cannot be reduced to any of its components or boiled down to the sum of its parts. Moreover, it only holds together as long as its members remain associated in their common enterprise.

Taylor's perspective falls under a singular and inspired ontological and metaphysical perspective, and, as such, it may appear to contradict its own reading of secularity according to which, in a context of profound diversity, one must renounce the founding of a political ethic on any metaphysical or secular basis. Is this position contradictory? Maybe, from the skeptical viewpoint that no other form of reconciliation is possible. But from a Taylorian standpoint, it is important to bear in mind that a strong collective identity cannot be summed up as a mere agreement on principles or norms. The question is not whether a "special" kind of solidarity is needed for democratic life – it is – but rather to find an articulation of this solidarity that does not reproduce various forms of democratic exclusion. When it comes to the issue of solidarity, on the one hand, we cannot conceive of a viable collective life in which any spiritual or metaphysical perspectives are excluded from the public debate; and yet, on the other, we need a strong collective identity. This apparent paradox between diversity and solidarity is inherent to the democratic experience in a secular age. As Taylor clarifies:

> The relationships are agonistic (...) because we're not in the business of trying to make some kind of middle, compromised solution or synthesis – no. We're in the business of friendship, which incorporates the kind of understanding where each can come to be moved by what moves the other. (Taylor 2010c: 320)

In my view, Taylor's answer to the skeptic is not to affirm the ontological primacy of his views about collective identity, harmony and unity, whose singularity he is the first to acknowledge, but rather to underline the negative effects of negating the diversity to which our modern secularity leads us.

Part II

From theory to practice

Religion and the European Court of Human Rights

7 Religious pluralism

The case of the European Court of Human Rights

Javier Martínez-Torrón[1]

Religious pluralism: indissociable from democratic society

Since its very first judgment on Article 9 of the European Convention on Human Rights (hereinafter ECHR or 'the Convention'), the European Court of Human Rights (hereinafter ECtHR or 'the Court') has attached great importance to the recognition and guarantee of pluralism, in close connection with the protection of freedom of thought, conscience and religion:

> As enshrined in Article 9 …, freedom of thought, conscience and religion is one of the foundations of a 'democratic society' within the meaning of the Convention. It is, in its religious dimension, one of the most vital elements that go to make up the identity of believers and their conception of life, but it is also a precious asset for atheists, agnostics, sceptics and the unconcerned. The pluralism indissociable from a democratic society, which has been dearly won over the centuries, depends on it.[2]

In subsequent judgments, the Court has often reiterated its position on the significance of guaranteeing pluralism, even when the plurality of religious positions in society is the cause of social tensions, which are normally derived from disputes about religious leadership or from splits within a church. In such cases, the ECtHR has always insisted that the right stance for the state is not to reduce social tension by eliminating or impairing pluralism. On the contrary, the state is not competent to intervene in strictly religious matters, even for the sake of social peace, and its role should be limited to acting as an impartial arbiter and to guaranteeing pluralism by ensuring that different religious groups can live together. Thus, the principle of *pluralism* seems to go hand in hand with state *neutrality* on religious issues:

> Although the Court recognises that it is possible that tension is created in situations where a religious or any other community becomes divided, it considers that this is one of the unavoidable consequences of pluralism. The role of the authorities in such circumstances is not to remove the cause of tension by eliminating pluralism, but to ensure that the competing groups tolerate each other.[3]

While the European Court has attributed a high value to pluralism, it has never considered it necessary to explain why. It is interesting to note this, for pluralism can be understood in at least two different ways: as a mere social fact and as a sign of freedom.

On the one hand, pluralism can be viewed as a *fact*, i.e. as the plurality of religious and belief positions actually existing in a given society at a given time. In this respect, European national societies offer many diverse levels of pluralism – some of them are more religiously homogeneous (and therefore less pluralistic) than others. Understood merely as a sociological datum, it is difficult to see pluralism as a value per se, for it is simply a variable fact that is a consequence of the historical circumstances of each nation. Moreover, how pluralistic should a society be in order to be accepted as 'truly democratic'? From a legal perspective – which in the area of religious freedom is supposed to be neutral[4] – it would make no sense to think that a society is worse or better than another because it is more religiously homogenous or heterogeneous. The principle 'the more plural the better' would imply that disagreement among people about the basic questions of life is better than agreement. Ultimately, affirming that pluralism as a fact is a positive value would imply that the state must have a preconception of pluralism in society, i.e. a specific type of pluralism conceived as a result that should be achieved by state intervention. The consequence would be the transformation of factual data into a normative notion of pluralism, which in my view would certainly not be neutral and therefore illegitimate.

For these reasons, it seems that, when the European Court mentions pluralism as a paramount value in democratic societies, we must understand it as referring to a different concept of pluralism: namely, to pluralism as an *effect or reflection of freedom*. Indeed, understood in this way it is very reasonable to consider pluralism as a positive value, for we assume – and it is a very realistic assumption – that in a free society there is necessarily a plurality of religious stances. Such plurality can be larger or smaller, but pluralism is always a sign of freedom. When there is no pluralism, we can say that there is no real freedom. And when there is freedom, there is always some pluralism and the possibility of a higher degree of pluralism. These observations have always been true but they are even truer nowadays because of the social mobility inherent in globalization.

If we agree that this is the notion of pluralism that the ECtHR must be referring to, what is positive per se is not pluralism but the freedom that pluralism reflects and is the result of. The Court can affirm that pluralism is 'indissociable from a democratic society'[5] because religious pluralism is a very *visible sign of the freedom* reigning in a democratic society, in which *some degree* of pluralism necessarily exists (indeed, because of the characteristics of contemporary societies, a *high* degree of pluralism is to be expected, especially in the West). Therefore, the emphasis – again, from a legal perspective – should be on the *protection of freedom* rather than on pluralism as such, which is just one of the results of freedom.

In other words, if we follow what is apparently the implicit approach of the ECtHR, the conclusion is that *the best way to guarantee pluralism would be a high degree of protection of the freedom of thought, conscience and religion* enshrined in Article 9 ECHR, for individuals and groups, in its internal and external dimensions, i.e. freedom to believe and freedom to act in accordance with one's beliefs. This, as in the rest of the rights recognized by the Convention, entails an extensive interpretation of the scope of protection of freedom of religion or belief and, in parallel, a restrictive interpretation of the limitations that can be legitimately imposed on that right – especially, a restrictive interpretation of which limitations can be deemed 'necessary in a democratic society'.[6]

State neutrality and freedom of conscience

Nevertheless, in contradiction with its own statements on the high value of pluralism, the case law of the European Court of Strasbourg has not always followed that track and has considered that the discretionary margin of appreciation at the disposal of national authorities should prevail over a broad interpretation of religious freedom. This has occurred especially with regard to the Court's interpretation of two interconnected notions: the scope of protection of freedom of thought, conscience and religion; and the principle of state neutrality, which, as noted above, is closely connected with pluralism.

Protection of individual religious identity, and not only collective or group religious identity, is an integral part of the guarantee of religious pluralism in society. On the other hand, individual religious identity is not expressed exclusively through choosing one's personal beliefs or experiencing a sense of *belonging* to a community or tradition. Religious or moral beliefs tend to be manifested in *practical conduct* and therefore religious identity finds its normal development in personal actions of a different nature, which go beyond mere compliance with certain rites or acts of worship. In other words, individual actions that are perceived by the individual as a moral obligation constitute a definite manifestation of religion or belief and therefore of the freedom of conscience protected by Article 9 ECHR. As a consequence, restricting these actions implies a limitation on religious identity, and this is something that may be done only under the conditions stated in Article 9.2 ECHR – only when a limitation is 'necessary in a democratic society' can it be acceptable or legitimate.[7] However, the Strasbourg jurisdiction, despite its above-mentioned emphasis on the significance of freedom of religion or belief, has at times interpreted the consequences of religious identity restrictively, in two different ways.

In the first place, the Court (and prior to it the now extinct European Commission of Human Rights)[8] has avoided the test imposed by the limitation clause of Article 9.2 ECHR by denying that, in cases of *conflict between moral obligations and neutral laws*, there is any state interference with the exercise of freedom of thought, conscience and religion. In such cases, the Strasbourg jurisdiction has sometimes held that Article 9.1 ECHR does not offer any protection to the exercise of religious freedom against obligations stemming from a legal provision that pursues a legitimate secular interest and is not aimed directly at restricting the freedom of religious choice of individuals or imposing limitations on religious practices. The state's neutral law must automatically prevail, without the need to justify it under Article 9.2 ECHR.[9]

In the second place, even in the case of laws that are unambiguously aimed at restricting certain religious expressions, the Court has held that those legal restrictions are reasonable when they seek to *guarantee the 'neutrality' of the public sphere*, understood as synonymous with 'secularity', i.e. as implying the absence of visible signs of religion. The consequence is that limitations on manifestations of religion – for instance the prohibition of religious symbols or clothing – have been easily justified under Article 9.2 ECHR, with the implication that religion cannot be a part of the public sphere, which should be presided over by a 'secularity' that permits the presence of non-religious ideas or signs but not their religious equivalent.

I will analyse the first type of cases in the third section of this paper and the second type in the fourth section.

Conflicts between moral obligations and neutral laws

Practice of religion or belief, forum internum *and* forum externum

With respect to the first type of situations, part of the problem arises from the interpretation given in Strasbourg to the European Convention's terms that describe the protectable content of freedom of thought, conscience and religion.

Among them, Article 9.1 ECHR mentions the right to manifest one's religion or belief in *practice*. The most obvious interpretation of this term seems to be that Article 9 guarantees the right of individuals to behave in accordance with the dictates – and prohibitions – of their own consciences. It would not be accurate to interpret the word *practice* as the mere practice of rites, considering that the ritual dimension of religious freedom is present in other words used by Article 9, in particular the terms *worship* and *observance*.[10] On the other hand, the protection of *practice* of religion or belief should be recognized in the same manner, irrespective of whether it is based on the tenets of an institutional religion or derives from strictly personal beliefs, and regardless of whether the individual's conscience is grounded on religious or on non-religious beliefs. The only substantial requirement would be that such practice is an expression of religion or belief, understanding the latter not as any type of opinion – which is protected by other rights included in the Convention, e.g. freedom of expression – but as 'views that attain a certain level of cogency, seriousness, cohesion and importance'.[11]

This broad construction of the right to manifest one's belief in *practice* was proposed by the General Comment of the Committee of Human Rights on Article 18 of the 1966 UN International Covenant on Human Rights.[12] I am afraid, however, that the attitude of the Strasbourg jurisdiction has been different.[13]

For many years, the European Commission of Human Rights has distinguished between two different and complementary aspects of the right recognized by Article 9 ECHR. One is the internal aspect (*forum internum*), which consists of the freedom to *choose* one's religion or beliefs; the other is the external aspect (*forum externum*), which consists of the freedom to *manifest* one's religion or belief 'in worship, teaching, practice and observance', 'either alone or in community with others and in public or private'. Such a distinction seems reasonable in principle, especially as later understood by the Court following the letter of Article 9 ECHR – only the *forum externum* or freedom to manifest was subject to the limitations stated in Article 9.2 ECHR, while freedom of choice or *forum internum* was granted absolute protection.[14]

However, it seems that the intention of the European Commission was not so much to reinforce the absolute character of freedom of choice in matters of religion or belief but, on the contrary, to relativize the protection of the freedom of manifestation, which should be circumscribed to the 'practice of religion or belief in a generally recognized form'. Such was the statement of the Commission in the first decision that used the term *forum internum*, and has been reiterated many times subsequently:

> Article 9 primarily protects the sphere of personal beliefs and religious creeds, i.e. the area which is sometimes called the *forum internum*. In addition, it protects acts which are intimately linked to these attitudes, such as acts of worship or devotion which are aspects of the practice of a religion or belief in a generally recognised form.[15]

Manifestation and motivation with respect to religion or belief

Understood in this way, the distinction between *forum internum* and *forum externum* paved the way for a minimalist interpretation of the freedom of individuals to act or behave according to the dictates of their own conscience, especially if viewed in the light of a former doctrine of the Commission, which drew a line between the concepts of *manifestation* and *motivation* with respect to religion or belief:

> The Commission considers that the term 'practice' as employed in Art. 9 (1) does not cover each act which is motivated or influenced by a religion or a belief.... [W]hen the actions of individuals do not actually express the belief concerned they cannot be considered to be as such protected by Art. 9 (1), even when they are motivated or influenced by it.[16]

In subsequent years, the foregoing approach of the Commission has been explicitly accepted by the Court.[17] Such an approach seems reasonable in the abstract, for behaviour *obliged* by conscience – which seems to be the behaviour protected by Article 9 ECHR – is different from behaviour simply *permitted* or *encouraged* by conscience. However, one of the problems it raises is that it could be understood as giving the Court too much discretion to decide when there is a proper manifestation of belief, thus replacing the individual's judgment of conscience.[18]

This was indeed the case in the twin decisions *Efstratiou* and *Valsamis*,[19] which had their origin in the applications of two Greek secondary school students, both Jehovah's Witnesses, who refused, for religious reasons, to participate in the school parades organized during the national festival to commemorate the outbreak of war between Greece and Fascist Italy in 1940; the students were punished with one day's suspension from school. When the ECtHR examined the arguments of the applicants, it declared that the parades that the Jehovah's Witnesses morally disapproved of were merely civic acts without any particular political or ideological connotation and, consequently, they could not offend the pacifist convictions of the students.[20] Thus, the Court substituted its judgment for the conscience of the persons involved, defining what was *reasonable* for them to believe with regard to their participation in a national commemorative ceremony. In my opinion, this is a gross mistake.[21] In assessing claims arising from individual conscience, it is unacceptable for a secular court to determine which beliefs are reasonable and which are not. Naturally, it is necessary to verify – as far as possible – that the parties are sincere; that they are not deceitfully alleging moral convictions they do not actually or genuinely hold in order to avoid fulfilling a legal duty. But this does not mean that a secular court is competent to elucidate when the beliefs of a person are sufficiently consistent from an objective point of view. Religious viewpoints do not need to meet a reasonableness threshold in order to qualify as a basis for asserting rights under Article 9 ECHR. Moreover, this is in contradiction with what the ECtHR itself declared, the very same year of *Efstratiou* and *Valsamis*, reflecting a deeply-rooted notion of Western legal culture, about the incompetence of public authorities to pronounce on the truth or falsity of a religious dogma or a moral belief:

> [B]ut for very exceptional cases, the right to freedom of religion as guaranteed under the Convention excludes any discretion on the part of the State to determine whether religious beliefs or the means used to express such beliefs are legitimate.[22]

Direct and indirect restrictions on freedom of conscience

An additional problem is that the Strasbourg case law has traditionally adopted a rather restrictive attitude in interpreting the distinction between manifestation and motivation vis-à-vis defining the scope of protection of Article 9.1 ECHR.[23] It has tended to consider that the protective umbrella of the Convention does not necessarily extend to people's behaviour that is imposed by their own conscience, especially when a person attempts to adapt his conduct to his moral obligations in ordinary life, but his behaviour does not strictly consist of religious teaching or directly correspond to specific ceremonial practices. And, however, there is little doubt that behaviour obliged by conscience is certainly a manifestation of religion or belief – and indeed a very important one – even if it does not strictly correspond to the 'practice of religion or belief in a generally recognized form'.[24]

With respect to the protection of conscientiously motivated behaviour, the ECtHR has often distinguished implicitly between a state's actions that have a *direct* and an *indirect* impact on freedom of religion and conscience.

The Court has recognized that the state interferes with the exercise of freedom of religion or belief when an individual's behaviour is prevented or punished by a law or by another state activity *directly* aimed at restricting the manifestation, the worship or the expansion of certain or of all religions. In such situations, the state must justify the interference in accordance with Article 9.2 ECHR and prove that the restrictive measures are 'necessary in a democratic society'. This has been the approach of the ECtHR, for instance, in cases relating to laws prohibiting religious proselytism[25] and the imposition of a religious oath as a legal condition to take a public office.[26]

Very different has been Strasbourg's approach to *indirect* restrictions on religious freedom caused by seemingly *neutral* laws of general applicability that pursue legitimate secular goals. The Court, following a previous doctrine held by the Commission, has apparently tended to deny that Article 9 ECHR offers any protection in those situations, indicating that there is no state interference with religious freedom. As a result, state action is relieved of being subject to the scrutiny of the limitation clause of Article 9.2 ECHR. The Court's analysis can be summarized as follows: it is not necessary to judge whether the state has provided a legitimate justification (according to Article 9.2 ECHR) for the legislation under attack because the right to freedom of thought, conscience and religion (according to the description of its content in Article 9.1 ECHR) has not actually been restricted. On these grounds, the Court has rejected a variety of applications in which freedom of conscience was alleged to claim the right to be exempted from neutral state norms. In *Kjeldsen*, the ECtHR decided against parents who expressed conscientious objection to having their children exposed to purportedly neutral sex education in state schools, arguing that the state was free to organize the educational system, and particularly the curricula of state schools, even if the religious or philosophical convictions of parents were disregarded, as long as there was no aim to indoctrinate students.[27] In *Efstratiou* and *Valsamis*, the Court denied that punishing two secondary school students for not attending – on religious grounds – a school parade to commemorate a national holiday was in violation of the conscience rights of the students or their parents.[28] In *Kalaç*, the Court concluded that the compulsory retirement of an officer of the Turkish army for his religious ideas – allegedly contrary to the constitutional principle of secularism – did not amount to an interference with his freedom of conscience, for he was permitted to observe the *normal* religious duties of Islam.[29] In *Cha'are Shalom Ve Tsedek*, the Court refused to accept that an ultra-orthodox minority Jewish community had the right to obtain a special permit for the slaughter of animals according to its interpretation of the Hebrew tradition, similar to the one that had been granted to the organization representing the majority of Jewish communities – in the Court's view, there was no interference with the freedom of conscience of the members of the ultra-orthodox community because they could easily obtain *glatt* meat by importing it from Belgium.[30]

Such a slant on the part of the ECtHR is unrealistic and bound to end up legitimizing unjustified limitations on freedom of conscience. Although by definition neutral laws are not designed to interfere with a particular religion or belief, in practice the legal duties they impose may clash with moral obligations that govern the lives of certain individuals, and consequently they may cause, as an *indirect* but unavoidable effect, a restriction on these persons' right to practice their religion or belief.[31] The immediate consequence is that a moral burden is placed upon the shoulders of these people, as they must choose between disobedience to the law and disobedience to their conscience – one receives a worldly punishment, the other entails a spiritual sanction.

In my opinion, interpreting Article 9 ECHR in a way that implies that neutral laws cannot cause an interference with individual freedom of conscience inverts the logical order of concepts in this matter. It is universally accepted that human rights must be construed broadly. Therefore, in order to understand the exact meaning of the freedom to manifest one's religion or belief in *practice*, it seems that we should approach the question in the following sequence: (1) according to Article 9.1 ECHR, freedom to practice one's religion or belief must be understood as protecting, in principle, every act of the individual when he obeys the dictates of his own conscience; but (2) Article 9.2 ECHR – limitations on freedom of religion or belief – shall be utilized, when necessary, as a corrective element for a freedom that, by its own nature, tends to be exercised in an undefined and unpredictable way.

Thus, we manage to reconcile two paramount interests that are inclined to conflict with each other: the maximum degree of initial protection of the freedom of belief and the security that the legal order demands. Furthermore, we introduce an important assumption: *the state has the burden of proof with regard to the necessity of a restrictive measure*, i.e. it must affirmatively prove that, in a particular case of conflict, it is 'necessary in a democratic society' to restrict the exercise of religious freedom. Following this approach would obstruct the development of policies that ignore the needs of religious freedom and that are harmful not only to individuals but also to minority groups and in general to groups with distinctive beliefs – ultimately, harmful to religious pluralism.

New light in the Strasbourg case law

A Grand Chamber decision of 2011, *Bayatyan*,[32] adopted the perspective suggested in this paper as most appropriate for the protection of freedom of conscience vis-à-vis state laws that pursue legitimate secular goals. The case had its origin in the application of an Armenian citizen, a Jehovah's Witness, who refused to comply with his military service for reasons of conscience and, although prepared to perform alternative civil service, was sentenced to two-and-a-half years in prison. The ECtHR's Grand Chamber, abandoning the prior and well-established case law of both the European Commission and the European Court of Human Rights,[33] held that the clause of 4.3.b ECHR, providing that neither military service nor alternative civilian service could be considered 'forced or compulsory labour', did not preclude that conscientious objection to military service could – and should – be judged in the light of Article 9 ECHR.[34] Deciding in favour of the applicant, the Court used two arguments that are particularly relevant here. First, although Article 9 ECHR does not specifically mention conscientious objection, freedom of conscience is protected by that article when there is 'a serious and insurmountable conflict' with legal duties, based on a 'conviction or belief of sufficient cogency, seriousness, cohesion and importance'.[35] Second, the penalties imposed on the applicant could not be deemed a measure 'necessary in a democratic society', especially taking into account that *there were other alternatives* to accommodate the competing interests of the state and the conscientious objector.[36]

Although the Court referred those arguments to the particular situation of an objector to military service, we should understand them as applicable to all other types of conflicts between individual conscience duties and neutral laws, provided that these moral obligations are grounded on a 'conviction or belief of sufficient cogency, seriousness, cohesion and importance'. In my opinion, it would be unsustainable to affirm that the ECtHR's reasoning is valid only for objection to military service or for other convictions that the Court decides to select in the future as *deserving* of a qualified protection by Article 9 ECHR, among other reasons because the Court itself has declared repeatedly that states are not competent to assess the legitimacy of beliefs and the means to express them.[37] If the state cannot make such an assessment, the Court is even less qualified to do so. The relevant factor is not to count on the sympathy or acquiescence of the ECtHR, but to verify that the conflict of conscience is grounded on beliefs – religious or not – 'of sufficient cogency, seriousness, cohesion and importance'.

Unfortunately, the expectations created by *Bayatyan* about a possible shift in the Court's case law with respect to freedom of conscience experienced a setback, less than one year later, with the *Sessa* judgment.[38] The case related to the religious objection of a Jewish lawyer who had been refused, due to alleged organizational reasons of the court, his – timely – request for a change of the date of a hearing in a criminal procedure because it coincided with Jewish festivities of prescriptive rest.[39] The ECtHR, in a four-to-three judgment strongly contested in a joint dissenting opinion of three judges, did not find any interference with the applicant's religious freedom, arguing that he could have been replaced by another colleague in the hearing and he 'did not prove that he had suffered pressure to change his religious belief or to prevent him from manifesting his religion or belief'.[40]

However, not long after *Sessa*, a new judgment of the European Court – *Eweida*[41] – seems to have returned to the principles that drew the path commenced by *Bayatyan*. In *Eweida*, the ECtHR decided four different applications that had in common the fact that religious practices, which the applicants understood as serious obligations of conscience, had a negative impact on the applicant's labour relations with public or private employers. Indeed, in three of the four applications the applicants had been dismissed.[42] I will not go into the details of the judgment,[43] part of whose rationale I cannot share. I will merely note that the approach of the Court can be summarized as follows: an employer's rule that prevents an employee from complying with a moral obligation constitutes an interference in the employee's rights under Article 9 ECHR, provided that such an obligation derives from 'views that attain a certain level of cogency, seriousness, cohesion and importance' and that there is 'a sufficiently close and direct nexus between the act and the underlying belief'.[44] The consequence is that the state must provide a sound justification for permitting that interference under Article 9.2 ECHR and must prove that it was 'necessary in a democratic society'. With this approach, the Court rejects the idea that freedom of conscience is not protected against neutral rules in the work- place, and that such rules do not properly constitute restrictions on individual freedom that fall under the limitation clause of Article 9.2 ECHR, because the employee can *easily* avoid the pressure on his conscience by resigning his job.[45]

State neutrality and the visibility of religion in the public sphere: prohibition of personal religious symbols

As mentioned above, further restrictions of individual expressions of religious beliefs have been legitimized by the ECtHR as a consequence of its understanding of state neutrality and, more generally, the neutrality of the public sphere. To consider that state neutrality towards religious ideas is a requirement of the protection of religious freedom seems reasonable when neutrality is conceived as the state's incompetence to judge the truth or falsity of religious doctrines. But it is less reasonable when the Court tends to understand neutrality as excluding, or at least easily justifying, state prohibitions of personal expressions of religious belief in public, particularly in educational environments (surprisingly such prohibitions are sometimes adopted, allegedly, in the interests of peace and tolerance).[46]

Dahlab*: prohibiting a state primary school teacher from wearing an Islamic headscarf*

We can see expressions of this attitude of the European Court in cases regarding the use of personal religious symbols in state schools decided since the beginning of the 2000s. In *Dahlab*, in 2001,[47] the ECtHR declared inadmissible the application of a Swiss teacher in a state primary school, who had converted to Islam, and who had been prohibited from wearing the veil on her head – which she considered prescriptive when teaching her students – in application of a cantonal law aimed at preserving the secular character of state schools. Although the Court recognized that the cantonal prohibition of 'powerful' religious symbols at school constituted an interference with the applicant's religious freedom, and that the state had therefore to provide a sound justification under Article 9.2 ECHR, it shared the opinion of the Swiss courts about the consequences of the neutrality principle. In particular, the ECtHR accepted that neutrality entailed some restrictions on teachers' rights to manifest their religion or belief, especially in the educational environment, where students may be more easily influenced and 'religious peace' must be protected with extreme care.

What seems surprising in the *Dahlab* case is the loose analysis of the facts, in parallel with too much respect for the state's margin of appreciation in interpreting the limitation clause of Article 9.2 ECHR. The 'religious peace' at the school did not seem to have suffered any serious threat, for there was no evidence of even a single complaint by the students or the students' parents or other colleagues in the five years that the applicant had been wearing the Islamic headscarf, until she was prohibited from doing so by the new (female) general director of primary schools of Geneva's canton. In addition, if we look at the underlying concepts of the decision, it is not easy to understand why a country enjoying religious peace like Switzerland should require that the state, to be neutral, must ban the visibility of religious personal symbols on teachers' clothing. At no time did the Court question if such an exclusive notion of neutrality could, and should, for the sake of a higher protection of freedom of conscience, be replaced by an inclusive notion of neutrality that would permit students to see in their own school a reflection of the religious pluralism existing in Swiss society. It is not unreasonable to think that, as long as teachers respect the students' belief and there is no attempted proselytism or indoctrination, the visibility of religious pluralism in school is more consistent with a neutral attitude of the state and therefore more respectful of religious freedom – in addition to being probably more instructive for students than the fictional absence of religion on the part of school personnel.

Leyla Şahin: *the preservation of a secular atmosphere in Turkish universities*

A few years after *Dahlab*, and in relation to the same notion of neutrality, arose the most important case until now on the use of personal religious symbols in the educational environment: *Leyla Şahin*, first decided by a Chamber of seven judges and later by the Grand Chamber of seventeen judges, confirming the Chamber's decision.[48] The applicant was a female Muslim medical student who had been subjected to disciplinary proceedings by the university authorities, based on rules that prohibited the use of headscarves by women with the aim of reducing the visibility of Islam on the premises of public universities, thereby allegedly guaranteeing their *secular atmosphere*. The disciplinary measures adopted against her included denying her access to written examinations and suspension from the university for a semester. After an eighteen-month legal battle to have her right to dress according to what she considered a religious and moral duty recognized, she abandoned her medical studies in Turkey and pursued them at the University of Vienna, in Austria.

The ECtHR sustained the validity of the student's sanctions, affirming that the Turkish authorities had acted within their legitimate margin of discretion when they imposed certain policies contrary to the wearing of religious clothing at the university. In the eyes of the Court, those policies constituted, no doubt, a restriction on the students' religious freedom, but they could be deemed 'necessary in a democratic' society, in the meaning of Article 9.2 ECHR, for the protection of the constitutional principle of secularism (*laïcité*), conceived as a guarantee of democracy and a safeguard against a possible advance of Muslim radicalism in Turkey. As in *Dahlab*, the Court applied in a lenient way its traditional doctrine of the national margin of appreciation and performed a poor assessment of the factual evidence presented by the parties.

It is not my intention to deal with the various deficiencies of the judgment in detail.[49] Here, it is sufficient to note that the ECtHR made use of bizarre and hypothetical arguments such as 'the impact which wearing such a symbol, which is presented or perceived as a compulsory religious duty, may have on those who choose not to wear it'[50] (curiously, the Court did not mention the same reasoning in the opposite direction, i.e. the impact of the ban on headscarves on those who do choose to wear it – obviously a massively more intrusive restraint). That argument implies, ultimately, a view that perceives religion predominantly as a potential factor of conflict, especially considering that there was no evidence (let alone sufficient evidence) of the intolerant atmosphere that wearing headscarves would allegedly generate at the university, or of any real pressure on uncovered female students on the part of their female or male schoolmates. As in *Dahlab*, the Court seemed to take for granted that the neutrality of the public sphere is best served when religion is absent or at least 'invisible'. The paradoxical consequence of this reasoning is to assume that a climate of tolerance and respect can be achieved through intolerance towards a particular form of religious expression, and then to conclude on the basis of mere hypotheses that there is clear evidence of a 'pressing social need'.

Sequels of **Leyla Şahin***: the justification of the French ban on religious garments in public schools*

In spite of its flaws and of the many criticisms it has received, the principles and perspective present in *Leyla Şahin* have subsequently been used by the Court to decide against the applicants in other cases of students or teachers that have had diverse sanctions imposed on them for wearing Islamic headscarves at school in Turkey[51] and also in France, where the restrictive policies on the use of religious clothing in state schools (but not at university) were confirmed and reinforced by the 2004 law on religious symbols.[52] The judgments relating to France make even less sense, because the hypothetical argument of the threat to the principle of *laïcité* that could stem from the visibility of a predominant Muslim majority is not applicable to that country.

Thus, in the *Dogru* and *Kervanci* judgments, in 2008,[53] the ECtHR declared legitimate, by a unanimous decision, the expulsion of two twelve-year-old female students from their state school because they had refused to remove their headscarves in physical education classes; the school authorities justified the decision alleging health and safety reasons. In addition to the reiteration of and continuous references to the arguments present in *Leyla Şahin*, the Court, surprisingly enough, seemed to share the perspective of some French courts, which attributed to the applicants the creation of a climate of tension at the school with their 'intransigent' attitude.[54] This is particularly shocking taking into account the fact that, apparently, the school authorities had rejected, without providing any reason at all, the applicants' offer to wear a hat or balaclava instead of a headscarf, in order to make their religious obligations compatible with the school's safety rules.[55] There is nothing in these judgments reflecting the sensible criteria of the *least restrictive means* proposed by the authorities in the United States,[56] or of the *minimal impairment* doctrine elaborated by Canadian jurisprudence,[57] which require, when a limitation on religious freedom is inevitable, a search for the least invasive alternative.[58] Nor is it comparable to the approach of the ECtHR's Grand Chamber in the *Bayatyan* case, as we have already seen.[59]

The *Dogru* and *Kervanci* judgments soon influenced the subsequent case law of the ECtHR on the use of personal religious clothing in the school environment, as we can see in six decisions of 2009, rendered on the same date, related to similar factual circumstances, and with an almost identical text. In all of them the applicants were students who had been expelled from schools in different French towns, and in application of the 2004 law against personal religious symbols in state schools, for persistently wearing religious clothing.[60] The ECtHR found that the disciplinary measures against the students were justified, despite the fact that, now, the prohibition on religious clothing was not limited to sports classes, but extended to all school hours and premises. Moreover, the fact that the Court did not consider it necessary to deal with those six applications in a full judgment on their merits and chose the more expeditious way of declaring them inadmissible as 'manifestly ill-founded', implies, in practice, a total and unconditional endorsement of the controversial French law of 2004.

Ahmet Arslan: *the prohibition of religious symbols in the public sphere is not sustained*

It is at least a relief that, in recent years, the European Court has declined to support strict secularist policies, *outside the educational milieu*, aimed at erasing the visibility of religion in the public sphere, as the case of *Ahmet Arslan* demonstrates.[61] In this case, the ECtHR held that forbidding the wearing of religious garments in public, and sanctioning the applicants – members of a religious Muslim group called *Aczimendi tarikatı* – for infringing this prohibition, constituted a disproportionate limitation on religious freedom. The ECtHR, though recognizing and emphasizing the importance of the secularity principle for Turkish democracy, decided in favour of the applicants, considering that the government had not proved the alleged existence of a threat to democratic principles and public order, because the applicants were ordinary citizens, without any specific public position of representation or responsibility, who had simply worn their religious dress in public streets and places open to all. The Court noted that this circumstance was essential to distinguish this case from other cases – especially *Leyla Şahin* – in which the applicants had worn religious garments in the specific environment of educational institutions.

Concluding remarks

An analysis of the Strasbourg case law reveals that, in the past, the Court has sometimes denied that Article 9 ECHR protects conscientious objections against *neutral* laws and, some other times, it has justified national policies aimed at imposing a conception of the public sphere that excludes, in the alleged interest of neutrality, the visibility of religion. It is not easy to avoid the impression that former references by the ECtHR to pluralism, and to the central role that pluralism plays in a democracy, risk yielding to such an exclusive concept of neutrality. By nature, pluralism is inclusive, and tends to reflect the plurality of positions – religious or not – actually existing in society.[62] Consequently, pluralism, which is so highly valued – at least on the level of solemn declarations – by the ECtHR, should require a corresponding legal notion of state religious neutrality inspired by inclusiveness, instead of exclusiveness. Such a notion, in turn, would have a positive impact on the actual protection of religious pluralism and should influence the case law of the Court on the two issues analysed in this paper: conflicts between freedom of conscience and neutral laws, and the visibility of religion in the public sphere.

In the first type of issues, after the *Bayatyan* case, the European Court appears to be somewhat more inclined to accept that states must make an effort to accommodate the moral obligations of individuals – if they are grounded on 'views that attain a certain level of cogency, seriousness, cohesion and importance' – when they clash with legal obligations imposed, directly or indirectly, by neutral laws. *Eweida* suggests that line of analysis, although it applies it with a reasoning that is partly questionable. On the contrary, *Sessa*, a few months before, returned to the old approach, which easily rejects that states are bound by any duty of accommodation of citizens' behaviour that is in accordance with their religious or moral beliefs. If we relate this with some other recent judgments regarding conflicts between churches and individuals in the area of labour relations, and which show a certain tendency to invade part of the traditionally recognized autonomy of religious communities,[63] we could draw the conclusion that perhaps the European Court is hesitating about how to define the boundaries between the legitimate powers of state and religion (or belief). And its hesitation may be caused by the fear of granting *too much protection* to freedom of religion or belief, in its individual and collective dimensions, to the detriment of the authority and power of a secular state that continues to be considered as the only solid ground on which a democratic system can be built.

Such fear – if we now pass to the second type of issues – is noticeable in the notion of neutrality proposed by the Turkish and French interpretations of *laïcité*, and ratified by the Court, which excludes the visibility of religion in some areas of public life and particularly in educational settings – virtually any ideological or philosophical position may be visible as long as it is not religious. The result of these policies can be described as *mutilated* pluralism and does not seem compatible with real *neutrality*, but rather with that deformation of neutrality that makes it, always and necessarily, synonymous with *secularism*. It is true that the European Court has not actively supported this exclusive notion of neutrality and has only applied the traditional margin of appreciation doctrine, trying not to impose unnecessary uniform European patterns on national systems of relations between the state and religion. However, the mere fact that the ECtHR justified the French and Turkish secularist policies that limit expressions of religious identity, without enough evidence of a danger to public order, might denote a certain agreement with the philosophy underlying those policies – that the public sphere is better organized, and *less problematic*, when religion is absent.

It has sometimes been suggested that this attitude could be explained by the declared interest of French and Turkish secularist policies in restricting the visibility of some symbols of Islam that may be understood as offensive to women (the female headscarf especially), or even as expressions of Islamic extremism, and that could exert pressure on people, especially on Muslims that refuse to wear these symbols.[64] But the fact is that a similar notion of neutrality inspired the Chamber's decision in the *Lautsi* case (2009),[65] apparently implying that the neutral organization of the state school system compels the state to eliminate all visible religious symbols, and the crucifix in particular, out of respect for the secularist convictions of some parents or students. Fortunately, the Grand Chamber judgment on the same case, in 2011, overruling the Chamber's judgment, denied that such an exclusive notion of neutrality was the only acceptable one and pointed out that neutrality could also be achieved by a school environment that is inclusive and therefore open to visible expressions of both majority and minority religions or worldviews.[66] The subjective feeling of some students about the crucifix – the Court added – was not enough to challenge the legitimacy of a school setting that was objectively based on an open and inclusive concept of neutrality.[67]

On the other hand, we should note that the ECtHR's past support for active secularist policies, as well as its doctrine on the automatic supremacy of neutral laws over religious objections, mainly applies to education cases.[68] It is certainly justifiable, and desirable, that the Court has a particular sensitivity regarding education issues, probably keeping in mind that minors tend to be more vulnerable and there is a greater need to guarantee their protection against indoctrination or religious pressure. However, in my opinion, and precisely because the realm of education is so special, the Court should put particular emphasis on construing an inclusive concept of pluralism and neutrality that protects, in practice, the religious identity of all and not only of those who identify themselves with strictly secular positions. Moreover, the recent French and Belgian laws banning the use of a full veil in public spaces shows that secularist policies exclusive of religious symbols tend to expand easily beyond the educational environment.[69]

At present it is not possible to judge if the European Court's recent decisions on *Ahmet Arslan*, *Lautsi* (GC), *Bayatyan* and *Eweida* are opening the door in

Strasbourg to a deeper understanding of religious and ideological pluralism that includes a higher protection of individual conscience rights and a more inclusive notion of the neutrality of the public sphere, or if these judgments merely reflect the uncertainties of an international court that navigates without clear points of reference through the increasing complexities of the relationship between religion, law and society. Personally, I hope they are indeed indicative of a change of direction in the ECtHR's jurisprudence, which would be applicable also to education cases. And, in the particular case of conflicts between conscience and neutral laws, we should not lose sight of the fact that the so-called *neutral* laws are not so neutral, for they normally correspond to, and are based on, the ethical values of the political and social majority, and therefore it is easy for them to impinge on the rights of people belonging to minority groups with distinctive beliefs.

Notes

1 Professor of Law and Director of the Department of Law and Religion, Complutense University (Madrid, Spain). Doctor *utroque iure* (of Law and of Canon Law). Vice-President of the Section of Canon Law and Church–State Relations of the Spanish Royal Academy of Jurisprudence and Legislation. Member of the Spanish Advisory Commission for Religious Freedom within the Ministry of Justice. This paper has been written within the Project DER2011–29385, of the Spanish Ministry of Science and Innovation. The author wishes to express his gratitude to Dr Camil Ungureanu for his insightful comments during the editing process of this chapter.

2 *Kokkinakis v. Greece*, 25 May 1993, para. 31. The case originated in the application of a Jehovah's Witness who had been found guilty of religious proselytism, as established in an old Greek law. This judgment marked a turning point in the history of the ECtHR's case law, which until then had never ruled on any application based upon Article 9 ECHR and had touched only incidentally on religious freedom issues (by a tacit unwritten rule, these issues were implicitly understood as an exclusive competence of national authorities and almost always declared inadmissible by the European Commission on Human Rights). Since then, the Court has been adjudicating regularly on religious freedom issues, as on any other right recognized by the Convention. See, for a detailed analysis of this transcendental judgment, J. Gunn (1966) 'Adjudicating Rights of Conscience Under the European Convention on Human Rights', in J. van der Vyver and J. Witte (eds), *Religious Human Rights in Global Perspective: Legal Perspectives*, Martinus Nijhoff: Boston, pp. 317–330; J. Martínez-Torrón (1994) 'Libertad de proselitismo en Europa. A propósito de una reciente sentencia del Tribunal europeo de derechos humanos', in *Quaderni di diritto e politica ecclesiastica*, 1: 59–71.

3 *Serif v. Greece*, 14 December 1999, para. 53. The case related to the government's intervention in the appointment of a Mufti in the region of Thrace, which has a significant Muslim population of Turkish origin, in a situation in which there was strong opposition between two rival factions in the Islamic community. A similar doctrine expressed by the Court shortly afterwards in *Hasan and Chaush v. Bulgaria*, 26 October 2000, also related to the religious disputes between two different factions of the Islamic community, this time in Bulgaria, and the intervention of state authorities in the election and appointment of a Muslim leader. See also *Metropolitan Church of Bessarabia v. Moldova*, 13 December 2001 (government's intervention in a church schism), and *Agga v. Greece*, 17 October 2002, which offers many analogies with *Serif*.

4 Cf. the doctrine of the ECtHR in the cases cited supra, in note 2.

5 *Kokkinakis*, para. 31, quoted in note 2.

6 Article 9.2 ECHR requires that limitations on religious freedom, to be legitimate, comply with three requirements: they must be 'prescribed by law'; they must pursue one of the aims mentioned in Article 9.2 (namely, public safety, order, health or morals, or the protection of the rights and freedoms of others); and they must be 'necessary in a democratic society'. See, for a more detailed analysis of this issue, J. Martínez-Torrón (2005) 'Limitations on Religious Freedom in the Case Law of the European Court of Human Rights', in *Emory International Law Review* 19: 587–636.

7 See note 6.

8 The European Commission of Human Rights acted, in the original design of the Strasbourg jurisdiction, as a filter to select which applications could arrive to the European Court to be decided on their merits. The Court could adjudicate only on those applications declared admissible by the Commission – the vast majority of applications were declared inadmissible as ill-founded, i.e. as not offering a prima facie appearance of possible violation of a human right. The Commission disappeared in 1998, when the Protocol No. 11 to the European Convention came into force. Since then, applications are declared admissible or inadmissible by the Court itself.

9 See J. Martínez-Torrón and R. Navarro-Valls (2004) 'The Protection of Religious Freedom in the System of the Council of Europe', in T. Lindholm, W.C. Durham and B.G. Tahzib-Lie (eds), *Facilitating Freedom of Religion or Belief: A Deskbook*, Martinus Nijhoff: Leiden, pp. 228–236.

10 The French version of Article 9 ECHR is even clearer in this respect, for it refers explicitly to 'le culte, l'enseignement, les pratiques et l'accomplissement des rites'.

11 *Campbell and Cosans v. United Kingdom*, 25 February 1982, para. 36. The same paragraph adds that such a concept of beliefs 'is not synonymous with the words "opinions" and "ideas", such as those utilised in Article 10 ... of the Convention, which guarantees freedom of expression'. This notion of beliefs has been subsequently used by the European Court. See recently, for example, *Eweida and others v. United Kingdom*, 15 January 2013, para. 81.

12 See General Comment No. 22: The right to freedom of thought, conscience and religion (Article 18): 30/07/93; CCPR/C/21/Rev.1/Add.4, General Comment No. 22. The General Comment on Article 18 was adopted by the Committee on 20 July 1993. For a detailed analysis of the text, see B.G. Tahzib (1996) *Freedom of Religion or Belief: Ensuring Effective International Legal Protection*, Martinus Nijhoff: The Hague, pp. 307–375.

13 See also M.D. Evans (1997) *Religious Liberty and International Law in Europe*, Cambridge University Press: Cambridge (reprinted in 2008), pp. 293–314; C. Evans (2001) *Freedom of Religion under the European Convention on Human Rights*, Oxford University Press: Oxford, pp. 110–132.

14 See *Kokkinakis*, paras 31 and 33.

15 *C. v. United Kingdom*, Decision on the admissibility of Appl. No. 10358/83, The Law, para. 1. The case related to a Quaker's conscientious objection to paying the percentage of taxes corresponding to the part of the state budget used in armament and weapons research. Among the most significant decisions reiterating this doctrine, see *Vereniging Rechtswinkels Utrecht v. The Netherlands*, Decision on the admissibility of Appl. No. 11308/84, The Law, para. 1. See also the Commission's report in the important case *Kalaç v. Turkey* (Appl. No. 20704/92), which would be decided by the Court on 1 July 1997.

16 *Arrowsmith v. United Kingdom*, Commission's report on Appl. No. 7050/75 (5 December 1978), para. 71. The case concerned a British pacifist sentenced to a term of imprisonment for having distributed illegal leaflets among English soldiers in Northern Ireland

17 See *Kalaç v. Turkey*, 1 July 1997, para. 27; and *Hasan and Chaush v. Bulgaria*, 26 October 2000, para. 60.

18 In addition, it raises the question of a possible biased understanding of what a proper manifestation of religion or belief is, for the expression 'practice of religion or belief in a generally recognized form' can easily be influenced by the Christian conceptions that are predominant in Europe.

19 *Efstratiou v. Greece*, 18 December 1996, and *Valsamis v. Greece*, 18 December 1996. The texts of both decisions are almost identical, as indeed were the facts at issue.

20 See *Valsamis*, paras 31 and 37; *Efstratiou*, paras 32 and 38.

21 See also C. Evans (2001: 120–124) *Freedom of Religion*, cited in note 13.

22 *Hasan and Chaush v. Bulgaria*, 26 October 2000, para. 78. See also, four years before, *Manoussakis v. Greece*, 26 September 1996, para. 47. The only difference between those two paragraphs is the reference to 'exceptional cases' contained in *Hasan*. This statement has been reiterated later by the Court. See, for instance, recently, *Eweida and others v. United Kingdom*, 15 January 2013, para. 81.

23 For further details on this approach of the Strasbourg jurisdiction, see J. Martínez-Torrón (1993) 'La giurisprudenza degli organi di Strasburgo sulla libertà religiosa', in *Rivista internazionale di diritti dell'uomo*, 335 et seq.

24 See note 15 and accompanying text.

25 *Kokkinakis v. Greece*, cited in note 1. The Court decided in favour of the applicant because the Greek courts, based on the national laws against religious proselytism, had sentenced a Jehovah's Witness without enough evidence that he had been engaged in 'improper proselytism', i.e. in trying to convert people through abusive or deceitful means. For the ECtHR, to apply the law indiscriminately against all types of religious proselytism was equivalent to restricting, without due justification, the freedom to manifest one's religion or beliefs in teaching.

26 *Buscarini et al. v. San Marino*, 18 February 1999. The Court held that requiring newly elected members of Parliament to swear allegiance to the Constitution on the Gospels, on pain of forfeiting their parliamentary seats, was contrary to the provisions of Article 9 ECHR, which 'entails, *inter alia*, freedom to hold or not to hold religious beliefs and to practise or not to practise a religion'. In the ECtHR's view, the religious oath requirement could not be considered 'necessary in a democratic society', for it amounted to imposing on the applicants an obligation to declare their belief in a religion that was not their own.

27 *Kjeldsen, Busk Madsen and Pedersen v. Denmark*, 7 December 1976. See R. Navarro-Valls and J. Martínez-Torrón (2011) *Conflictos entre conciencia y ley: las objeciones de conciencia* (2nd edn) Iustel: Madrid, pp. 253–255; M.D. Evans (1997: 342–343, 355–356) *Religious Liberty*, cited in note 13; C. Evans (2001: 90–93) *Freedom of Religion*, cited in note 13. A similar doctrine was reiterated in two more recent cases related to conscientious objection to some educational contents, in particular to mandatory courses of supposedly neutral religious instruction; the Court applied the same criteria but found that in these cases the courses of religious instruction were not sufficiently neutral and decided in favour of the applicants. See *Folgerø v. Norway*, 29 June 2007 and *Zengin v. Turkey*, 9 October 2007. See, for a detailed analysis of these two judgments, M.A. Jusdado and S. Cañamares (2007) 'La objeción de conciencia en el ámbito educativo. Comentario a la Sentencia del Tribunal Europeo de Derechos Humanos Folgerø v. Noruega'; and J. Martínez-Torrón (2007) *'La objeción de conciencia a la enseñanza religiosa y moral en la reciente jurisprudencia de Estrasburgo'*, both in *Revista General de Derecho Canónico y Derecho Eclesiástico del Estado*, 15. See www.iustel.com (accessed 5 May 2014).

28 See supra, notes 19–20 and corresponding text.

29 *Kalaç v. Turkey*, 1 July 1997. The case related to the compulsory retirement of an officer of the Turkish army for his alleged membership of an Islamic fundamentalist movement supporting ideas contrary to the constitutional principle of secularism. The

Court held that the applicant had not been punished because of his religious beliefs or practices but rather because his 'conduct breached military discipline and infringed the principle of secularism' (ibid. para. 30); there was no need to justify his retirement under Article 9.2 ECHR because 'the applicant's compulsory retirement did not amount to an interference with the right guaranteed by article 9 since it was not prompted by the way the applicant manifested his religion' (ibid. para. 31). The Court seemed to be satisfied with the fact that the applicant:

> was able to fulfil the obligations which constitute the normal forms through which a Muslim practises his religion. For example, he was in particular permitted to pray five times a day and to perform his other religious duties, such as keeping the fast of Ramadan and attending Friday prayers at the mosque.
>
> (Ibid. para. 29)

For a more extensive and critical comment on this case, very poorly reasoned by the ECtHR, see J. Martínez-Torrón (2010) 'Islam in Strasbourg: Can Politics Substitute for Law?', in W.C. Durham, R. Torfs, D.M. Kirkham and C. Scott (eds), *Islam, Europe and Emerging Legal Issues*, Ashgate: Aldershot, pp. 41–44.

30 *The Jewish Liturgical Association Cha'are Shalom Ve Tsedek v. France*, 27 June 2000. The problem arose from the fact that the ultra-orthodox community was more demanding than the rest of Jewish communities with respect to the conditions in which ritual slaughter had to be performed. In this case, the ECtHR focussed on the interpretation of the equality principle rather than on the neutrality of the challenged measure. The Court took into account the fact that the *glatt* meat imported from Belgium had a higher price, but considered that the unequal treatment of members of the ultra-orthodox community was justified under Article 14 ECHR on the ground of the protection of public health and public order. Seven of the seventeen judges of the Grand Chamber wrote a joint dissenting opinion considering that the principle of equality had been violated.

31 This is in fact the case of the different types of conscientious objection. For a recent extensive analysis of conscientious objections in international and comparative law, with numerous bibliographical and case law references, see R. Navarro-Valls and J. Martínez-Torrón (2011) 'Conflictos entre conciencia y ley', cited in note 27. At the same time, we should not forget that significant religious persecutions have been carried out in the past two centuries under the pretext of laws that were formally neutral and of general applicability. See W.C. Durham, *Perspectives On Religious Liberty: A Comparative Framework*, in "Religious Human Rights in Global Perspective", p. 33 cited in note 2.

32 *Bayatyan v. Armenia* (GC), 7 July 2011. The Grand Chamber overruled the previous Chamber decision, of 27 October 2009. Let us note, incidentally, that the only dissenting opinion in *Bayatyan* Chamber's decision was written by Judge Power. In *Bayatyan*, the Grand Chamber essentially accepted Judge Power's analysis.

33 See, for further details, R. Navarro-Valls and J. Martínez-Torrón (2011: 102–105) 'Conflictos entre conciencia y ley', cited in note 27. See also, for the European Commission and the European Court's case law on conscientious objection to military service prior to *Bayatyan*, C. Evans (2001: 170–179) *Freedom of Religion*, cited in note 13.

34 See especially *Bayatyan* (GC), paras 100–103.

35 See ibid., para. 110.

36 See ibid., para. 125.

37 See supra, note 22 and accompanying text.

38 *Francesco Sessa v. Italy*, 3 April 2012.

39 The applicant's request had been made several months in advance, immediately after he was told about two new alternative dates – they were fixed to replace the original date of the hearing, in which the applicant was present but not the instructor judge.

Both alternative dates were important Jewish festivities, namely Yom Kippur and Succoth, respectively.

40 *Francesco Sessa*, para. 37.

41 *Eweida and others v. United Kingdom*, 15 January 2013, para. 81.

42 In brief, the conflicts of conscience were the following. In *Eweida*, an employee of British Airways insisted on wearing a visible necklace with a golden cross, as a symbol of her commitment to her Christian faith, against the uniform rules of the airline (which allowed for exemptions for Muslim headscarves but not for crosses). In *Chaplin*, a nurse working on a geriatric ward claimed her right to wear a necklace with a cross and the management of the hospital found this to be unsafe after the new hospital uniform introduced V-necked tunics for nurses. In *Ladele*, a registrar of births, marriages and deaths expressed a conscientious objection to registering civil partnerships between persons of the same sex – her borough had decided in 2005 to designate all existing registrars of births, marriages and deaths as civil partnership registrars. In *McFarlane*, a psycho-sexual therapist working for a private organization providing a relationship counselling service had conscience scruples with regard to providing counselling to homosexual and bi-sexual couples. Only in the case of *Eweida* did the ECtHR find a violation of Article 9 ECHR.

43 For an analysis on this decision, see M. Hill (2013) 'Religious Symbolism and Conscientious Objection in the Workplace: An Evaluation of Strasbourg's Judgment in *Eweida and others v. United Kingdom'*, in *Ecclesiastical Law Journal*, 15: 191–203. See also H. Hall and J.G. Oliva (2013) 'Simbología religiosa en el ámbito laboral. A propósito del caso Chaplin y sus implicaciones en el derecho británico'; F. Pérez-Madrid (2013) 'Objeción de conciencia y uniones civiles entre personas del mismo sexo: comentarios acerca del caso Ladele c. Reino Unido'; and A. González-Varas (2013) 'Objeción de conciencia al tratamiento psicológico de homosexuales', all of them in *Revista General de Derecho Canónico y Derecho Eclesiástico del Estado*, 32. See www.iustel.com (accessed 5 May 2014).

44 See *Eweida*, paras 81–82.

45

> Given the importance in a democratic society of freedom of religion, the Court considers that, where an individual complains of a restriction on freedom of religion in the workplace, rather than holding that the possibility of changing job would negate any interference with the right, the better approach would be to weigh that possibility in the overall balance when considering whether or not the restriction was proportionate.
>
> (Ibid., para. 83)

46 For an interesting recent reflection on the different notions of state neutrality, in scholarship as well as in comparative law, and the difficulties of finding an operative definition of this principle, see R. Palomino (2011) 'Religion and Neutrality: Myth, Principle, and Meaning', in *Brigham Young University Law Review*, 3: 657–689.

47 *Dahlab v. Switzerland*, Decision on the admissibility of Appl. No. 42393/98, 15 February 2001. *Dahlab* was declared inadmissible by the Court as 'manifestly ill-founded' in a lengthy decision that, as sometimes occurs, actually went into the merits of the case.

48 *Leyla Şahin v. Turkey*, 29 June 2004 (Chamber's decision), and *Leyla Şahin v. Turkey*, 10 November 2005 (Grand Chamber's decision). The Chamber's decision was adopted unanimously and the Grand Chamber's decision was adopted by sixteen votes to one.

49 This judgment of the ECtHR has been extensively commented upon by scholars. See, for instance, the chapters by T.J. Gunn, N. Hostmaelingen, T. Lindholm and I.T. Plesner (2012) in the collective book *Islam, Europe and Emerging Legal Issues*, cited in note 29. See also N. Lerner (2005) 'How Wide the Margin of Appreciation? The Turkish Headscarf Case, the Strasbourg Court, and Secularist Tolerance', in

Willamette Journal of International Law and Dispute Resolutions, 13: 65–85; B. Chelini-Pont and E. Tawil(2006–2007) 'Brèves remarques sur l'arrêt Leyla Sahin', in *Annuaire Droit et Religions*, 2: 607–611; T. Lewis (2007) 'What Not to Wear: Religious Rights, the European Court, and the Margin of Appreciation', in *International and Comparative Law Quarterly*, 56: 395 et seq. Among Spanish legal literature, see S. Cañamares (2005) *Libertad religiosa, simbología y laicidad del Estado*, Thomson-Aranzadi: Pamplona, pp. 179–180; J. Martínez-Torrón (2009) 'La cuestión del velo islámico en la jurisprudencia de Estrasburgo', in *Derecho y Religión*, 4: 94–98. See also the dissenting opinion of Judge Tulkens to the Grand Chamber decision.

50 *Leyla Şahin* (C 2004), para. 108, and *Leyla Şahin* (GC 2005), para. 115.

51 Cf. *Köse and 93 other applicants v. Turkey*, Decision on the admissibility of Appl. No. 26625/02, 24 January 2006; *Kurtulmus v. Turkey*, Decision on the admissibility of Appl. No. 65500/01, 24 January 2006. See J. Martínez-Torrón (2009: 98–101) 'La cuestión del velo', cited in note 49.

52 *Loi*, No. 2008–224, 15 March 2004. The ECtHR provides a general overview of the debate, as well as of the most relevant legislation and case-law, in paras 17–32 of the 'twin' decisions *Dogru* and *Kervanci*, cited below, in note 53. For an analysis of the situation in the first years of the public debate about the Islamic headscarf in France, see D. Le Tourneau (1997) 'La laïcité à l'épreuve de l'Islam: le cas du port du "foulard islamique" dans l'école publique en France', in *Revue Générale de Droit*, 28: 275–306. For a critical assessment of the 2004 law in France, see A. Garay 'Laïcité, école et appartenance religieuse: pour un bilan exigeant de la loi n° 2004–228 du 15 Mars 2004', in *Cahiers de la Recherche sur les Droits Fondamentaux 4: Quel avenir pour la laïcité cent ans après la loi de 1905?*, Caen 2005, 33–47; B. Chelini-Pont & T.J. Gunn, *Dieu en France et aux Etat-Unis. Quand les mythes font la loi*, Berg International: Paris 2005. The issue has also attracted the attention of Spanish scholars; see, among others, S. Cañamares Arribas (2005: 70) *Libertad religiosa, simbología*, cited in note 49; A. González-Varas Ibáñez (2005) *Confessioni religiose, diritto e scuola pubblica in Italia. Insegnamento, culto e simbologia religiosa nelle scuole pubbliche*, CLUEB: Bologna, pp. 229 et seq.; M.J. Ciáurriz (2009) '*Laicidad y ley sobre los símbolos religiosos en Francia*', in *El pañuelo islámico en Europa* (coord. by A. Motilla), Marcual Pons: Madrid, pp. 91 et seq.

53 *Dogru v. France*, and *Kervanci v. France*, both of 4 December 2008. For a comment on those decisions, see B. Chelini-Pont and D. Girard (2009) 'Le voile musulman et la conception française de l'Etat laïc', in *Revista General de Derecho Canónico y Derecho Eclesiástico del Estado*, 19: 1–11; J. Martínez-Torrón (2009: 103–107) 'La cuestión del velo', cited in note 49.

54 See *Dogru* and *Kervanci*, paras 13 and 74.

55 Cf. ibid., para. 75.

56 There has been a tendency to assume that the 'least restrictive means' test died along with the 'compelling state interest test' in the aftermath of the US Supreme Court's decision in *Employment Division, Dep't of Human Resources v. Smith*, 494 US 872 (1990). However, reinstatement of that test remains in effect in federal settings, See *Gonzales v. O Centro Espirita Beneficente Uniao Do Vegetal*, 546 US 418 (2006). In fact, a majority of jurisdictions within the United States have retained heightened scrutiny, typically including a variant of the least restrictive means or narrow tailoring requirements. See W.C. Durham Jr and R.T. Smith (2010) 'Religion and State in the United States at the Turn of the Twenty-First Century', in *Law and Religion in the 21st Century: Relations between States and Religious Communities* by S. Ferrari and R. Cristofori (eds) Ashgate: Farnham, UK, pp. 79–110; W.W. Bassett, W.C. Durham Jr and R.T. Smith (2010) *Religious Organizations and the Law*, West, Weagan: Mason, US, §2.66.

57 See N. Lerner (2005: 84–85) *'How Wide the Margin of Appreciation?'*, cited in note 49; J. Woehrling (1998) 'L'obligation d'accommodement raisonnable et l'adaptation

de la societé à la diversitá religieuse', in *McGill Law Journal*, 43: 325 et seq.; W.C. Durham Jr (1994) 'Freedom of Religion: The United States Model', in *American Journal of Comparative Law Supplement*, 42: 624 et seq. The issue of the least restrictive alternatives for religious freedom, in the context of a deep analysis of the use of the principle of proportionality, has been studied by J. Gunn (2005) 'Deconstructing Proportionality in Limitations Analysis', in *Emory International Law Review*, 19: 465–498. For an interesting application of this criterion by the Canadian Supreme Court, see the decision *Multani v. Commission scolaire Marguerite Bourgeoys*, 2006 SCC 6, JE 2006–508, related to the wearing of a Sikh *kirpan* (a religious object that resembles a small dagger) within the school premises. For a comment on this decision, see A. Decroix (2006–2007) 'Les symboles religieux au sein des établissements scolaires: l'exemple du port du kirpan dans les écoles canadiennes', in *Annuaire Droit et Religions*, 2: 337–343; S. Cañamares Arribas (2006) 'Simbología religiosa en la escuela. Comentario a la sentencia del Tribunal Supremo de Canadá Singh-Multani c. Marguerite-Bourgeoys (Commission Scolaire)', in *Revista General de Derecho Canónico y Derecho Eclesiástico del Estado*, 11: 1–11.

58 On the contrary, the ECtHR's permissive attitude towards the state margin of appreciation was already present in three other cases declared inadmissible by the ECtHR, following the trail left by *Leyla Şahin*, which related also to conflicts caused by the wearing of religious clothing but this time with regard to rules or procedures of public safety instead of rules on school clothing. Those rules imposed indirectly a limitation on certain religious practices, but they had a lesser actual impact on the lives of the applicants. In two of these cases the conflict was caused by the refusal of male Sikhs to remove their turban from their heads, either to pass security controls before entering the boarding area at Strasbourg airport (*Phull v. France*, Decision on the admissibility of Appl. No. 35753/03, 11 January 2005), or to take an identity photo that could be considered valid for the renewal of a driving licence (*Mann Singh v. France*, Decision on the admissibility of Appl. No. 24479/07, 13 November 2008). In the third case, the applicant was a Moroccan Muslim woman who was refused a visa to travel to France and join her husband because, when asked to remove her headscarf at the French consulate for identification purposes, she declined to do so in the presence of an agent other than a woman (*El Morsli v. France*, Decision on the admissibility of Appl. No. 15585/06, 4 March 2008). In all these cases the applicants had suggested different ways to make their religious duties compatible with security rules, but the ECtHR did not even consider the possibility that the French authorities had exceeded their margin of appreciation when they rejected those suggestions *tout court* and without any possible alternative.

59 See supra, note 36 and accompanying text.

60 In four of these decisions the applicants were female Muslim students who felt morally obliged to wear a headscarf: *Aktas v. France*, Decision on the admissibility of Appl. No. 43563/08; *Bayrak v. France*, Decision on the admissibility of Appl. No. 14308/08; *Gamaleddyn v. France*, Decision on the admissibility of Appl. No. 18527/08; *Ghazal v. France*, Decision on the admissibility of Appl. No. 29134/08. In the other two, the applicants were male Sikh students who had been expelled for wearing a *keski* – a more discreet garment that is usually worn under the turban characteristic of Sikhs (*Jasvir Singh v. France*, Decision on the admissibility of Appl. No. 25463/08, and *Ranjit Singh v. France*, Decision on the admissibility of Appl. No. 27561/08). The six decisions were rendered on 30 June 2009.

61 *Ahmet Arslan et al. v. Turkey*, 23 February 2010. We could also recall other cases in which the ECtHR considered disproportionate and unjustified some sanctions imposed by the Turkish authorities on parliamentary representatives, politicians, religious leaders or journalists for publicly defending the use of female Islamic headscarf and openly criticizing the restrictions imposed by Turkish law. These decisions are: *Kavakçi v. Turkey*, *Ilicak v. Turkey*, and *Silay v. Turkey*, all of them decided on

5 April 2007 with almost identical reasoning; *Gündüz v. Turkey*, 4 December 2003; *Erbakan v. Turkey*, 6 July 2006; *Güzel v. Turkey*, 27 July 2006; and *Kutlular v. Turkey*, 29 April 2008. See J. Martínez-Torrón (2009: 101–103) 'La cuestión del velo', cited in note 49.

62 See S. Ferrari (1997) *'The New Wine and the Old Cask: Tolerance, Religion and the Law in Contemporary Europe'*, in *Ratio Juris* 10: 75–89.

63 Cf. *Schüth v. Germany* and *Obst v. Germany*, both 23 September 2010; *Siebenhaar v. Germany*, 3 February 2011; and *Sindicatul "Păstorul Cel Bun" v. Romania*, 31 January 2012 (the latter case is currently on appeal before the Grand Chamber). For a comment on the two first judgments, see J. Martínez-Torrón (2012) 'Freedom of religion in the European Convention on Human Rights under the Influence of Different European Traditions', in H. Zacher and M.A. Glendon (eds), *Universal Rights in a World of Diversity. The Case of Religious Freedom*, Pontifical Academy of Social Sciences: Vatican City, pp. 336–342.

64 See, for further details, J. Martínez-Torrón (2012: 49) *'Islam in Strasbourg'*, cited in note 29.

65 See especially *Lautsi v. Italy*, 3 November 2009, paras 56–57. Significantly, the Chamber cited some of the relevant decisions in which the Strasbourg jurisdiction justified the prohibitions of Islamic headscarf in the educational environment.

66 See especially *Lautsi v. Italy* (GC), 18 March 2011, para. 74. The *Lautsi* case has been – and continues to be – commented upon by scholars from very diverse positions. See, on the *Lautsi* Grand Chamber decision, and from different perspectives, V. Turchi (2011) 'La pronuncia della Grande Chambre della Corte di Strasburgo sul caso Lautsi C. Italia: post nubila Phoebus', in *Stato, Chiese e pluralismo confessionale*, October (see www.statoechiese.it, accessed 5 May 2014), where further bibliographical references, especially to Italian legal literature, can be found; and P. Ronchi (2011) 'Crucifixes, Margin of Appreciation and Consensus: The Grand Chamber Ruling in Lautsi v. Italy', in *Ecclesiastical Law Journal*, 13: 287–297. See also, comparing the Strasbourg and the US approach to institutional religious symbols, J. Witte, Jr and N.L. Arold, '"Lift High the Cross"? Contrasting the New European and American Cases on Religious Symbols on Government Property', in *Emory International Law Review*, 25: 5–55; and a critical view of *Lausti GC*, in the light of Canadian law and putting the European case law into a socio-cultural perspective, L. Beaman (2012–2013) 'Battles over Symbols: The "Religion" of the Minority versus the "Culture" of the Majority', in *The Journal of Law and Religion*, 28: 67 et seq. In Spain, see S. Cañamares Arribas (2011) 'Los símbolos religiosos en el espacio público: entre la amenaza real y la mera sospecha', in El *Cronista del Estado Social y Democrático de Derecho*, 20: 60–67; S. Meseguer Velasco (2011) 'Símbolos religiosos en colegios públicos: ¿hacia dónde camina la jurisprudencia europea?', in *Anuario Jurídico Villanueva*, 5: 202–213.

67 See *Lautsi* (GC), para. 66. In my opinion, *Lautsi* (GC) would have been even better if it had elaborated more on some points remarked in the concurring opinions of two judges (Power and Bonello). In particular, the idea that coercion should be the test to a violation of freedom of religion or belief, and not the *subjective feeling* of offence experienced by some persons in the presence of some religious symbols.

68 And, to a lesser extent, to public safety cases. See supra, note 29 and corresponding text, and note 58.

69 See, on this controversial issue, among the writings of Spanish legal scholars, V. Camarero (2012) *El velo integral y su respuesta en democracias europeas*, Tirant Lo Blanch: Valencia; R. Navarro-Valls and J. Martínez-Torrón (2011) *Conflictos entre conciencia y ley: las objeciones de conciencia*, 2nd edn, Iustel: Madrid, pp. 378–384; and B. Aláez (forthcoming) 'Some constitutional thoughts about the Islamic full veil ban in Europe', in *Vienna Journal of International Constitutional Law*, 7–3. On the developments of this issue in municipal by-laws in Spain and the recent judicial

reaction to them, see M.T. Areces (2013) 'La prohibición del velo integral islámico. A propósito de la sentencia del Tribunal Supremo'; V. Camarero (2013) 'Análisis de la primera decision del Tribunal Supremo respecto del velo integral'; and A. López-Sidro(2013) 'Restricciones al velo integral en Europa y en España: la pugna legislativa por prohibir un símbolo', all of them in *Revista General de Derecho Canónico y Derecho Eclesiástico del Estado* 32. See www.iustel.com (accessed 5 May 2014).

8 A marriage made in heaven?

The relationship between religious pluralism and secularism

Lorenzo Zucca

Britain lives in the age of equal marriage: most forms of discrimination have been removed and the state recognizes the union between two persons rather than that between a man and a woman. It is therefore not surprising that religious marriage should be open and pluralist: the Church Of Scientology, for example, has just been allowed to celebrate valid religious marriages on its premises by the UK Supreme Court in the landmark case of *Hodkin v. Registrar*.[1] The decision is particularly important because it squarely moves away from a Judeo-Christian theistic definition of religion and embraces a much more open test that is broadly in line with religious pluralism.

Part of the problem comes from the fact that England recognizes in religious marriage the same legal effects as for standard civil marriage. The state would have an easier life if the only legally recognized marriage was the civil form. This would not limit the possibility of people marrying in their own church, as happens in France. Religious marriage, in this framework, is open to all people and all beliefs. Religious authorities do not have to seek the recognition of the state, which is required in the UK. Indeed no civil or religious marriage can take place in a site that has not been duly registered: the Places of Worship Registration Act (1855) (PWRA) sets out the conditions.

The PWRA 1855 is pluralistic: the point is to recognize equal freedom of religion. The Act is the end point of a progressive liberation of all faiths in Britain – a process that started with the Toleration Act of 1688, which made religion free for dissenting Protestants. The second step was the Catholic Relief Act of 1791, extending toleration to Catholics, then the Religious Disabilities Act 1846, which included the Jews. Since 1855, all religious denominations can come forth to have their churches recognized as places of worship, in which they can celebrate religious weddings.

Religious pluralism must be capacious, but it cannot be all-inclusive. In order to determine where the limits are, it is necessary for the state to define religion so as to discriminate between religious and non-religious phenomena. However, there is no accepted secular definition of religion that can suit the purposes of the state. Theories of freedom of religion do not help in that quest: they either take religion for granted or they reduce religion to other phenomena. The main contrast is between liberty-based and equality-based theories of freedom of religion.

Liberty-based theories of freedom of religion believe that the state is to be suspected of unduly interfering with consciences. This means that freedom of religion should be conceptualized as freedom of conscience, and, as such, it has super protected status. Equality-based theories of freedom of religion argue that the state can provide a scheme of fair liberties to all citizens. Within such a framework, freedom of religion is but another freedom, like free speech or assembly. This means that freedom of religion does not qualify for special protection. At best, it provides equivalent protection to that already afforded under other rights. Crucially, it also means that freedom of religion can be equated or reduced to other types of freedom.

Both theories share the impossibility of defining religion in a satisfactory way. The Scientology case is there to exemplify this problem. Lord Toulson accepts that a court cannot provide a strict legal definition of religion. At best, it can spell out a few guidelines that help to reach an empirically verifiable description. Needless to say, such a description will tend to be over-inclusive, but courts will be there to guard the boundaries on a case-by-case basis. This is especially important when a religion does not claim economic benefits, but only wishes to be recognized as performing a spiritual mission like any other religion. In this case, the state should have less rather than more discretion as to whether to recognize a group of people as being religious. This case should be distinguished from scenarios in which state and church collaborate on an economic basis. Religions provide important public and social services; when they do so, they should be equated with and evaluated on the basis of the criteria used for other charities and service providers. In the UK, Scientology, for example, already benefits from tax breaks on the basis that it provides a certain number of services.

In areas such as religious marriage, religious pluralism should be as broad and over-inclusive as possible. The state should be distrusted and religions should be protected in the performance of their worship. In other words, a liberty-based conception of freedom of religion prevails in this case. However, when the state distributes economic benefits, religious and non-religious providers should be treated fairly on the basis of analogous criteria. In this case, the state has the role of distributing economic benefits fairly and equally, and an equality-based conception of religion applies.

In what follows, I will take the Scientology case as an illustration of one of the key questions that faces a state committed to religious pluralism: the impossibility of defining religion in general, or religious worship in particular (pp. 149–153). Given such an impossibility, the state – and its judiciary – should extend freedom of religion as much as possible when it does not involve economic benefits (pp. 153–157). On the other hand, it should treat religious and non-religious organizations equally when they provide social and public services on an economic basis; this leads us to realize that secularism should not be understood as strict separation, but as a multi-faceted collaboration instead (pp. 157–160).

The impossibility of defining religion

The practical importance of this issue cannot be underestimated: to be defined as a religion comes with important legal benefits, ranging from tax breaks to exemptions from legal duties. More generally, the very limit of religious pluralism depends on the definition of religion. There are two extremes that may make freedom of religion either over-inclusive or under-inclusive. Religion is defined over-inclusively when it is nothing else than the free exercise of one's own conscience. Every individual exercises free conscience and, on this basis, every individual could claim to be covered by freedom of religion. Religion is defined under-inclusively when the majority groups of a limited number of religious communities can claim the benefits of the protection of freedom of religion.

In this chapter, there is no attempt to find a middle ground between under-inclusive and over-inclusive definitions of religion. I believe that there is no objective definition that can be adopted by the state, or by a judge. What is clear is that the state should not be in the business of handing out badges of religious acceptability. In particular when it recognizes to a religious function the consequences of the law, as in the case of religious marriage, it should not be choosy when it comes to granting this privilege to new religions. In this case, it should take the declaration of a group as being constitutive of the group's nature. After all, the very Places of Religious Worship Act of 1855 was meant to introduce more pluralism rather than less. On the one hand, the state has an interest in that all groups who practice a religion should register themselves as religious groups. On the other hand, religious groups have an incentive to register themselves as such.

Where the state should be stricter is on the range of benefits attached to the status of religion. I believe that non-economic benefits should clearly be protected, while economic benefits can only be protected if the religion performs duties that are valuable for the whole society, such as the assistance of poor people. In other words, charitable status should be decoupled from religious status. Also, tax breaks should be granted on the basis of the non-profit nature of the gathering. The status of religion is better linked with benefits that have to do with the spiritual mission of each religion. To limit the right to marry according to one's own convictions does not seem to be justifiable. Scientology has an equal right to celebrate religious weddings as any other religious organization.

It is true that non-economic benefits can include exemptions from the ordinary law. On this point I would draw a further distinction. When the state singles out a special power for a religious organization (e.g. the power to celebrate marriage, which is going to have legal consequences) it can make sure that those who officiate are trusted individuals and groups, but has no way of testing whether what they are doing is *really* religious, since there is no settled legal definition of religion. On the other hand, if the state has to decide on a claim to be exempted from a law, it can evaluate conscientious claims on various grounds: its depth, its sincerity, etc. In order for a conscientious claim to be eligible for an exemption of ordinary law, the claim does not have to be religious. My point is that the label "religious" should be considered as making a difference only when the state decides to confer on religious groups a special benefit as a matter of law. This benefit should be granted as widely as possible and it is the burden of the state to indicate precisely when the burden cannot be extended to religious groups. So, in the present case, if the state creates a benefit for all religious groups that consists of the power to celebrate marriage, any group that presents itself as religious should, in principle, have this power. If the state does not want a group to benefit from it, it will have the burden of proof: it will have to demonstrate that the group is not religious.

The spirit of the Places of Worship Registration Act 1855 is pluralistic: the Act controversially requires that a place be certified to the Registrar General. However, it is unclear whether the Registrar General has a duty to register or whether she can exercise a measure of judgment as to what qualifies as a place for religious worship. Lord Denning asserts in his usual sharp way: " I think that the Registrar General has only jurisdiction to register a place so long as it is *truly a place of meeting* for religious worship."[2] In other words, the Registrar General has to check whether the place's main function is to meet for religious worship, otherwise there would be too many abuses taking place. To establish that, however, it is necessary to know what amounts to religious worship; then we can decide whether a place is truly a place for religious worship.

Segerdal has now been overruled by the UK Supreme Court. Justice Ousely, who heard the *Hodkin* case in the first instance, concluded his judgment by giving an advise to the higher court: "Forty years on from Segerdal, the Court of Appeal may find the route at least to reconsider its decision in Segerdal, with the fuller material now available."[3] It is not the Court of Appeal that has decided, but the Supreme Court (directly), since the case has leapfrogged to the highest court, which is a sign of its importance. It is clear from Ousely's words that the precedent has to be re-thought. *Segerdal* was the leading precedent on the point of whether Scientology engages in "religious worship." The answer of the Court was negative, but the *ratio* was unclear: Was it because Scientology is not a religion or was it because Scientology does not worship? The first argument was simple: if Scientology is not a religion, then it can hardly engage in religious worship. It is nevertheless very problematic: what is a religion and why is scientology not one? The second argument is more complex: courts are to be agnostic as to whether Scientology is a religion; instead they are to rely on empirical evidence that shows that the practice of Scientology is not comparable to any other form of worship. The argument is severed from the question of what is religion, but it is equally problematic: it assumes that worship can be defined and compared across religious faiths. It is unclear, however, why there should be a paradigmatic way of worshipping.

Lord Denning, possibly the most famous judge in recent British legal history, gave a simple answer. Religion is about worshipping a god. He did not mince his words in *Segerdal* and was happy to offer his own definition in order to settle the problem. Needless to say, in *Segerdal*, Lord Denning put forward his personal convictions: to him Scientology is not a religion. Moreover, Scientology does not worship in a way that is comparable to any other religion he knows. The kernel of his position is contained in the following passage:

> [a place of meeting for religious worship] connotes to my mind a place of which the principal use is as a place where people come together as a congregation or assembly to do reverence to God. It need not be the God which the Christians worship. It may be another God, or an unknown God, *but it must be reverence to a deity.*
>
> (*R v. Registrar General, Ex parte Segerdal* [1970] p. 707)[4]

In this short sentence, Lord Denning provides his definition of religious worship rooted in his theistic understanding of religion: it must be reverence to a deity. It does not require much extrapolation to say that religion seems to be defined here in a theistic way. If you apply this definition to Scientology, it rules it out of the spectrum, since it does not believe in a deity and thus it is not a religion. Indeed, for Lord Denning, Scientology was "more a philosophy of the existence of man or life, rather than a religion". If one applied that definition strictly, other recognized religions such as Buddhism would not pass the test, for Buddhism does not entail a reverence to God. At this point, Lord Denning was even more puzzling, since he added to his original definition a few exceptions, which he did not define. He simply stated: "there may be exceptions", but did not specify which ones. Denning added a passing remark: "For instance, Buddhist temples are properly described as places of meeting for religious worship." Nothing else is added. There is no explanation of why Buddhism can be considered as a religion and Scientology cannot. There is no further elaboration of the exception. Lord Denning first asserts a bold definition of religion, and then smuggles in an exception to make room for widely accepted religious practices.

Justice Ousely made it clear that "a useful elaboration of Lord Denning's thoughts would not have lengthened his judgment unduly". In the case of *Hodkin v. Registrar*, Lord Lester, who was advising Miss Hodkin, rightly questioned the nature of the exception. The point here is that the definition of religion does not hold. It leaks water badly, and it is not capable of accounting for the exception.

The Supreme Court acknowledged the limits of *Segerdal*'s definition of religion. In fact, Lord Toulson, writing for the majority, admitted that no legal definition offered in the past by any common law jurisdiction is apt to do the job. Instead of a legal definition, Lord Toulson offers a set of guidelines that form a description, which needs to be verified empirically on a case-by-case basis. As far as the present case is concerned, the Supreme Court provided an ad hoc recognition of Scientology as a religion for the purposes of the 1855 Act and the Marriage Act of 1949. But is it, then, just that? For a religion to be recognized as such, it simply takes time and acceptance on the part of society. Is that the conclusion of this saga? In truth, the central legal problem will not wither away. Another group of people will request the same benefit in light of its religious nature. What should the Registrar General do then? Armed with the new description provided by the Supreme Court, the Registrar General will have to do her investigations. She will then form a view as to whether a new religion can be analogized with already existing religions. If her decision is negative, the adherents of the new religion have the chance to apply for a judicial review of the Registrar General. The ultimate word will be that of the judge, even though a judgment will never provide a clear-cut boundary between religion and non-religion.

In *Segerdal*, Lord Justice Winn and Lord Justice Buckley concurred with the conclusion of Lord Denning, but preferred to remain agnostic as to the nature of Scientology. They focused on the practice of religious worship. They consulted Scientology's booklet and heard the affidavit of one of its ministers. On this basis, they decided that Scientology was not using prayers, attitudes of piety or threats of damnation like all the other religions. I stop here for a second, as I find it particularly ironic that, in order to be worthy of the title of religion, one has to engage in "threats of damnation". Besides the involuntary comic effect of this statement, there lies a more general lesson. Worship seems to be tied with religious practices. Lawyers would like to claim that it is possible to sever the concept of worship from that of religion. This conceptual move allows them to define worship in a more empirical way – singling out factual criteria by reference to paradigmatic examples.

The impossibility of defining religious worship

Is it possible to sever worship from religion? Isn't worship a central dimension of religious practice? English courts have attempted to do just that in the past: namely, to claim that the question raised by the Places of Religious Worship Act is not about religion, but about worship. Accordingly, Scientology was not regarded in the past as engaging in worship. What was prohibited before, and is allowed by the PRWA, is the chance to meet as a religious group and worship in one's own preferred way. Strictly speaking, the Act protects freedom of worship as one of the central points of religious freedom. It is therefore particularly hard to treat worship independently from religion.

In the Court of First Instance, Justice Ashworth gave a tentative definition of worship. He claimed that worship is an act of veneration that requires a subject engaged in such action and an object of veneration. For Ashworth, Scientology is hardly a religion: it is more like a venting place where people of different faiths can exchange views on their spiritual character. Even so, Ashworth believes that it would be possible for Scientology to be engaged in religious worship; Scientology has to be seen to be doing acts of worship. Ashworth's position betrays a typical mistake of legal officials. They first abstract from religious practices familiar to them some common elements that are then presented as essential to the definition of religion. In the case of worship, it is clear that the relation between the worshipper and the worshipped is prefaced by a monotheistic (or simply theistic) understanding of religion. Buddhism would not pass the muster of the definition proposed by Ashworth, since it does not single out an object of worship.[5] The irony of this definition is in the suggestion that despite being defined by reference to religious practices, worship can also be practised by non-religious entities. Of course, this does not happen to be the case for Scientology, but the reason, for Ashworth, does not seem to flow directly from the fact that Scientology was not regarded as being comparable to mainstream religions.

The legal move to separate religion from worship – conceptually – is spurious. There may be worship without religion. However, the suggested definition of worship in *Segerdal* would lead us to think that there is no worship without theistic religion. Lawyers often engage in reductive explanations so as to simplify their gathering of evidence. In the specific case, Ashworth moves on to consider whether the booklet that describes the practices of Scientology could provide any evidence as to the fact that Scientologists engage in worship. He concluded that Scientology did not engage in practices that amount to acts of worship in a conventional sense. That move nevertheless opened the door for a more sociological approach. In its struggle for recognition, Scientology enlisted an Emeritus Reader of Sociology from Oxford University: Dr Wilson. The attitude of the court in *Segerdal* prompted the correct response by the Church of Scientology. The idea is to show that the legal definition of worship is factually incorrect. If you embark on a comparative study of religions, you will find that there are many more attitudes than those listed by the English judiciary (prayer, threat of damnation, etc.). Moreover, a comparative study of the sort calls for a subtler definition of worship. Dr Wilson suggested that worship can be defined as "practices designed to bring a person into communication with the basic spiritual reality". This definition does not solve the problem of the definition of religion, but at least re-orients the discussion towards a more general idea of basic spiritual reality, which could be theistic or non-theistic.

Dr Wilson's report was dismissed on the grounds that it did not deal with the evidentiary question of whether or not the practices of Scientology have changed from 1970. His report aimed to show that the definition of worship in *Segerdal* was too narrow to start with. But even with such a narrow and conventional definition, Scientology could still be defined as being engaged in worship. Justice Ousely believed that the only possible way to follow the precedent was by showing that practices have changed considerably. In *Hodkin v. Registrar*, the Supreme Court decided to overrule *Segerdal*.

The decision of the Supreme Court

Scientology is a religion: this much is clear in the UK Supreme Court's Declaration 11 ruling in the high profile case of *Hodkin v. Registrar*. The facts of the case were simple. Mrs Hodkin wanted to get married to her fiancé in church. The only problem was that the Church of Scientology was not registered as a place of worship according to the Place of Worship Registration Act of 1855 (PWRA). Moreover, a 1970 precedent of the Court of Appeal (*Segerdal*) ruled that Scientology was not a religion because it did not believe in any God (Lord Denning), and in any case it did not worship in a manner that could be compared to any other established religion (Lord Justices Winn and Buckley).

The UK Supreme Court overruled its precedent in a clear and forceful way. Scientology is a religion and its premises should be registered for the purpose of solemnizing a religious marriage. This result is not surprising and was largely expected. It seems to be the correct result, since there was no readily available principled reason to exclude Scientology from a religious benefit that applies to all other religions.

In the case of *Segerdal* (1970) Lord Denning honestly confessed that Scientology was not a religion for him. It was more like a philosophy. Implicit in Lord Denning's position is a theistic definition of religion: religion has to coincide with a belief in a supranatural divinity. This poses immediate problems: what about widely practiced religions such as Buddhism or Jainism? They do not worship a god: are they religions then? Lord Denning had to grant an exception for Buddhism and for few other religions. He does not explain what justifies the exception. He just asserts that Buddhism is in and Scientology is out.

The UK Supreme Court moved away from a theistic definition of religion. Lord Toulson, writing for the majority, argues that a theistic definition of religion does not capture a great number of cases. It would merely impose a Judeo-Christian definition upon the rest of the world's religious experiences. But is it possible to come up with a watertight definition of religion? Lord Toulson is adamant that lawyers are not fully equipped with the appropriate tools to settle this question. However, he still believes that it is possible to give empirically grounded indicia, so as to give an idea of what religion looks like.

Lord Toulson is quick to admit that his is not a legal definition but merely a *description.* To buttress his point, Lord Toulson looked at other comparative attempts to define religion, only to conclude that: "experience across the common law world over many years has shown the pitfalls of attempting to attach a narrowly circumscribed meaning to the word". That said, Lord Toulson singles out two main comparative points of reference: the judgment of Chief Justice Adams in *Malnak v. Yogi* (1979) and the judgment of the High Court of Australia in the *Victoria* case (1983). Judge Adams convinces Lord Toulson on the methodology: a judge needs to move away from a Judeo-Christian definition of religion and embrace "a *comparative approach* to the identification of a religion" (italics added). Concretely, a judge should proceed by analogy; to do so he needs to single out a number of indicia that will, in turn, inform the investigation. Lord Toulson, however, does not believe that a new legal definition can emerge by the application of those indicia. Instead he follows Justices Wilson and Deane of the High Court of Australia, who suggest that at best a judge can formulate a set of guidelines, the importance of which will have to be evaluated in the cultural context and on a case-by-case basis. A description is meant to be informative, but it cannot be used as a stringent legal test.

So what is his description? In his words:

> For the purpose of PWRA I would *describe* religion in summary as a spiritual or non-secular belief system, held by a group of adherents, which claims to explain mankind's place in the universe and relationship with the infinite, and to teach its adherents how they are to live their lives in conformity with the spiritual understanding associated with the belief system.
>
> (*R v. Registrar General of Births, Deaths and Marriages* [2013] italics added)[6]

Toulson's description has four elements:

1 religion is a spiritual or non-secular belief system;
2 adherents to the belief system form a group;
3 the belief system claims to explain mankind's place in the universe and his relationship with the infinite;
4 there is a code of behaviour consistent with the belief system.

None of these guidelines is meant to be exhaustive of the idea of religion; they are purely offered as aids to figure out what religion looks like. Needless to say, most leading religions easily meet all the criteria. So the problem remains – what is not to be considered as religion? One thing alone seems to be excluded according to the first indicium: secular beliefs squarely fall outside of the realm of religion; as if it was easy to tell apart secular beliefs from religious beliefs. Most secular beliefs are formed against the background of Judeo-Christian roots. Think of human dignity: is it a secular or a religious value?

Lord Toulson understands that this distinction is problematic: it imposes a dichotomy between secular and spiritual beliefs. The latter is the realm of religion. The former is, according to Toulson, whatever "can be perceived by the senses or ascertained by the application of science". This reinforces the well-trodden dichotomy between science and faith, which is much less staunch than one believes. Moreover, it also suggests that to be a secularist is incompatible with having spiritual beliefs. This is clearly wrong. To have a secular outlook simply means that political institutions should not be directly influenced by religious arguments that can only be understood by one group of the community that happens to sign up to the relevant religious beliefs. It is important to stress that it is in the interest of religious pluralism to have political institutions that do not favour one religion over another. A secularist can indeed have spiritual beliefs. In the end, the description provided by Lord Toulson is not going to dispel the greatest problem of all: how do we draw the boundary between religion and everything else?

The description Lord Toulson provides is painted with a very broad brush: it gives an impressionist view of the cathedral, and leaves the contours completely blurry. Perhaps a court cannot do more than that: it just gives us an impression of religion but not a legal definition. The latter is impossible: it would take much more expertise in theological and sociological debates as well as in comparative religious studies. In conclusion, the decision does not provide a new legal definition of religion. It shifts away from a very narrow Judeo-Christian definition of religion to a much more sociological, empirically responsive and open description that claims to be more suited to a pluralist society. The Supreme Court welcomes Scientology in the pantheon of accepted religions and leaves the door open for new religions to come forth and ask for the registration of their place of worship. New cases will come up. The English Registrar will have to conduct her investigations on the basis of the guidelines provided by the court. Her negative response will always be reviewable by the courts.

The only real fear concerns the power of the courts. Lord Toulson would like to lower the heat of the debate and tone down the disagreement. He wishes to be modest as to what judges can say about religion, but the truth is that the last word on this matter will always be theirs.

The Scientology saga teaches us something about the legal struggle to define religion. Failing to provide a rigorous definition that would draw distinct lines, lawyers resort to various strategies to either avoid or play down the religious question. The easiest route is to dodge the religious questions and pretend that other concepts can be freely defined in isolation from religion – the example being used here is that of worship. This escape route is fraught with problems, as worship turns out to be as difficult to define and impossible to severe. Assuming that worship can be understood in isolation from religion, lawyers pretend to rely on empirical evidence and fact-finding. It is not clear what evidence is there to prove, since judges have not provided clear tests to meet. But at least their conscience will be assuaged, and perhaps they will be forgiven for dodging the methodological problem.

So what if it is impossible to define religion or religious worship? Does this mean that we should do away with any religious test? I believe that the state should start by distinguishing two scenarios: on the one side, those cases where the label of religion attaches to economic benefits; on the other, those cases where the label of religion attaches to non-economic benefits. There are two broad types of non-economic benefits: on the one hand, the state does recognize claims of religious conscience to exempt individuals from the regular application of the law; on the other, the state itself may create special legal benefits that apply exclusively to religious groups. The legal status of religious marriage falls exactly into that category. It is important to stress that in the case of religious marriage, religion is special and deserves a special privilege because the state says so in the first place. The state need not recognize a special privilege to religion in this form, but elects to do so. The state could just as well decide that the only marriage with legal force is civil marriage. By singling out a privilege that only applies to religious groups, the state indirectly recognizes the central importance of religion in society. By the same token, the state also recognizes a special aspect of freedom of religion: religious groups are free to celebrate marriage as they see fit.

Now, if the state recognizes an area of special privilege for religion, it also means that the state recognizes religion as being special – at least in this area.

But if that is true from the viewpoint of the state – that is, religion deserves some kind of special benefits – then the state is also implicitly recognizing that the right to religious freedom is (at times, at least) special. It follows from this that having created an area of special protection for religion, the state must have special reasons to limit the application of that special benefit. It must have special reasons to offer to religious groups if it is to deny them the same benefits accorded to other religions. More specifically, the state must provide special reasons to deny Scientology the benefit that is enjoyed by other religions.

So, in the specific case where the state itself recognizes a special benefit for religion, then religion must be treated as having a special right, meaning that the state should be distrusted with any type of limitation of that right. In all other cases, freedom of religion can be treated as a general right. This means that freedom of religion in other cases does not call for special protection for religion alone, but calls for equal protection of whoever is in a comparable situation. So, for example, whenever someone calls for an exemption from the law, the state should be prepared to take equally seriously religious and non-religious arguments to conscientious objection.

Finally, the same will be true for economic benefits granted by the state. The state should not grant special economic advantages to religions because they are religions. They should grant economic benefits if someone is providing a service or a function that is in the public or social interest. Religions can apply for charitable status or they can provide all other types of services. In these cases, the state should constantly monitor the way in which religious and non-religious actors use public funds.

Freedom of religion can be treated as a special right in the case of religious marriage, for example. This is because the state itself decides to treat religion specially in the first place. This being the starting point, the state should then be unable to limit that special benefit. In all other cases, the state should treat religions fairly in a way that does not burden them unfairly or create special benefits.

A fresh start: secularism enhances religious pluralism

Secularism should be thought of differently. It is not about the separation between Church and state. Church and state collaborate on many fronts. The Church provides important public and social services. When it provides such services it should be equated and evaluated on the basis of other charities and service providers. Scientology, for example, benefits from tax breaks on the basis that it provides a certain number of services. The point of secularism is not to draw boundaries between Church and State, but is instead to suggest fair terms of collaboration on the one hand, and, on the other, to protect and promote religious pluralism.

Perhaps the best term of collaboration should follow the old motto: "Render therefore unto Caesar the things which are Caesar's; and unto God the things that are God's." This should not be interpreted as reinforcing the separation.

Collaboration is possible when there is a clear repartition of the task. Religious marriage for example is the business of religion. The state should not intrude into that business. Just to be clear: the problem in the UK lies in the fact that the state equates religious marriage with civil marriage. Thus, for the purpose of marriage, the religious minister becomes the equivalent of the public servant. This means that the state has an interest in the identity and qualification of the religious minister. But things should not follow this pattern. In many other modern secular states, civil marriage is celebrated independently from religious marriage. The only one that has legal validity is the former. Religious marriage has a great symbolic value, but no legal consequences are attached to it. In my mind, this is the appropriate way of secularizing an institution such as marriage, where discriminations based on sex, gender and religion have always been predominant. To fully secularize marriage would minimize the possibility of discrimination of the state towards the minority.

To fully secularize marriage does not mean at all to dismantle religious marriage. On the contrary, religions would be in full control of how to celebrate it and with whom. Religious marriage would preserve all its symbolic force in the eyes of the people who believe in the religion of their choice. Certain functions performed by religions acquire a particular meaning in the eyes of the faithful. For example, religious marriage – for some – has a special significance, and I don't see why the state should be in the business of deciding which marriages are religious marriages and which are not. This may require the state to withdraw the legal seal from all religious marriages. If this is to be true to the respect of religious pluralism, then so be it!

It is possible to see in this context the way in which secularism can protect and promote religious pluralism. I hasten to add that this type of secularism is perfectly compatible with the idea of collaboration between state and Church. In all the areas of interaction, where religions are helping the state by performing certain crucial services, such as education and charity work, the state is perfectly entitled to give tax breaks and benefits to religious groups in ways that are equal to other providers. Of course, in these cases, the state will have an interest in keeping religion under control.

Collaboration means two separate attitudes of the state vis-à-vis religion. At times, the state will recognize that religions are better left alone performing their religious functions. As long as they do not silently break the law in the performance of their rites, religions should be left alone and the state should not intervene. At other times, when religions seek support for the performance of secular functions, the state can recognize their role as being beneficial to everyone and grant them economic advantages similar to those granted to other service providers.

Does this mean that we can live without a state definition of religion? The answer is yes, we can. The state will have to recognize religious functions, rites, holidays and other religious phenomena. The state can practice a devolutionary approach towards religions. Religious groups can be afforded a wide margin of self-rule. Wherever the state has attempted to turn religious institutions into secular ones – as in the case of religious marriage – it should simply back down. In those cases, religion will be recognized as having the full right to self-determination. Does this leave the door open to abuse? This should not be the case. The state can review globally the sets of benefits attached to religion. One thing that is clearly not costly is to recognize the privilege of symbolism for religion.

Where does this leave us in terms of having a coherent theory of freedom of religion? Much ink has been spilled in the last ten years to develop theories that would explain or dismiss the special status of religion. The chief mistake of all these theories is to want to come up with one single formula on how to treat religion. The basic point is that the relationship between state and religions has many different facets. A one-size-fits-all theory will never do the job of singling out the proper attitude of the state towards religion. At times, the state should be hands-off, when the functions performed by religion are exclusively religious. Religious marriage can only be celebrated by religions. At other times, the state should be fair to both religious and non-religious groups. Thus the state will oscillate between the best liberty-based theory of religious freedom and the best equality-based theory of religious freedom. The exact boundary between the two is not that important. The state can decide that, but it cannot decide to supplant all religion's functions, because it would never succeed; but also because it is incapable of performing the same functions that religions perform and, finally, because it would end up minimizing religious pluralism by monopolizing all the functions performed by religions.

Coda

Religious pluralism and secularism can go hand in hand very comfortably. The secularization of some institutions can create a greater space for religious pluralism rather than less. To fully secularize marriage – by making civil marriage the only valid legal marriage in the country – the state would promote a greater measure of freedom between religions. Any religion would be enabled to celebrate marriage in its preferred way. The state, from its vantage point, would not have to monitor whether or not the religion is a real religion. It is sufficient that the religion be regarded as a religion from the vantage point of its believers.

The spirit of the Place of Worship Act is to promote religious pluralism. The idea is to bring into the light all religious groups that regard themselves as such. A mere declaration could suffice and the Registrar would be under an obligation to recognize every declaration, even those that were scarcely believable. The advantage of this system would be to give an incentive to all religions to come out of the closet, and to prevent the existence of a black market of religions that could offer religious services to vulnerable people. To this extent, and only to this extent, the state could peep into the life of religions of one country, but only to acknowledge their fundamental freedom of exercise, including the freedom to call themselves religions. Scientology should absolutely be free to call itself a religion without having the state handing down a badge of recognition.

If this means that Scientology will be entitled to celebrate religious marriages that have the legal force of civil marriage, then so be it. The state decides to give religious marriages this force; it can just as well decide to withdraw it. But as long as it does recognize the legal effect of a religious function, it cannot allow itself to decide which religion is state-supported and which is not. For all other issues, the state should be open and equal. There are various forms of engagement between Church and state. Each one of them can be assessed on a different basis. If the function provided is identified as religious by the state, then religions have the exclusive competence to it. If the function provided is secular, then religions can enter the competition on fair and equal terms with non-religious providers.

Secularism and religious pluralism are mutually supportive. The more a state withdraws from religious institutions, the more it increases the freedom of religions to organize themselves as they please. This does not mean that it has to leave religions alone altogether. Whenever religions want to participate in the life of society by providing their services, they will be allowed to do so by being given an opportunity that is comparable to non-religious providers. If they do receive public funding, or if they do perform public functions, religions will have to accept that they are accountable to the state and to the whole society at large, and not only to their own restricted community.

Notes

1 *Registrar General of Births, Deaths and Marriages* [2013] UKSC 77.
2 *R v. Registrar General ex parte Segerdal and another* [1970] 2 QB 697, 3 All ER 886, Para. 102.
3 *R (on the application of Hodkin and another) v. Registrar General of Births, Deaths and Marriages* [2012] EWHC 3635.
4 *R v. Registrar General, Ex parte Segerdal* [1970] 2 QB 697 (p 707).
5 This can be qualified: Buddhism may be interpreted as worshipping gods, according to some scholars.
6 *R (on the application of Hodkin and another) v. Registrar General of Births, Deaths and Marriages* [2013] UKSC 77 at p. 58.

9 Conscientious objection to same-sex marriage

Politics by other means

Daniel Gamper[1]

Introduction

Most Western countries recognize the right to conscientious objection to compulsory military service.[2] Traditionally, conflicts between obligations of conscience and civil obligations are considered to be so insurmountable that institutions should offer alternative paths to guarantee freedom of conscience for potential objectors. In general, it might be said that provisions for conscientious objection are a sign of refinement of a legal system as a community expresses its self-restraint when individuals are faced with an intolerable moral dilemma (Cohen 1968). In these cases people tend to offer motivations of a religious nature, although secular motivations, such as pacifism, are also taken into account. However, if the state is thought of as secular, then why should religion be deemed special? What religious demands deserve accommodation by state institutions? For political philosophy this matter is closely linked to the alleged primacy of religious freedom. What is at stake here is *laïcité*, secularism, i.e. how should the state respect freedom of conscience for all, while remaining religiously unbiased or neutral?

Recent decades have witnessed an increase in cases of conscientious objection to compulsory military service. This has led some authors to distinguish between a classic conscientious objection and a post-modern conscientious objection (Bertolino 1994: 10), or even to state that a "big bang" of conscientious objections has occurred (Navarro-Valls and Martínez-Torrón 2012: 29). Citizens increasingly apply for the recognition of the right to conscientious objection in various areas, each with its specific casuistry that hinders the coherent systematic and normative presentation of the phenomenon in its entirety. One of the common features of the new forms of conscientious objection is that they are not directly related to the provision of an alternative service. There is no alternative route for doctors that object to practising abortions, or for pharmacists that refuse to sell the abortion pill.

The surge in the number of applications for exemption for reasons of conscience is one of the current challenges of liberalism: namely, that of recognizing cultural–religious particularities. Classical liberal neutrality is no longer appropriate to respond to requests for recognition. When confronted with such requests, the Rawlsian overlapping consensus appears to be biased in favour of secular citizens. Rawls states that, for a society to be well ordered, citizens should be reasonable, they should be capable of distinguishing between those elements of their comprehensive doctrine, which everybody should be able to understand and maybe also share, and those that are only applicable in their private or intimate world. According to Rawls, very religious persons that think that life is sacred, if they act reasonably, should be able to suspend this belief or to translate it into a language or into concepts available to all. If they are not able to do so, then they cannot be counted as reasonable citizens. Therefore, the overlapping consensus does not seem to include these new kinds of requests for conscientious objection based on religious beliefs, due to the uneven burden placed on religious citizens (Rawls 1997).

It is, consequently, not surprising that some scholars advocate a *modus vivendi*, a juridical pluralism that permits effective individual and collective manifestation (as a cult or a way of life) of one's religion (Gray 2000). However the problem with this *modus vivendi* is that it is more appropriate for common law countries than for those whose legal system is based on civil law. While studying the new cases of conscientious objection, one may choose between one of these two approaches: either try to find a general model applicable to all contexts; or let each legal system find the most appropriate solution according to the circumstances of the case.

The overall context of the present study is what one may call the post-secular debate. Once the ideology behind the theory of secularization has been exposed, and hence any enlightened dream of a society free of religion abandoned, political institutions must accept the vitality of religious communities and eventually their powerful political influence. The dividing line in the post-secular debate is not between the majority religion (Catholicism and Protestantism in Europe) and minority religions (in particular Islam), but between secularized citizens and secular institutions on the one hand and religion on the other. The post-secular society, the society that does not coercively privatize religion, imposes demands that challenge the non-religious nature of public reason, as normatively defined by Rawls and Habermas.

Some obvious problems arise in the post-secular society. If religious reasons may be advocated in the public arena, and if respect for religious freedom directly imposes the burden of accommodation on state institutions, then the secular nature of the law may be at risk. In this chapter, I intend to argue that the "big bang" of conscientious objections may have political consequences, especially when this right is used for political purposes. In the case analysed, conscientious objection can be likened to civil disobedience, thereby losing its primordial function as a protective mechanism of the individual's conscience. By disguising civil disobedience as conscientious objection, religious individuals and communities participate in the public debate, and even in the legislative process, not through public reasoning but through demanding, on the basis of exclusively religious motivations, exemptions and individualized recognition. I will therefore argue against the inflation of conscientious objection and defend a more restrictive definition of it in order to preserve the secular nature of the law.

The following pages focus on the request for conscientious objection by registrars and political agents (mayors, councillors, etc.) motivated by their refusal to participate in the celebration of same-sex marriages. In the second section (pp. 163–165), I will present the legal case raised by a British civil servant (*Eweida and others v. UK*, 15 January 2013). The third section (pp. 165–167) will compare the classic definitions of conscientious objection and civil disobedience, with emphasis on their eventual political role. The fourth section (pp. 168–172) analyses the challenges that the new forms of conscientious objection impose on secularism and the final section (pp. 173–174) proposes a more restrictive definition of conscientious objection.

Conscientious objection to same-sex marriage: the *Ladele* case

Why would a public servant refuse to register a marriage between people of the same sex? These are of course still marginal cases, but the reason mainly adduced is a religious one. What some public employees are declaring in their demands for conscientious objection is that their religious beliefs prevent them from collaborating in something they consider to be wrong. They do not say why it is wrong, or how it is damaging to society. They merely state that collaborating with this practice presents them with a serious conflict of conscience. Is it advisable to find an arrangement that allows some registrars to be exempted from celebrating same-sex marriages? Alternatively, should the state, as a matter of principle, not allow any exemptions that entail a discriminatory bias?

After the passing of laws on same-sex marriage with a legislative process that involved mass mobilizations (Spain 2005, France 2013), the debate has shifted in some cases, but not many, to demands for exemption from the celebration of same-sex marriages.[3] The argument on the following pages is that these conscientious objections are a way of continuing the legislative debate about the legitimacy of same-sex marriage laws by other means. These requests for exemption perform a dual function: on the one hand, they seek the protection of individual conscience and, on the other, they serve to continue the political debate concerning the law that recognizes equal treatment for homosexual couples. In other words, they function as a denunciation of the injustice of the law.[4]

Although to date, the number of these types of conscientious objection requests has not been significant, they can help us clarify why the secular city must, as a matter of principle, prevent religion from determining the normal functions of state institutions. By setting this limit on accommodation policies or recognition of objection, state institutions try to find a balance between religious equality and non-discrimination policies on the basis of sexual orientation.

The case that serves as my starting point is a judicial process that ended in January 2013 with a sentence issued by the European Court of Human Rights (ECtHR).[5] The main character in the case was Ms Ladele, employed by the London Borough of Islington, a local public authority that had a "Dignity for

All" equality and diversity policy, which stated that Islington should promote fair treatment for everyone without discrimination. All employers were expected to promote these values, and work against discrimination. From 2002, Ms Ladele was a registrar of births, deaths and marriages. Two years later, the Civil Partnership Act came into force in the United Kingdom, whereby civil partnership between people of the same sex was allowed and they were accorded the same rights and obligations as those of a married couple.

Ms Ladele, in accordance with the requirements of her job, found herself obliged to register such marriages, but given that she "sincerely believes that same-sex civil partnerships are contrary to God's law" (*Eweida and others v. UK*, 15 January 2013, par. 23), according to "the orthodox view that marriage is the union of one man and one woman for life",[6] she refused to carry out her duties as a registrar when same-sex couples were involved. As a result of her refusal, she was dismissed from her position, which is why she took legal action.

Ms Ladele :

> submitted that her acts, for which she was disciplined, were a manifestation of her religion [...] and that in failing to treat her differently from those staff who did not have a conscientious objection to registering civil partnerships, the local authority indirectly discriminated against her.
>
> (*Eweida and others v. UK*, 15 January 2013, par. 70)

Ladele argued that she was discriminated against because of her beliefs, and that:

> the local authority did not adequately take into account its duty of neutrality. It failed to strike a balance between delivering a service in a way which would not discriminate on grounds of sexual orientation, while avoiding discriminating against its own employees on grounds of religion.
>
> (Ibid. par. 72)

However, and as indicated by the ECtHR sentence, the crux of the problem is that the person in question represents the state, and has to implement a service that should not only be effective but should also comply "with the overarching policy of being an employer and a public authority wholly committed to the promotion of equal opportunities and to requiring all its employees to act in a way which does not discriminate against others" (*Eweida and others v. UK*, 15 January 2013, par. 105).

Against granting an exemption to Ms Ladele, one could argue that if she cannot comply with her obligations, she should resign from her position, as "the possibility of changing job would negate any interference with [freedom of religion]" (*Eweida and others v. UK*, 15 January 2013, par. 83). The ECtHR does not share this view and affirms instead that it is necessary to find a balance in the workplace, because the possibility of resigning from one's job is too burdensome.[7] In favour of accommodating Ms. Ladele's needs, one could also argue that the relevant outcome is that all same-sex marriages are registered without any delay and that, simultaneously, her religious freedom remains untouched. This outcome can easily be achieved if there are other co-workers ready to handle all requests.[8]

These two favourable motives for accommodation could be countered as follows. There is no alternative duty for the objector, so this could easily be considered a case of undue disadvantages between co-workers. Another legal reason for not granting accommodation is the Court's use of the margin of appreciation, by which states are better positioned to regulate the legal matrimonial figure and to establish the requirements that civil servants must comply with in performing their functions. Moreover, the ECtHR "has also held that same-sex couples are in a relevantly similar situation to different-sex couples as regards their need for legal recognition and protection of their relationship" (ECtHR, *Eweida and others v. UK*, par. 105). In other words, for same-sex couples, many European countries tend to recognize the right to establish legal ties, be that marriage, or be that registered partnership status.

However, the definitive argument to refuse exemption is that the local authorities were pursuing a legitimate objective. At the end of the day pragmatic, prudential or instrumental considerations give way to the matter of principle: public servants must treat all marriages equally, irrespective of the sex of the partners.[9]

By refusing to recognize Ms Ladele's right to conscientious objection, the ECtHR implicitly adopts a restrictive view of freedom of conscience. State officials in exercising their duties might be asked to suspend some of their religious or ideological convictions, if this appears to be necessary in order to implement non-discriminatory policies. Each state has the right to legitimately impose on its civil servants obligations that they might find burdensome, but that are justified by the duty of the institutions to treat all citizens without discrimination. I take this ECtHR decision as a paradigmatic example of how to cope with the new extended versions of conscientious objection, the political scope of which may jeopardize the liberal state's commitment to secularism.

The blurring of the distinction between conscientious objection and civil disobedience

In recent decades there has been an increase in conscientious objection in new areas: pharmacists who refuse to sell contraceptives or abortion pills, doctors who express their desire not to participate in abortions and also civil servants or mayors who do not want to celebrate same-sex marriages. In the next section, I argue that these cases of conscientious objection should be seen as a disguised form of civil disobedience, and that they could be seen as an illegitimate way to participate in the legislative process. While, traditionally, conscientious objection was thought of as a protection of the individual conscience, these new forms also have a political scope. That is why I deem it necessary to draw a dividing line between conscientious objection and civil disobedience.

There is conscientious objection when an individual requests exemption from a duty, because compliance with it imposes on his or her conscience an insurmountable conflict with his or her religious or philosophical convictions. Such conflict is relevant from the legal point of view when it is specified as the "rejection of a regulation by a subject that should observe it" (Rodotà 1993: 56).[10] The characteristic features of conscientious objection are: the imposition of a duty on all citizens; the request for non-compliance with the duty by the objector; and the link between non-compliance and faith in one's own convictions. Conscientious objection is therefore considered to be a contrast between two duties: a duty to conscience and a public duty. Conscientious objection is one of the external manifestations of a freedom of conscience that can no longer be limited to the possibility of believing or not believing *in foro interno*, but extends to that of behaving in accordance with one's own convictions.

The classic understanding of conscientious objection links it to the necessary existence of an alternative service. Today this link has been broken because the new areas in which objection applies, no longer imply any kind of alternatives. Doctors or pharmacists, or registrars that refuse to celebrate marriages between same-sex couples, cannot perform an alternative duty. These new forms adopted by conscientious objectors should be studied under a new profile, avoiding their homologation with classic conscientious objection to military service.

The universal validity of the law, i.e. the fact that it applies equally to everybody, clashes here with the demands for a differentiated, non-egalitarian treatment. Freedom of conscience as a negative freedom, as institutional respect for the beliefs of each individual and non-interference with them, is by nature an egalitarian freedom because it does not require, in principle and from a theoretical perspective, the distribution of assets. It is a freedom that is by nature already distributed, or more precisely, satisfied.

However, in the effective guarantee of this freedom, which is in principle indivisible, problems arise when considering one of its constituent elements, namely the manifestation of this freedom: the exercise of public religious cults, the bearing of religious symbols or even the participation of organized religious communities in political rallies.[11] This manifestation of the freedom of conscience can lead to the request for recognition of the right not to comply with public duties. In other words, not only to be exempted from certain actions required by the state or by contractual relations with the institution, but also the recognition of the right not to do these things, i.e. the state in this case cannot remain neutral with regard to people's convictions, but rather it is obliged to consider valid the religion-based reasons adduced by individuals seeking exemption.

It is worth noting that, from a political and juridical point of view, the question of conscientious objection has never been completely established: "it is a social phenomenon whose sense mutates, its scope is dynamic, and its manifestations are diverse in extension and depth" (Bertolino 1990: 1). Nevertheless we can try to identify some of its features. In *A Theory of Justice*, John Rawls does so by comparing conscientious objection to civil disobedience. While the former "is not a form of address appealing to the sense of justice of the majority, [...] is not an act in the public forum", civil disobedience "invokes the commonly shared conception of justice that underlies the political order" (Rawls 1971: 365, 369). Moreover, "conscientious refusal is not necessarily based on political principles; it may be founded on religious or other principles at variance with the constitutional order" (ibid.: 369). We can thus conclude that, traditionally, civil disobedience is political, indicates the community's sense of justice, ultimately pursues the modification of laws because they are considered unjust and can be both individual and collective, while conscientious objection does not aspire to the modification of laws, but rather to allow an individual not to comply with some laws in order to avoid profound conflicts with his or her conscience.

Rawls' comparison, however, does not clearly separate both concepts. While conscientious objection was solely a right related to military service, there was no need to trace analytically its differences to civil disobedience. The problem has arisen with the new and extended forms of conscientious objection, which may encompass not only individuals but also groups (as was the case with Civic Education in Spain), who demand the recognition of their right to conscientious objection not only because of the conflict they experience in their consciences when obliged to perform certain civic duties, but because they believe that there is something unjust in the law.[12] Hence, conscientious objection can be a way of expressing the state's failure to impose a policy that complies with its mandatory neutrality. By objecting to an obligation, the citizen is not only claiming that his or her religious freedom is being unduly restricted or limited, but also that the law is unreasonable, unjust, and goes beyond what the state can ask citizens to do. Conscientious objection thus acquires a public character, as does civil disobedience, and also a political scope: not only protecting the individual's conscience by demanding alternative treatment or an exemption, but also instigating a change in law or policy. While conscientious objection in its primal sense did not directly raise the question of the injustice of the law, but of the inner conflict experienced by the individual, it is increasingly becoming a collective action with a political scope, rather than a legal tool to preserve the integrity of one's conscience.

The main motivation for adopting a more restrictive view of conscientious objection lies in the necessity to safeguard state institutions from undue religious influence, and to avoid unjustifiable inequalities in the legislative process. The recognition of the right to conscientious objection was never thought of as a way to permit religious citizens to indirectly influence political discussion in society. It was a way to protect the citizen's conscience from state interference, and hence to allow for an effective freedom of conscience. A conscientious objector was not someone questioning the legitimacy of the law, nor a martyr prepared to face punishment for his or her opposition to the status quo, as was the attitude of the civil disobedient. Conscientious objection is mainly an attitude that should be managed legally, granting exemptions and a different treatment. Objectors are not necessarily critical of a state policy. The only thing we can know for sure about them is that they are experiencing an insurmountable moral dilemma.

Political secularism and conscientious objection in post-secular societies

Today's new inflationist forms of conscientious objection pose new problems, which must be faced from the point of view of political secularism, i.e. of the way the state regulates religious freedom. This is because objectors aim at a religiously motivated modification of the law and, instead of arguing for their critical point of view, ask for recognition of their disagreement. To put it bluntly: the alleged moral conflict is instrumentalized for political reasons, introducing religious motivations to a debate which should be based on public reasons and not on the protection of an individual's conscience.[13]

The extended version of conscientious objection challenges the secular state's commitment to religious neutrality. Such neutrality does not imply that there should be a wall of separation, as Jefferson wanted, between politics and religion. Rather, it means that there should be no connivance between the state and churches, and that the interventions of religious confessions in the legislative debate should ultimately be filtered in order for the final legislation not to be biased towards certain citizens and exclude any minorities.[14]

This concept of political secularism is outlined in Habermas' considerations regarding the public role of religions: specifically, the threshold that religions cannot cross in order to guarantee the *weltanschaulich* neutrality of state institutions. Not only do laws have to be drafted in such a way that nobody is excluded, but the behaviour of state representatives, of those that "hold a public office or [are] candidate[s] for such", must be "subject to the obligation to remain neutral in the face of competing world views" (Habermas 2006b: 9; see also Ferrara 2009; Lafont 2009). The question concerning the *Ladele* case relates to how we should interpret this restriction on the religious freedom of civil servants and people working in public positions, at least when carrying out their duties. How much room for manoeuvre do these people have if they find themselves in a situation of having to collaborate with a legal act that goes against their personal convictions?

What concerns us here is the procedure for public employees that are not involved in the legislative process, but that have to attend to the citizens that come to state offices and have to do so under the terms established by the law.[15] Defenders of conscientious objection hold that this restriction imposes burdens on civil servants, as if their consciences should not be treated equally to those of other people. To reach a conclusion in this respect, it is important to heed the motivations adduced by those who demand exemptions. By looking at these motivations it may be possible to clarify where the acceptable limits of such exemptions lie.

Conscientious objectors to registering same-sex marriages cannot convincingly argue that the laws extending marriage to homosexual couples cause them harm. The reasons of same-sex marriage opponents lie elsewhere: the consequences that this might have for society as these are couples whose primordial purpose is not reproduction; the fostering of a message that children do not need a mother and father; and also the fact that they do not share this new definition of marriage (Gallagher 2010).[16] In other words, their motivations tend to highlight the negative consequences for society of the legal recognition of homosexual marriages, as well as the belief that this is threatening the integrity of the traditional concept of marriage.

It could be expected that those who think that gay marriage is a bad thing, acted in a tolerant way. Toleration has been historically the instrument for achieving peaceful coexistence in diverse societies. In some contexts, homosexuality was allowed even though most people had a negative view of it. However, over time, the balance of this tolerance has shifted. Those who formerly tolerated are the ones who must now be tolerated, as the majority represented indirectly in the positive law has turned those who were formerly tolerated, homosexuals, into subjects with rights under the same conditions as heterosexuals.[17] Toleration here should be understood as "coping with", living with the undesirable consequences of a certain situation, agreeing to live in a society whose rules do not fully correspond to one's own worldview. This is what a reasonable citizen would do, i.e. acknowledge that not everyone thinks as he or she does, and accept the existence of a social pluralism that will not disappear, as it is a consequence of the free exercise of individual rights.

If being tolerant requires collaborating with what one considers to be wrong, then it is no longer limited to "coping with", but also requires the individual to become an agent in an action he or she deplores. The internal conflict suffered by the individual is intensified. Maybe the proper reaction, then, should be disobeying legal imperatives, and accepting the punishment associated with that disobedience, as Thoreau did. The civil disobedient expresses a political denunciation by appealing to a justice that is not positive, and renounces the claim for state protection, as do those who demand recognition for their conscientious objection.

This is a similar situation to the one Ms Ladele is facing. What she claims is not just that same-sex marriages go against her convictions, but also that this act, in her opinion, is wrong.[18] It would therefore be logical for her to stop collaborating and to assume the consequences of her refusal. There is no question that this would be a heroic deed, not only heroic because the state would fail to offer another solution, but also because it is her own conscience that has led her to act that way and to carry a substantial burden.[19]

However, if the individual experiencing the conflict decides not to leave his or her job, but instead demands an adaptation of the law to his or her situation, it would then be relevant to attend to the reasonability of the beliefs to which the objector wishes to stay faithful in contraposition to the legal obligation. It is not the role of judicial bodies that are confronted by demands for the recognition of conscientious objection to evaluate the reasonability of the beliefs adduced to in this quest for exemption. Neither can they accept everything that is said to them, for it is essential for the conflict of conscience to be insuperable, profound, serious and sincere, and to therefore distinguish it from cases of individuals simply looking to cheat the system. That is why conscientious objections of religious believers who can make reference to the doctrinal content of their confessions are easier to accommodate than those that might be presented by somebody by mere virtue of their personal and secular beliefs.[20] Catholics can, for example, refer to the stipulations of the Congregation for the Doctrine of Faith:

> In those situations where homosexual unions have been legally recognized or have been given the legal status and rights belonging to marriage, clear and emphatic opposition is a duty. One must refrain from any kind of formal cooperation in the enactment or application of such gravely unjust laws and, as far as possible, from material cooperation on the level of their application. In this area, everyone can exercise the right to conscientious objection.[21]

In this way, the Catholic Church offered its members a document that they could brandish in support of their refusal to cooperate with the application of the law. It is important to stress here that these doctrinal texts serve the explicit function of providing objectors with arguments in order to promote religious freedom understood in the broadest sense as active participation in democratic deliberation.

From this Catholic point of view, the extension of the right to marry to homosexual couples is not seen as an anti-discrimination policy, but as something that might jeopardize the religious freedom of all believers whose duty is to solemnize or register marriages.[22] I think that by stressing the negative effects of gay marriage on believers, the Catholic Church is trying to divert our attention from what is really at stake here, namely the fact that requests for exemptions are mainly "religiously motivated discrimination against lesbians and gay men" (NeJaime 2012: 1188). The demand for recognition of conscientious objection, in this specific case, not only entails opposition to a specific piece of legislation that places its opponents at an alleged disadvantage, but also implies a refusal to participate in a legal marriage ceremony, i.e. blocking the enforcement of a law.

We get a better understanding of the peculiar nature of demands for objection to the celebration of same-sex marriages if we compare them with the opposition to voluntary interruption of pregnancy. Pro-life advocates that those who refuse to practise abortions do not wish to collaborate with the exercise by women of their right to decide. However, in this case it could be adduced in defence of doctors that by objecting to the practice of abortions they are protecting the life of the embryo, i.e. their objection is based on the defence of a publicly recognized value. In the case of opposition to homosexual marriages, there is no such value that justifies objection, other than the traditional understanding of the concept of marriage and the family, which would, strictly speaking, also oblige them to oppose divorce. In fact, what is really being defended here, are a series of stereotypes about sexual orientations, and although these may tend to be accommodated in common law, it is shameful that this should be the case, as one of the commitments of the rule of law is the avoidance of all kinds of discrimination, which requires critical revision of such stereotypes (Widiss *et al.* 2007: 462).

All that we know about what motivated Ms Ladele to initiate an expensive legal process that doubtlessly shows, among other things, how sincere her beliefs are, is that her religious convictions prevented her from recognizing the legitimacy of homosexual marriages. As for her motivations, we have no further information. However, given that she is a state representative, and given that her attitude performatively shows discrimination against homosexuals, there can be no doubting that she must have had major motivations. When Ms Ladele says that civil unions between homosexuals oppose the divine commandments, she is also saying that in her mind, some citizens are not deserving of equal treatment in terms of the administrative, economic and social benefits of marriage and civil partnerships. The law that recognizes these unions does not place Ms Ladele, or the members of her religion, at a disadvantage, so she cannot argue in terms of discrimination, but merely in terms of what her conscience says to her. She is a member of a minority that does not identify with this specific law that was passed by the country's authorities, something that is all too common in democracies, and when she finds herself obliged to collaborate with the application of the law, she is faced with a conflict of conscience. The conflict in this case is not solely religious but also political, as it arises from her opposition to a state law that she considers unjust because it deteriorates and perverts the nature of an institution that she holds in very high esteem, namely marriage. It becomes clear here how conscientious objection, when it is religiously motivated, can suppose collusion between religion and politics, and not just a conflict between the duty to be loyal to one's own conscience and certain civil or labour obligations.

It may be true that the claimant has no legal obligation to explain the scruples that are causing such an uncomfortable situation, for it is enough to sincerely hold that a conflict is being experienced first-hand. But it does seem reasonable that the political motivations of the affair should be made explicit. Someone demanding recognition of their conscientious objection should make it clear, in this specific case, why they believe that some people should not be recognized as having the same rights as others. As Lafont so poignantly puts it in this same volume:

> Secular citizens do not have to address justifications based on religious reasons concerning the sinful nature of homosexuality – reasons that they do not share – in order to meaningfully participate in that debate. A perfectly appropriate way of engaging in that debate is to offer counter-arguments in order to show why the proposed policy is wrong if they think it is. Objecting to the unequal treatment involved in denying the right to marriage to a group of citizens seems a perfectly meaningful way to participate in that debate.
>
> (Lafont, this volume)

In the previous section, we have seen the Rawlsian distinction between conscientious objection and civil disobedience. The former tends to be individual and based on motivations that need not be shared, while the latter is public and is politically and constitutionally motivated. The *Ladele* case, taken as representative of the new forms of conscientious objection that are being adopted in the wake of certain recent legislative changes, illustrates how hard it is to maintain the distinction proposed by Rawls. When the Catholic Church advises believers not to collaborate with the state in the implementation of certain laws, it is not saying that these laws impose a profound conflict on the consciences of believers, but that believers should not collaborate: i.e. that they should boycott the application of the law and demand recognition of the right to conscientious objection.

The scenario we have described above illustrates how conscientious objection leans towards civil disobedience when used with a political scope. Through their attitude, objectors participate in the legislative debate, although *by means* that are not strictly deliberative, but that surreptitiously infiltrate democratic debate. We certainly should not become anchored to the unquestionably fuzzy distinction between conscientious objection and civil disobedience. If I stress the importance of the distinction between both concepts, it is to underline that the political weight of the conscientious objection cases at hand surpass their allegedly exclusive legal nature.

However, this political intent concealed behind the demand for conscientious objection does not imply that institutional arrangements should not be found to enable civil servants or people in public positions to be exempted from celebrating same-sex marriages or registered partnerships. So, for example, in Denmark, after recognizing the right for homosexual couples also to be able to marry in church, a clause was introduced whereby pastors, who also act as official registrars, could avoid having to officiate at such ceremonies.[23] However, this clause is only applicable to church pastors and to no other public employees. As already commented (see note 3), in the United States the problem has focused on "religious non-profit organizations and affiliated non-profits" that are exempt "from civil liability or punishment by local and state agencies for refusing to provide services or facilities for the solemnization of a marriage" (Dickson 2012: 183).[24] Spain also contemplated the possibility of introducing a conscience-based clause that was finally omitted from the law (López-Sidro 2009: 4). A similar situation can be observed in Holland (MacDougall *et al.* 2012: 150). In the UK, as the *Ladele* case shows, there are some "local authorities [that] allowed registrars with a sincerely held religious objection to the formation of civil partnerships to opt out of designation as civil partnership registrars" (*Eweida and others v. UK*, 15 January 2013, par. 25).[25]

Thus there are proposals and arrangements that permit certain civil servants or political agents to resort to conscientious objection. Most of these alternative treatments are based on the supposition that freedom of conscience is important. The most widely used justifications are pragmatic: the institution must ensure that at all times, there are public employees that can provide the required service in order for there to be no discrimination against homosexual couples.

A more restrictive understanding of conscientious objection

The legal recognition of same-sex marriages implies the "moral neutrality of homosexuality and bisexuality" (Feldblum 2006: 87). If the state's own representatives falter in the implementation of this policy, this undermines the state's basic commitment to gender equality. Pragmatic considerations may solve certain problems. However, when equality before the law is at stake, acting on grounds of principle must be the overriding concern (Feldblum 2006: 120; Parkinson 2011: 292).

That is what was declared in the decision of the Saskatchewan Court of Queen's Bench in relation to a marriage commissioner who claimed the right to decide on whether or not he should perform his governmental duties in accordance with his religious beliefs. The court maintained that the marriage commissioner is "government" and that when he acts as a marriage commissioner, his "freedom of religion ought to be limited to exclude discrimination on the basis of sexual orientation".[26] This same question of principle can be found in the decision of the Spanish Supreme Court regarding the request by a judge to conscientiously object to registering same-sex marriages:

> It is not a case of whether or not it is possible to replace the person responsible for the Civil Register in a specific case, or whether there are ways of avoiding damages to third parties, but of the principle that subjects the judge to the law in any of his attributed duties and makes his intervention, precisely because of this subjection [...], a warranty of the legitimate rights and interests of everybody.[27]

Secularism, the political structure of the state that does not allow for arbitrary discrimination, must be protected by public institutions, and given that these are governed and managed by citizens exercising their public functions (judges, civil servants, politicians), these citizens have to accept limitations to their religious freedom, at least in those situations in which they are performing their duties. The obligation to respect laws is one of the main requirements of state institutions, which are based on the rule of law, so what is relevant here is not the conscience of those individuals, but how these people serve the general public.[28] The egalitarian policy that makes differences in sexual orientation morally irrelevant should be contested on political grounds, as those are the rules of the legislative game. This is Habermas' position, as Lafont puts it, according to which "non-religious reasons must be offered to justify coercive policies in political deliberation at the institutional level of parliaments, courts, ministries and administrations, that is, in the *formal* public sphere" (Lafont 2008). Marriage registrars, such as Ms Ladele, find themselves in the "formal public sphere", but in the executive part of it, not the legislative. This means that they are not allowed to advocate against the policy with which they are supposed to treat other citizens, at least not while they are performing this task. While performing their duties, civil servants are not supposed to deliberate about state policies, but to execute them fairly when equal rights are at stake. Accepting that registrars object on religious grounds to a policy that extends marriage rights to homosexuals is a breach of the contract between state institutions and society. This unspoken liberal contract states that institutions should be blind to the morally irrelevant features of citizens. It is not up to the state official to decide whether someone deserves to get married. Their duty is, on the contrary, not to discriminate, and this imposes on them the obligation to treat all equally. The Rawlsian demands to "apply the principle of toleration to philosophy itself" (Rawls 1985: 231) should be imitated by civil servants: they should process citizens' paperwork solely on the basis of secular terms, of political reasons, leaving aside their comprehensive doctrines while at work. Otherwise the danger of undue discrimination and legal insecurity may become more apparent.

To summarize, I do not advocate the closeting of believers within the public sphere. The public deliberative arena can be undoubtedly enriched by religious contributions. However, if laws are to be applied to all citizens equally, they must be formulated in the formal stages of the legislative process solely on terms understandable to everybody; they cannot have an exclusively religious motivation. This is what political secularism is about. Ms Ladele did not need to rationally justify her opposition to the law because she was not formally criticising it; she was asking to be exempted from some of her duties. Granting her a special status would have not only given the impression of a religious bias in state policy, but would also have meant the approval of the use of conscientious objection as a shortcut in the legislative process.

Notes

1 The research reported in this paper has received financial support from the Spanish Ministerio de Ciencia e Innovación (*La religión en el espacio público. Formas de laicidad*, FFI2009–07433).

2 Also sustained by the ECtHR, modifying its own opinion. While in 2009 it stated that "Article 9 [of the European Convention of Human Rights] does not guarantee the right to conscientious objection" (*Bayatyan v. Armenia*, 10 May 2010, par. 60), the Grand Chamber later noted that:

> opposition to military service, where it is motivated by serious and insurmountable conflict between the obligation to serve in the army and a person's conscience or his deeply and genuinely held religious beliefs, constitutes a conviction or belief of sufficient cogency, cohesion and importance to attract the guarantees of Article 9.
>
> (*Bayatyan v. Armenia*, 7 July 2011, par. 110)

3 In the United States, the debate has mainly focused on exemptions for religious organizations that might be required to offer "services, accommodations, advantages, facilities, goods, or privileges for the solemnization or celebration of a marriage" (State of New York, Marriage Equality Act, 24 June 2011). Religious exceptions addressed to the activities developed around marriage are as follows:

> No individual … shall be liable, penalized or denied benefits under the law of this state or any subdivision … including but not limited to laws regarding employment discrimination, housing, public accommodations, licensing, government contracts or grants, or tax exempt status, for refusing to provide services …

> related to the solemnization of any marriage ... or for refusing to treat as valid any marriage, where such providing ... or treating as valid would cause such individual ... to violate their sincerely held religious beliefs.
>
> (Stern 2010 : 307)

Some scholars have proposed a pragmatic extension of these exemptions to government employees with religious objections, claiming that they "should be permitted to step aside from facilitating same-sex marriages when it poses no hardship for same-sex couples" (Wilson 2010: 321).

4 As Brian Barry radically puts it: "either the case for the law (or some version of it) is strong enough to rule out exemptions, or the case that can be made for exemptions is strong enough to suggest that there should be no law anyway" (Barry 2001: 39). The latter of Barry's alternatives dramatically shows the subversive function of conscientious objection, which then becomes no longer a request for exemption but rather for a change in the law, blurring definitively the distinction between conscientious objection and civil disobedience. However, the radical alternative of Barry's quote fails to take into account the existence of "tragic choices" (abortion, euthanasia, etc.).

5 *Eweida and others v. UK*, 15 January 2013.

6 Court of Appeal (Civil Division) on Appeal from Employment Appeal Tribunal, [2009] EWCA Civ 1357, par. 7.

7 The reasoning is similar to that used by Rawls when arguing about the freedom to leave the country, a freedom whose existence does not automatically make state institutions fair: if people continue to live in the state it is not because they consider their institutions to be fair, but because the price to pay, namely exile or emigration, is excessively high (Rawls 1993: 222). Moreover, conscientious objection, where it is closest to civil disobedience, also implies the willingness "to undergo significant hardship rather than do that thing" (Greenawalt 2007: 1625).

8 There have been several proposals from scholars of religious freedom seeking methods for accommodating requests for conscientious objection to same-sex marriages. For a usual reasoning in favour of accommodation, see Wilson, who holds that the number of same-sex marriages is low – as would also be the number of conscientious objectors to it – so these could easily be accommodated without any form of sexual orientation discrimination. Conscientious protection in the United States has mainly focused on religious or charity organizations that directly or indirectly participate in the celebration of marriages. However, Wilson goes further and in her proposal for a "Marriage Conscience Protection" also puts forward a protection of government employees or officials that consider participation in the solemnization of same-sex marriages to go against their convictions. She combines arguments of principle (pre-eminent defence of religious and conscientious freedom), with prudential reasoning, such that one can only be forced to officiate a homosexual marriage "in the case of an individual who is a government employee or official, if another employee or official is not promptly available and willing to provide the requested government service without inconvenience or delay" (Wilson 2010: 368).

9 As the ECtHR points out, "some other United Kingdom local authorities took a different approach, and allowed registrars with a sincerely held religious objection to the formation of civil partnerships to opt out of designation as civil partnership registrars" (*Eweida and others v. UK*, 15 January 2013, par. 25). So the case of the London Borough of Islington is one of a deliberately applied policy for non-discrimination against homosexual minorities, and firmly committed to equal rights among all citizens, that does not allow for exceptional agreements, but that should be respected in its totality.

10 I prefer this definition because it does not make explicit the type of authority imposing the obedience, thus also including those cases of objection that occur in relations of a private nature, namely in the employment sphere. Rather than concerning

conscientious objection, these are instead cases of accommodation, such as the ones in which workers ask to be able to celebrate holidays in accordance with their religions, allowing them to work under conditions that do not compel them to abandon their religiously motivated behaviours.

11 One can point here to a "subtle shift in the role of the state from that of a potential violator of religious freedom to that of the primary decision-maker in the task of balancing conflicting rights" (Mawhinney 2013).

12 See Ruiz Miguel (2010); Cappuccio and Gamper (2010b).

13 I follow here Rawls' understanding of public reason (Rawls 1997: 779–780).

14 By political secularism, I mean the political arrangement that, with some important differences, is found in liberal democratic countries, and that is characterized by the "moral equality of persons, freedom of conscience and religion [...] and the institutional structures that are essential to achieve these purposes" (Bouchard and Taylor 2008: (2008).

15 An example of this is the law introduced in July 2009 in Denmark that forbade judges from appearing in trials in a way that "could be perceived as an expression of their possible religious or political affinities or their position in relation to religious or political matters" (*Retsplejeloven*, par. 55). This entails that they cannot wear any kind of religious symbol, not even crosses or head-cloths, or turbans or kippahs. It is hard to say that this is an unjustifiable limitation of the religious freedom of government employees, among other reasons because it affects all judges equally, regardless of their religion. It could be seen as a limitation on the religious freedom of government workers in comparison with other citizens, but this only makes sense if one ignores the representative role of judges in democracies, and the fact that they must apply the law regardless of their religious convictions.

16 Opponents of the recognition of same-sex marriages also adduce an objective and non-nominalist definition of the concept of 'marriage', such as for example, Glendon (1991); Macioce (2006: 82); Cartabia (2011: 638). For an objective defence of marriage, see Sandel (1989); Berg (2010). This is the view also found in the findings of the California Supreme Court arguing that "gay individuals are fully capable of entering into the kind of loving and enduring committed relationships that may serve as the foundation of a family and of responsibly caring for and raising children" *In re Marriage Cases*, 183 P.3d 384, 428 (Cal. 2006). Judge Kennedy holds also a non-essentialist view of marriage in the historical decision of the *Supreme Court, United States v. Windsor* (570 US, 2013).

17 See, for instance, the Spanish reform of the Civil Code: "Marriage shall have the same requirements and effects whether both spouses are of the same or different sex" (*Ley* 13/2005, 1 July 2005).

18 It should be noted in defence of Ms Ladele, that the law recognizing same-sex partnerships came into force after she started working as a registrar for the London Borough of Islington.

19 The question of the appropriateness of the burden is analysed by Feldblum, who concludes that:

> the reasons given by the State [to impose such a burden] must "reflect the public good". And ensuring that members of the public who have a morally neutral characteristic are able to live without fear or vulnerability of discrimination based on that characteristic seems to be a reason that reflects the public good.
>
> (Feldblum 2006: 120)

From the Catholic point of view, this burden can also be experienced as a witnessing of faith (Macioce 2011).

20 The predominance of religious reasons in requests for labour exemptions questions the way secularism works. I do not have space here to deal with this question, which

both Laborde and Lafont discuss in greater depth in this book (see Chapters 2 and 3). See also Nussbaum (2008: 165, 169).

21 *Considerations regarding proposals to give legal recognition to unions between homosexual persons*, 3 June 2003. See also the appeal of Benedict XVI to Catholic pharmacists:

> Your Federation is invited to address the issue of conscientious objection, which is a right your profession must recognize, permitting you not to collaborate either directly or indirectly by supplying products for the purpose of decisions that are clearly immoral such as, for example, abortion or euthanasia.
>
> (Address of His Holiness Benedict XVI to Members of the International Congress of Catholic Pharmacists, 29 October 2007)

A similar message was issued by the *Conferencia Episcopal Española*, according to which same-sex marriages are "a flagrant denial of fundamental anthropological data and a veritable subversion of the basic moral principles of social order", *Nota del Comité Ejecutivo de la Conferencia Episcopal Española*, 5 May 2005.

22 The language of discrimination and oppression is also used in support of conscientious objectors (Stychin 2009: 734). An insightful way of describing it:

> Given the unfortunate history of religious persecution, as well as American constitutional concern for preserving religious liberty, advocates' broad-based claim of religious injury has understandable resonance. For proponents to present this as a claim that pits the need for religious protection against other statutorily protected statuses (such as race, sex, and sexual orientation) has undoubted purchase – often despairingly referred to as that of "competing victimhoods".
>
> (Flynn 2010: 239)

23 Forslag til Lov om ændring af lov om medlemskab af folkekirken, kirkelig betjening og sognebåndsløsning (Præsters ret til at undlade at vie to personer af samme køn m.v.), 15 June 2012.

24 Dickson stresses the fact that the inseverability clause was decisive in the legislative bargaining process, allowing a compromise between anti-discrimination law and religious freedom.

25 In this context, I would like to point out one of the arguments given in a Memorandum (*Marriage, Same Sex Couples*, Memorandum submitted by Dr D. Cooper, Dr N. Barker and Dr E. Wilkinson (MB 54), www.publications.parliament.uk/pa/cm201213/cmpublic/marriage/memo/m54.htm (last retrieved 1 July 2013)), about the acceptability of exemptions exclusively to the celebration of same-sex partnerships:

> Within the context of secular public action, not everything identified [...] as the manifestation of a religious belief can be accepted as valid. Other interests and rights are also relevant. It is arguable that if registrars do not wish to conform to the provisions governing secular marriage, they should work in a more explicitly religious context governed by religious norms.

26 *Nichols v. Saskatchewan (Human Rights Commission)*, 2009 SKQB 299, [2009] 10 WWR 513, par. 53.

27 Tribunal Supremo, 69/2007, 11 June 2007. Cf. Cappuccio and Gamper (2010a), and a critical approach in López-Sidro (2009). See also the recent decision of the French *Conseil constitutionnel* in response to the request for recognition of conscientious objection to the celebration of same-sex marriages by some mayors. The Court argued that the state should remain neutral in the application of the law, and that this obligation means no violation of the mayor's liberty of conscience (*Décision* n. 2013–353 QPC, 18 October 2013).

28 It is evident that in the case of the law being clearly unjust, it would then be a virtue for public employees not to abide by it, so this thesis must be separated from radical

judicial positivism. But in the cases being dealt with here, and even more so considering that it is a conscientious objection, what is being adduced by those claiming objection is not that the law is unjust, but that compliance obliges them not to heed their own convictions. This is the claim that they have chosen, which takes away the political force that would be held by a disobedience grounded on a conviction that the law is unjust.

10 The conundrum of pluralism and the doctrine of the margin of appreciation

The crucifix "affair" and the ambivalence of the ECtHR

Marisa Iglesias and Camil Ungureanu

Introduction

The persistent manifestations of religion in the public sphere have created a conundrum for the European Court of Human Rights: how is it possible to square the development of a legal framework of protection of religious freedom and pluralism with the recognition of the, conflictive diversity of state-religion models in Europe? The European Court of Human Rights (ECtHR) tackles this conundrum as an international organization that has a subsidiary role with respect to nation-state jurisdictions; this subsidiary role, largely captured by the doctrine of the margin of appreciation, is not that of imposing a uniform state-religion *model* – be it secularist, (semi-)confessional, laicist or postsecularist – but that of developing a thin constitutional *framework* in order to interpret the European Convention of Human Rights (ECHR). This framework is open-secular in that, in conformity with the Convention, it should neither advance a uniform principle of rigid separation between state and religion (secularism), nor a privileged collaboration between majority religion(s) and state at the expense of pluralism (majoritarianism). Instead, it has/should have the double task of recognizing and, at the same time, establishing limitations on diverse models from French and Turkish *laïcité* to Greek and Russian semi-confessionalism.

However, the Court's "religious" jurisprudence and its understanding of the margin of appreciation in balancing freedom of religion, infra-state and inter-state pluralism have been ambivalent. The ECtHR has sometimes abandoned the construction of this open-secular minimal framework, and has oscillated between deferential attitudes towards nation-states – namely, granting too wide a margin of appreciation; and, more rarely, judicial interventionism – namely, glossing over its subsidiary role.[1] The *Lautsi v. Italy* case, dealing with the crucifix in Italian public schools is a good illustration of this ambivalence.[2] The Chamber's initial decision (in 2009) to ban the crucifix has been interpreted as an attempt to impose a uniform secularist model hostile to religion or – alternatively – as a victory of reason over religious obscurantism. As expected, the Grand Chamber's reversal of the initial decision in 2011, mainly on account of the doctrine of the margin of appreciation (a doctrine that is ignored in the initial decision), elicited mirror reactions from prominent supporters of secularism and (Christian) conservatism. Instead of entering the speculative terrain of ideological debate, in this chapter we discuss the crucifix "affair" in relation to the ECtHR's role in developing a consistent doctrine of the margin of appreciation (DMA) as part of a thin constitutional framework for approaching freedom of religion and pluralism in Europe. The *Lautsi* final decision represents, from our perspective, a missed opportunity for strengthening the Court's legitimacy, and developing a coherent DMA. In *Lautsi* 2011, the Court uncritically accepted the status quo based on a privileged relation between state and majority Church in Italy; in turn, the initial *Lautsi* in 2009 did not sit well with the subsidiary role of the ECtHR and the rationale of the DMA.

In the following, we shall deal with the DMA starting from the *Lautsi* controversy. We shall distinguish between a voluntarist and a rationalized view of the margin of appreciation, and defend the latter as a key element of the Court's legal framework. This exploration is all the more topical given the recent decision to incorporate a reference to the margin of appreciation in the preamble of the Convention itself, by means of a new Protocol.[3] We shall then analyse the consequences for cases such as *Lautsi*; we shall argue for a moderate stand between judicial interventionism and uncritical acceptance of a privileged relationship between state and majority religion. In this context, we shall examine the merits and demerits of intermediary or contextual solutions in the crucifix controversy.

The doctrine of the margin of appreciation and the accommodation of pluralism

Despite their opposition, *Lautsi* 2009 and 2011 mirror each other: the 2009 ban did not contain any reflection on the margin of appreciation; in turn, the Grand Chamber's all-too-brief reasoning in 2011 was massively based on the DMA, albeit without any sustained discussion of it. As a result of these oscillations, it is not surprising that the DMA has become a much-contested jurisprudential instrument. Critics have insisted that it hinders the generalization of the Court's legal solutions, leads to structural incoherencies, affects legal certainty and, in the end, prevents the ECHR from consolidating a reliable system for human rights protection in Europe (Hutchinson 1999; Brauch 2005; Kratochvíl 2011). By contrast, defenders welcome the use of the DMA as a legitimizing device. By means of the DMA, the Court's reasoning gains the flexibility needed to justify its authority vis-à-vis the will of secular states in matters of rights protection. In addition, the DMA is also truthful to the fact of pluralism in Europe (Mahoney 1998; Gerards 2011; McGoldrick 2011).

The ECtHR has used this hermeneutic tool since its very beginnings and, in a more elaborated way, since the seminal case *Handyside v. United Kingdom* (1976).[4] The DMA aims to acknowledge the role of the judgment of state authorities in cases of interference with a convention right (Arai-Takahashi 2002, Chapter 1; Brauch 2005: 114–121; Legg 2012). The Court has provided different reasons to justify the DMA. The very system for the protection of human rights in Europe is, on the one hand, the product of a division of labour between the member states of the Council of Europe and the ECtHR. The secular state is seen as the main actor responsible for securing these rights, and the Court has a subsidiary role: it becomes legitimately involved only through contentious proceedings, and once all domestic remedies have been exhausted. On the other hand, there is often no regulatory consensus among the member states for sensitive issues like those concerning morals or religion. State authorities have, in addition, direct contact with fundamental developments in their countries, and they are generally better placed than an international institution to decide the proper application of the Convention. However, according to the Court, this margin is limited; it goes hand in hand with European supervision, and its width varies depending on the type of right at stake, objectivity of the legitimate interests pursued by the state and the evolution of the European consensus in the field.

The judicial task of the ECtHR is, as the result of the DMA, not to examine *in abstracto* the compatibility of a given state decision with the ECHR, but to supervise whether the state has overstepped its margin of appreciation in the protection of convention rights. This results in a significant difference between the reasoning of the ECtHR and the sort of reasoning usually carried out by a national constitutional court. As we have suggested, the Strasbourg Court is not required to develop a constitutional model, but a minimal constitutional framework that proceeds by undertaking a contextual assessment of the impugned measure taking into account the national setting and its political, legal and social circumstances. ECtHR is meant to reach stable equilibriums amongst different reasons, values and rights that may come into tension, and to take into account citizens' expectations regarding the protection of their rights and democratic considerations in plural and changing settings, as well as the will of member states. The very preamble of the ECHR assumes such a need for balancing when it states that :

> those fundamental freedoms which are the foundation of justice and peace in the world are best maintained, on the one hand, by an effective political democracy and, on the other, by a common understanding and observance of the human rights upon which they depend.
>
> (Convention for the Protection of Human Rights and Fundamental Freedoms 4 November, 1950)

As some commentators have pointed out, this statement injects an axiological duality in the Convention regarding the desideratum of reaching a balance between rights and democracy (Arai-Takahashi 2002: 242–249). This duality justifies and even demands the ECtHR's granting of a national margin of appreciation, especially when the issue at stake is whether a particular restrictive measure is "necessary in a democratic society". The question, nevertheless, is how the DMA should be developed so as to become a useful device for this balancing exercise.

To address this question, we suggest a distinction between two versions of the DMA: a *voluntarist* version and a *rationalized* one. These versions are intermingled in the Court's case law. The voluntarist version of the DMA (hereafter VDMA) is grounded on the assumption that the Court is an international body with a subsidiary role and mere derivative legitimacy in comparison with that of member states.[5] In conformity with this logic, the Court endorses not only a procedural or chronological deference to the national judgment as to the interpretation of convention rights, but a normative view of the subsidiarity principle. The European supervision is carried out with an a priori strong presumption in favour of the state; as a consequence, the ECtHR should be reluctant to engage in an independent and detailed proportionality assessment of the impugned measure. From the perspective of the VDMA, factors such as the lack of European consensus or the assumption that the state is better placed than an international court become fundamentally important due to an institutional logic deferential to state sovereignty. In the case of religious conflicts, the jurisprudence of the ECtHR often relies on the VDMA, and this version was a key grounding argument in the widespread opposition and political controversy caused by *Lautsi* 2009. The VDMA has been used by some states and academics to support the Grand Chamber's final holding. Dominic McGoldrick stresses in defence of *Lautsi* 2011 that the ECtHR, as a judicial institution different from a constitutional court, should develop "political antennae". For him:

> judicial authority ultimately depends on the confidence of citizens and there is no real link between the European judges and the European population. If the Court's interpretations deeply differ from the convictions of the people, the people (and their governments) will start resisting judicial decisions.
>
> (McGoldrick 2011)

That is why, according to McGoldrick, a broad use of the doctrine of the margin is "a sensible and credible judicial strategy of self-restraint for the ECtHR to follow" (ibid.: 500–501). In the same vein, Janneke Gerards notes that the DMA is an appealing instrument "to negotiate between the court's task to protect human rights as effectively as possible, and its need to respect national sovereignty and make its judgments acceptable for national authorities" (Gerards 2011: 114).

Unlike the VDMA, a rationalized version of the doctrine (hereafter RDMA) does not start from a strong presumption in favour of the state, but takes the national margin of appreciation to be the result of balancing the values at stake in the protection of Convention rights. The Court focuses on examining whether the impugned measure has achieved a fair balance between individual rights and democratic values. From this viewpoint, the reasoning of the Court does not need to be mediated by general considerations of institutional legitimacy, and the state's will does *not* have independent value. The weight of the will of the state depends on the state's success in reaching an axiological equilibrium that is inherent to a democratic society. The aim of the RDMA is not simply to justify the "deference" to state sovereignty, but to assure a balanced recognition of democratic values within the framework of the ECHR.

The logic of the RDMA is present in the accommodation clauses of Articles 8 to 11 of the Convention,[6] and is consistent with the axiological duality that inspires this international treaty. However, when sensitive "religious" issues and conflicts are involved, the Court's tendency has been to resort to the VDMA. Yet granting broad discretion to states in the protection of the right to religious freedom is questionable at a principled level; in addition, instead of strengthening the Court's legitimacy vis-à-vis the states, such deference has resulted in the erosion of part of its jurisdictional role.[7] A jurisprudence dependent on national sovereignty prevents the Court from articulating a minimal constitutional framework stable enough to settle the contours of state autonomy regarding its ability to deal with its internal (religious) pluralism. Decisions such as *Lautsi* 2011 illustrate this concern. The Grand Chamber's short and abrupt argumentative turn, as well as its ad hoc distancing from the (otherwise questionable) criterion set in *Dahlab*, illustrates the absence of a well-grounded and consistent stand able to justify the margin granted to the Italian state without falling into mere political indulgence.[8]

The shortcomings of a VDMA in the Court's case law on religious freedom explain why experts and even judges of the ECtHR have been reluctant to take the DMA more seriously. From this sceptical perspective, the Court should abandon the doctrine since it only made sense in its early years in order to consolidate institutional stability, and in a context of more value homogeneity amongst an initially smaller number of states.[9] But this scepticism is justified *only* with respect to its voluntarist version. By contrast, the RDMA should have an important role to play in assessing the constraints exerted by the Convention on state sovereignty in matters involving religion. We have already noted that Article 9.2 mirrors the axiological duality of the Convention; this makes it reasonable to affirm that the extent of the right to freedom of religion shall be the product of a proportionality assessment in the pursuit of different social goals.

Still, for scholars such as George Letsas, something like the RDMA is not necessary to account for the relevance of proportionality. This version of the doctrine would only stress that the ECtHR should undertake a proportionality test, something already included in the accommodation clauses of the Convention; clauses that are the natural domain where the DMA is applicable (Letsas 2006: 709–715). In contrast to Letsas' opinion, we suggest that an RDMA may serve as a more general guide for the Court's judgment regarding interferences with the right to freedom of religion. Letsas bases his conclusion on a conception of rights as trumps – that is, a view of rights which, as he himself acknowledges, does not easily match the conventional provisions regarding rights in the first place.[10] Once a more flexible view is adopted, the RDMA may help to clarify both what is wrong with an abstract assessment of conventionality, and when a stringent proportionality test in the application of the Convention should be rejected. As we shall explain, an RDMA favours an assessment of state measures by taking into account the particular political, social and cultural situation, by attending to the general standard of rights protection provided by the state when dealing with its internal religious pluralism and by considering current inter-state or external pluralism in Europe.

The RDMA becomes more convincing as a general interpretive device in religious matters once we take into account fundamental elements concerning the jurisdictional role of the ECtHR. The aim of the Convention itself, as a complementary tool in the consolidation of constitutional democracy, is to assure a minimal threshold of formal and substantive quality in the standards of human rights protection within the Council of Europe. Yet this does not imply that the task of the Court is to specify, according to its own criteria, what this minimal threshold is. As Michael Hutchinson points out, if this were the case, the Court would not need to include in its judgment any consideration external to rights, and the previous balance carried out by the denounced state would not really have any impact. The difficulty is that this minimum cannot be settled *in abstracto*. This threshold implies a degree of flexibility: the contours of the Court's framework will remain dependent on a balance between rights and democracy (Hutchinson 1999: 642–644; Brems 2009: 358–359).

On the other hand, the logic of the Convention makes it difficult to endorse a legal characterization of the right to religious freedom as trump or side constraint – namely, as a reason that excludes other considerations external to rights. Again, this view is too restrictive to account for a judicially protected legal right that may openly compete with reasons of public interest – namely, public safety and order, health or morals. To account for the functioning of the ECHR, we need a weaker conception of rights, a conception that may have critical value and give priority to rights over the public interest without diluting the legal identity of the Convention as an international treaty.[11] Keeping these two elements in mind, the RDMA ascribes to the ECtHR the function of supervising the state's internal axiological balance in responding to demands for human rights protection. But the ECtHR has a systemic function too. The Court is required to consolidate a legal structure of human rights able to work as a general guide for member states and their citizens. The question, then, is how the RDMA could be implemented in the Court's reasoning so as to be faithful to these different functions. The *principle of proportionality* is a basic element in the assessment of a state measure restricting a right susceptible to balance by considerations of public interest. As we have noted, the ECtHR has a tendency to use the VDMA and to minimize the proportionality exam when religious conflicts are at stake. This results in a strong deference to the state in determining when a restriction to the right to religious freedom is "necessary in a democratic society". The question, however, is how the proportionality test should be carried out when we take the axiological duality of the ECHR seriously.

When a restrictive measure pursues a legitimate aim, the proportionality test is usually understood as the examination of three questions: (1) is the measure "suitable" to achieve such an aim? (2) Is it "necessary" to achieve that aim? (Were there other less restrictive options that could achieve the aim with similar efficacy?), and (3) is the measure proportional in the narrow sense? Does the measure achieve a balance between the degree in which the legitimate aim is satisfied and the restriction of the right? This structured assessment, called the "German test of proportionality" as well, has been used by many constitutional courts and, to some extent, by the Court of Justice of the European Union.[12] So far, the ECtHR has not engaged in such a structured test of proportionality when assessing whether a restrictive measure is necessary in a democratic society. Its proportionality assessment has revolved around considering whether there is a pressing social need, whether the right is impaired as little as possible taking into account the state's available alternatives, and whether the state has achieved a fair balance between the right and the legitimate aim.[13] However, the Strasbourg Court has not addressed all these questions simultaneously or in a sequential way.

The primary aim of the RDMA, unlike the VDMA, is that the ECtHR becomes really involved in a proportionality assessment. This would represent an important step in the effective protection of convention rights vis-à-vis the will of the state. Nevertheless, the RDMA requires that the Court engage in a proportionality test as a balancing exercise that includes both first-order and second-order reasons for action.[14] More specifically, when approaching a particular conflict between rights and collective interests, the Court may use, together with first-order reasons, second-order reasons that assign a certain degree of prominence to national standing and democratic considerations. Second-order reasons become relevant when analysing which level of restriction is conventionally acceptable as well as what are the options available to the state.

A first fundamental question to be considered in the proportionality test concerns the general level of protection of the right to religious freedom provided by the state. When a particular restriction is not strong and the state has a high standard of protection of this right, a "neutralization theory", such as the one used by the Grand Chamber in *Lautsi* 2011, may be considered.[15] In contrast, when the national level of protection is low, the Court may be justified in increasing the stringency of the proportionality test. The latter situation is a possible threat to the effective protection of Convention rights and, here, the Court will be constrained to compensate for the state's inaction in attending to its international commitments. Therefore, the higher the general level of protection displayed by the state, the higher the reliability of its opinions with regard to rights.

The Court may also resort to the "comparative method" in the proportionality test in order to assess whether the state makes use of the least restrictive measure and of alternative options (Arai-Takahashi 2002: 15). Since the ECHR was created to improve the overall level of rights protection in Europe, a reason to doubt that the denounced state lacked other less restrictive options is to show that other member states, in comparable situations, have pursued the same legitimate aim without affecting the right at issue.

The lack of a European consensus could be relevant as well in order to diminish the stringency of the proportionality test, but not for the reason provided by the VDMA. The relevance is conditional on the presence of a link between consensus building and the rationale of a gradual progress in the system of human rights protection in the region. The consensus standard should thus go hand in hand with the evolutive interpretation method, another important device in the Court's case law.[16] To consider the lack of consensus per se as a reason for deference to the state's measures is objectionable, since this could lead to a gradual decline in the general level of rights protection, as well as incoherence and arbitrariness. The degree of the European consensus becomes important insofar as it is useful to identify a gradual improvement in the quality of our European democracies while diminishing the "surprise effect" that an evolutive interpretation disassociated from the "state of the art" in Europe could entail. In this sense, the applicability of the consensus standard depends on a balance between substantive concerns and reasons of legal certainty, and the search for a mutual adjustment that supports the consolidation of human rights. When this mutual adjustment fails, which is to be determined by the ECtHR, the lack of consensus should lose its relevance in the balancing exercise.[17]

Furthermore, assessing whether the state is better placed to decide on the matter may be another key factor in guiding the proportionality test. If the Court finds, after careful consideration, that a conflict cannot be properly addressed without a deep knowledge of the life circumstances of a particular society, it has a strong reason to supervise the axiological balance carried out by the state under less strict scrutiny.[18] This factor gains in importance only when the state's impartiality in religious conflicts has not been compromised. Once the state has shown a tendency to privilege the majority religion or surrender to religious pressure, it is no longer reasonable to assume that it is better placed than an international body to handle conflicts raised by that lack of impartiality.[19] The same could be argued when such conflicts arise in a semi-confessional state or in a state endorsing a secularist worldview hostile to the presence of religion in the public sphere. In such cases, the ECtHR should undertake a more stringent scrutiny of proportionality since its task is then to ensure that the conventional requirements of state neutrality with respect to religion are met. This becomes clear when taking into account the Court's conception of the state responsibility in handling internal or infra-state religious pluralism. On the one hand, the ECtHR has long insisted on the instrumental relationship between freedom of religion and democracy, stressing that this freedom is one of the foundations of a democratic society due to its central role in warranting its inherent pluralism.[20] On the other hand, according to the Court, "states are responsible for ensuring, neutrally and impartially, the exercise of various religions, faiths and beliefs. Their role is to help maintain public order, religious harmony and tolerance in a democratic society, particularly between opposing groups".[21] In this sense, the idea that the state is better placed gains strength only when its institutional stance and previous practices allow it to exert that responsibility in a reliable way.

Finally, the RDMA becomes a suitable hermeneutic device in order to ensure a balance between rights and democracy insofar as it is coherently applied in the Court's case law, and with a view to offering general standards that may guide states and their citizens. Certainly, the proportionality test should be undertaken by considering the particular circumstances of the state in question. This is why the Court should not engage in a merely abstract analysis of compatibility between the individual right and the national regulation. Still, its function is to gradually articulate a thin constitutional framework for interpreting Convention rights. Following Steven Greer's terminology, we could distinguish between two types of axiological balancing assessments: (1) an ad hoc balancing, where the assessment is entirely focused on the particular case, and (2) a structured balancing, where the particular balancing between rights and collective interests is mediated by the aim of setting general standards of human rights protection in the region (Greer 2003: 413). This structured balancing is what various commentators demand from the Court in order to build a coherent regime for the realization of human rights and fundamental freedoms, the very goal of the Convention. Those who resist the idea that an international body should have the last word on rights may perceive as a virtue the fact that the Court constrains itself to finding reasonable solutions on a case-by-case basis rather than by articulating a general framework. However, this particularism erodes its jurisdictional function: as in *Lautsi* 2011, the Court's reasoning often ends up resembling that of an arbitration body. The ECtHR may only keep its institutional legitimacy as a judicial body if the production of reasonable particular results is as important as the production of doctrine at the European level (McHarg 1999: 696). This explains why the jurisprudence of the Court in religious matters has been so contested due to its axiological incoherence, its variability amongst cases and its lack of predictability (Brauch 2005: 125–147; Kratochvíl 2011: 343, 351–352).

Unlike the VDMA, the RDMA has the virtue of offering general standards of protection while attending to the axiological dualism of the Convention. If adopted by the Court, this conception of the margin would allow it to assess national regulations by more comparable parameters and with a view to designing a minimal constitutional framework for deciding legal conflicts involving religion. Such an open-secular minimal framework is necessary to settle the conventional value and specific purpose of the right to religious freedom in a manner comprehensive enough to include a plurality of legitimate aims while still preserving a minimal quality in the enjoyment of the right. The rest of the task in securing this Convention right and in determining the consistent standard of protection beyond that threshold is a question for each member state to decide.

The ECtHR has stressed the state responsibility of religious neutrality and impartiality, and has insisted on the link between religious freedom and democratic pluralism. The Court acknowledges both the legitimacy of semi-confessional states and secularist ones. The conventional reasonableness of these systems does not depend on the place afforded to religion in the public sphere, but on the impact of these systems on citizens' religious pluralism and on the right to freedom of religion that renders such internal pluralism possible. In this vein, states are asked to open up to expressions of religious diversity as a minimal constraint to their autonomy. According to this constraint, national authorities have the responsibility for handling religious conflicts in the least coercive way available and using, whenever possible, ways of settling disputes that encourage religious tolerance and harmony. Regarding religious conflicts at state schools, the jurisprudence of the Court has settled a few generic constraints, such as the principle of non-indoctrination and the idea that religious teaching has to be provided in an objective, critical and pluralistic way,[22] although such parameters have not always been applied with the same determination and strength.

The rationale of the RDMA offers, in our view, a good tool to critically assess the Court's argumentative strategies, and to strengthen its attempt to construct an open-secular framework – namely, a via media between imposing a specific state–religion model and the mere acceptance of the privileged relationship between state and religion. The RDMA is also enlightening with respect to the difficult *Lautsi* case. In the following section, we shall draw on the RDMA to justify why the Italian imposition of the crucifix in state schools should not have been deemed compatible with the ECHR, even when a national margin of appreciation is recognized.

The *Lautsi* "affair"

The main elements of the *Lautsi v. Italy* case are relatively well known. The *Lautsi* case concerned Ms Soile Lautsi, an Italian national living in Abano Terme (Italy), and her children. In 2001–2002, Ms Lautsi's children, aged 11 and 13 respectively, attended the state school "Istituto comprensivo statale Vittorino da Feltre" in Abano Terme. All of the classrooms had a crucifix on the wall, including those in which Ms Lautsi's children received lessons. The appellant argued that the presence of the crucifix went against Article 2 of Protocol No. 1 (the parents' right to educate their children according to their convictions and beliefs) and Article 9 (freedom of religion). The final *Lautsi* decision examined the conflict mainly under Article 2 of Protocol No. 1 as the *lex specialis* in the area of education. The Protocol reads as follows:

> [n]o person shall be denied the right to education. In the exercise of any functions which it assumes in relation to education and to teaching, the State shall respect the right of parents to ensure such education and teaching in conformity with their own religious and philosophical convictions.[23]

The Grand Chamber's decision in 2011 was, as we have pointed out, mainly based on the DMA. At the level of principles, the Court interpreted the articles, and taking them into account. It argued that the planning of the curriculum as well as the school environment falls, as a rule, within the competence of the Contracting States.[24] However, granting a wide margin of appreciation to the state's involvement in education has its limits. According to the Grand Chamber, the second sentence of Article 2 of Protocol No. 1 entails that the state "is forbidden to pursue an aim of indoctrination that might be considered as not respecting parents' religious and philosophical convictions".[25] The state should be neutral in that it is to avoid (religious) indoctrination. The state must also take care that "information or knowledge included in the curriculum is conveyed in an objective, critical and pluralistic manner".[26]

The Grand Chamber further maintained that the state had a positive obligation to recognize or respect religious and non-religious pluralism, and to foster a culture of mutual respect. This is the view of a state that is neutral and has positive obligations with regard to both the school curriculum and the school environment. Symbols such as the crucifix pertain, for the Grand Chamber, to the "school environment", which should also be in accordance with the principles of the Convention. The Grand Chamber argued – in agreement with the initial *Lautsi* decision – that the crucifix was not merely a cultural symbol, but a religious one. However, in contrast to the initial *Lautsi* decision, the Grand Chamber pointed out that the crucifix was "an essentially passive symbol".[27] Such a passive symbol is to be distinguished – argues the Grand Chamber – from "didactic teaching" or "participation in religious activities",[28] which can actively lead to indoctrination.

The Grand Chamber also sustained that there was no clear evidence that the crucifix may have an influence on pupils.[29] Moreover, it underscored that in the Italian context pluralism was respected, in particular at the school level.[30] Moreover, given the lack of consensus over the issue of the crucifix in Europe and the variety of interpretations of the concept of "respect", the Court concluded that granting a wide margin of appreciation to the Italian state was perfectly legitimate. As a result, the Grand Chamber reversed the 2009 ban.[31]

However, the Italian imposition of the crucifix on state school premises amounts to interference with the *forum internum* of freedom of religion (the right to maintain and change one's internal beliefs). Neither Article 9 nor Article 2 (Protocol 1) are compatible with this kind of state interference. Still, it is arguable that this limitation is not especially strong, since the indoctrinating effect of symbols is not obvious compared with the imposition of a religious practice or activity. The active or passive character of a symbol largely depends on its particular context of use. Do we then have reasons to support a strong deference to the state criterion in this case? Following the parameters of the RDMA, the consensus standard would not clearly favour such a deferential attitude. Even when there is no regulative consensus on religious symbols in the public sphere, the uniform imposition of displaying the crucifix in state schools suggests a bias of the Italian state in favour of the Catholic Church, but such a regime is rather exceptional in Europe. Only a small minority of member states impose the presence of the crucifix in state schools. In addition, the exceptional imposition of the crucifix is more related to the national aim of preserving religious traditions rather than to genuine value pluralism in protecting freedom of religion. Taking into account the special responsibility of the state in children's education, the lack of regulative homogeneity of symbols should play a minor role within the rationale of a gradual progress in the consolidation of the right to religious freedom in the region.

It is also reasonable to cast doubt on the argument that a state whose cultural traditions privilege the symbols of the majority religion in detriment to non-believers or other minority religions is better placed to impartially decide on the conflicts caused by the institutional use of the crucifix. Consequently, neither the lack of a consensus argument nor the idea that the state is better placed justify in this case granting a broad deference to the Italian state, keeping, moreover, in mind that the Italian regulation has a weak democratic pedigree (i.e. the obligation was not enacted by Parliament but was based on decrees of the 1920s, mainly from the Fascist period, and which have not been supervised by the Italian Constitutional Court).[32]

A further question is whether the Italian state has used the least restrictive means available when affecting the *forum internum* of religious freedom so as to preserve its traditions. As the ECtHR has correctly stressed, preserving cultural traditions is one of the legitimate aims of a democratic state.[33] The question is, however, whether the state could have pursued that aim by less coercive means. Using the comparative method, it turns out that other options to keeping the tradition of displaying the crucifix are available. In fact, in countries such as Spain, Greec, and San Marino, which do not have a specific regulation on the matter, the crucifix is still present in some state schools. Making the presence of crucifixes mandatory is not necessary or, at least, the Italian state has not demonstrated such a necessity in its social setting. In turn, juridification is probably not the most suitable way to preserve cultural and religious traditions in a democratic society. The persistence of traditions with religious roots is connected with a variety of intertwined factors and, to a large extent, depends on its popular support within a social setting based on tolerance and mutual respect. Since the Italian state had other less coercive options, the lack of proportion of a restrictive measure affecting the *forum internum* of religious freedom cannot easily be compensated for by the fact that the state is more protective of religious pluralism in other aspects of its educational system. That is why a theory of neutralization does not gain enough importance in this case. What is really at stake is, in the end, the will of the Italian state expressed in its appeal to *Lautsi* 2009, which is something without independent value from the viewpoint of an RDMA.

Arguing that the ECtHR should have found a violation of the Convention in the compulsory display of crucifixes in Italian state schools does not imply that *Lautsi* 2009 was right in its approach. The Chamber's ruling found a violation of the Convention by reasoning in abstract about the "possible" emotional distress for pupils, and without taking into account the national context of the application of rights. The Chamber simply pre-decided the significance and the impact of the crucifix as being incompatible with the Convention.

In 2011, the Grand Chamber was right to distinguish between "didactic teaching" and "participation in religious activities" and symbols,[34] since prima facie the former presuppose an "engaging relationship" with pupils.[35] Direct engagement – namely, by means of compulsory religion classes taught by priests in state schools – represents a clear-cut bias in educational practice, and an undermining of an open-secular framework. However, this is not so clear in the case of symbols. Since the impact is more imponderable in such cases, it is arguable that the Court should have manifested judicial restraint. It is noteworthy that, according to the jurisprudence of the Court, the secular and neutral character of the state should not be understood in "absolute" terms. On the contrary, from the perspective of an open-secular minimal framework, it is compatible with the active recognition granted to the majority religion, as long as this does not discriminate against other religious and non-religious alternatives. In other words, the development of a special relationship between the state and the majority religion – (namely, that expressed by the presence of majority religious symbols in public institutions) – may be acceptable within the Convention system.[36] Additionally, in the absence of expert empirical knowledge, the Court's decision in 2009 was ultimately based on conjecture, and did not comply with the principle of proportionality that is at the heart of the RDMA.[37] While its concern with minority rights was certainly legitimate, the Chamber did not engage in a fair balance of the conventional values involved in assessing the presence of the crucifix at school. Its judgment went beyond the minimal protection of Convention rights, since it ended up imposing a strict secularist model of managing religious diversity at the European level. The Chamber failed to explain why it had denied a margin of appreciation to the national criterion, even a limited one. No attention was paid to the range of legitimate ways in which a democratic society may reconcile freedom of religion with public symbols in countries where tradition and religion are intermingled. Overall, the mere fact that a religious symbol is displayed on the walls of a state school is, in our view, not enough to represent a breach of the Convention. The relevant issue is the role the state has played with regard to the presence of this symbol.

Lautsi 2009 also takes for granted (just like *Lautsi* 2011) that the only option compatible with the Convention is either banning the display of the crucifix, or imposing it. We turn now to examining a via media between *Lautsi* 2009 and *Lautsi* 2011 – namely, the merits and demerits of a contextual approach to the issue of the crucifix.

A contextual approach?

The contextual approach to the crucifix is an alternative to the all-or-nothing strategy. Since this approach avoids the top-down imposition (either of the Court or of the national state), it is prima facie more compatible with our defence of the RDMA – namely, with an approach that challenges the privileged relation between state and religion and, at the same time, grants a margin of appreciation to the state.

The contextual approach (CA) has so far been adopted only at the state level – namely, in Germany and Spain. There is no single solution under the heading of the CA. According to the emphasis on deliberation and/or decision, one can distinguish different contextual solutions. For example, a decision-based solution envisages that one parent's petition is enough for the school board to automatically remove the crucifix. We can call this *conditional removal*: taking down the crucifix is not to be implemented overnight in all state schools (as in *Lautsi* 2009), but is conditioned by the explicit demand of a parent. The minority is, thus, empowered. In turn, a *deliberation-oriented solution* aims at enhancing democratic participation and local deliberation in contexts of religious pluralism. The decision to keep or not to keep the crucifix is majoritarian, and it is premised on the internal dialogue within the governing organs of each school, provided that these local institutions are organized in inclusive-democratic terms and ensure representation, participation and a voice to all affected parties (parents, teachers, etc.).

The CA has significant merits, but it runs into difficulties as well. On the positive side, it does not "freeze" by legal means the dynamic of signification of the crucifix, given that decision-making is relegated to the level of the school council/board. The CA thus has the merit of recognizing that contexts are plural, conflictive and changing, and that an a priori stand on the significance and impact of a crucifix is not immediately warranted. The active or passive character of a religious symbol cannot be settled in advance without taking local circumstances into account. In contrast, both the *Lautsi* 2009 and 2011 cases pre-decided the meaning and impact of the crucifix, and imposed from the top their respective solutions. These impositions are misguided: first, granting a broad margin of appreciation to the Italian state so as to make the presence of crucifixes mandatory across-the-board amounts to a trivialization of the (latent) power of religious symbolism; second, as we have pointed out, in *Lautsi* 2009 the assessment of the Court that a religious symbol may be emotionally distressful for pupils was made in abstract, without empirical evidence, and without analysing the various contexts of the display of crucifixes in Italian state schools. *Lautsi* 2009 and 2011 are, from this perspective, at fault for not precluding the possibility of this case-by-case deliberation and decision according to the diversity of contexts of signification. In addition, without an *explicit* request to remove the crucifix, *Lautsi* 2009 adopted a uniform solution on account of the speculative and context-less assumption that there was a legal conflict. Especially when it comes to legal decisions taken by an international Court with a subsidiary role, entering the realm of speculation should be avoided.

The deliberation-based solution appears to have further inclusive and participatory-democratic merits. By not requiring the immediate exclusion of crucifixes from classrooms, this solution also gives a margin of reflection and discussion as to the way Italian citizens and residents interpret their rights and historical–religious traditions. The empowered citizens themselves are to take a decision by majority as to the presence of the crucifix. Being participants in the construction of rights, some Catholics may be willing to reach out to non-Catholics, and contribute to the public conversation. Likewise, both Catholics and non-Catholics would have the opportunity to reflect on the significance of the crucifix and, more broadly, on the inherited relationship between state and religion and the kind of society they would want to live in. Leaving the final decision to the school governing body after a reasoned dialogue and internal deliberation is, for its advocates, a democratic and participatory way to manage such religious controversies. From this perspective, *Lautsi* 2011 is disappointing in democratic terms because it amounts to an avoidable use of state coercion to handle conflicts that could be solved by less stringent and more participatory means. In effect, the ECtHR itself has long insisted on the instrumental relationship between freedom of religion and democracy, considering that freedom of religion is one of the foundations of a democratic society due to its central role in warranting its inherent pluralism[38]. If so, decisions from the school governing body should not simply be considered decisions of the public power, but decisions of the society itself.[39] In short, for the defenders of the CA, a mandatory solution coming from outside is less democratic because it rules out any possibility of local deliberation to obtain arrangements that could be accepted as reasonable by those whose daily life is affected by the fact of religious pluralism.

From this perspective, a further advantage of the CA is that it favours a double division of labour in the implementation of convention rights. The RDMA is based on the assumption that the protection and implementation of the Convention is the product of a division of labour between member states and the Court. The state has the first task of securing those rights and the Court intervenes to ensure that this task has been carried out in accordance with the ECHR.[40] The CA appears to be in tune with the via media of the RDMA: the flexibility of the contextual solutions formula aims at protecting (non-)religious minorities, while respecting, to a certain extent, the state's margin of appreciation to keep a special relationship with a particular religion. Furthermore, as part of a democracy-oriented plea for the RDMA, it is arguable that the proper implementation of Convention rights needs, when feasible, an *additional* division of labour, not only external but also internal – namely, between each member state and its citizens/residents. From a democratic perspective, citizens/residents should play an active role in the interpretation and implementation of rights.

The CA also appears to be consistent with the demand for state neutrality in religious matters.[41] In *Lautsi* 2011, the Court pointed out that "States have responsibility for ensuring, neutrally and impartially, the exercise of various religions, faiths and beliefs. Their role is to help maintain public order, religious harmony and tolerance in a democratic society, particularly between opposing groups", and "the State is forbidden to pursue an aim of indoctrination that might be considered as not respecting parent's religious and philosophical convictions".[42] According to these restrictions, the defenders of this solution argue that the state is in fact more neutral by renouncing the opportunity to settle a mandatory result on the removal of religious symbols from classrooms in advance, and leaving this decision to the particular context instead. The state's responsibility in keeping religious harmony and tolerance could be simply satisfied by ensuring that the local solution will be the product of a democratic and participatory process. The issue at hand in *Lautsi*-type cases is the displaying of crucifixes in *state* schools, where the state has a special responsibility to avoid any form of indoctrination in the organization of the educational system and environment.[43] However, the non-indoctrination requirement is clearly satisfied if the state refrains from imposing the presence of crucifixes in advance.[44]

Nonetheless, there are different objections to the CA. These objections carry different weights. First, for those who defend a strong constitutional secularism, any local solution should be dismissed as Trojan Horse, which undermine modern constitutionalism. According to Andras Sajó, decentralization and local negotiation result in uncertainty and perennial local conflicts (Sajó 2009: 519). However, in democratic contexts where we agree that it is legitimate for us to disagree, we need a procedure more than a definitive answer. While local solutions may be different depending on each school, in a pluralist democracy these differences may be legitimate if they are the result of reasonable deliberative and decision-making processes. Further, leaving the decision to the local context does not create "perennial conflicts", but keeps disagreement alive: no position on the crucifix will be safe from criticism and challenge, which is reasonable to expect in a pluralist democracy.

Second, one could argue that the CA tends to overburden minorities that are already in an inferior position of power and status. Think of an immigrant Muslim parent who does not know either the language or the rules regarding how to make a request. The CA appears to worsen his/her disadvantaged position. Furthermore, given that power structures and restraints are often constituted at the informal level, a minority parent might choose not to voice his/her discontent in order to avoid the possibility of bad treatment or marginalization of his/her child at school. If one parent chooses to go against the majority, this may result in subtle and informal mechanisms of marginalization in school – that is, to more domination and discrimination. Lack of knowledge, but also informal power mechanisms might be at the root of the fact that, in Bavaria, there have been so few requests to remove the crucifix. Therefore, while the contextual approach claims to consider societal pluralism more seriously, it might lead to its undermining. In order to assess the normative appeal of the CA, empirical studies that go beyond a strictly behaviouristic understanding of power relations (Lukes 2005) are necessary.

Third, to what extent is it realistic to expect that school councils could act as open arenas of deliberation and decision-making? When in place, school councils or governing bodies are neither based on procedures that support inclusive deliberations nor on a solid culture of deliberation. It is then an open questionas to whether the CA is not too idealistic about the role of deliberation and power relations at the school level.

In sum, there is no optimal or clear-cut solution to the crucifix affair. The contextual approach claims various merits, and it can be usefully connected to the via media inherent in the RDMA, but the implementation of a fully fledged contextual solution based on deliberation runs into difficulties. However, in the absence of expert knowledge as to the impact of the crucifix, and given the Court's subsidiary role and the importance of proportionality, the RDMA demands an intermediary solution based on the questioning and rejection of the Italian state's *unvarying* imposition of the presence of crucifixes in Italian public schools as being incompatible with the Convention.[45] Such a minimal contextual solution would have probably been preferable to any top-down uniform imposition.[46]

Conclusion

The ECtHR does not aim to construct a European secularist "wall of separation" between state and religion. Within an open-secular framework that grants recognition to systems as different as French laicism and Greek semi-confessionalism, the secular state is, from the Court's perspective, not purely neutral and separate; instead, the secular state can, depending on the context, build different forms of collaboration with religious communities and institutions, as long as it does not breach the ECHR. Furthermore, the secular state has the positive obligation to protect and enhance a pluralistic culture of mutual tolerance, respect and dialogue amongst citizens. For instance, in *Gorzelik v. Poland*, the Court argues that:

> proclaiming or teaching religion ... are also important to the proper functioning of democracy. For pluralism is also built on the genuine recognition of, and respect for, diversity and the dynamics of cultural traditions, ethnic and cultural identities, religious beliefs.[47]

This approach is consistent with the growing pluralization and individualization of the socio-religious landscape as well as with inter-state pluralism in the region. It is also part of a broader process of re-visiting the traditional compromises between state and religion in a more plural world where different (non-)religious communities and groups seek a place in the public sphere.

The ECtHR's jurisprudence remains, however, marked by ambiguity and inconsistency. By applying the DMA in its voluntaristic version, a Janus-faced ECtHR has often granted national states too much discretion; this has led to the over-protection of majority religious sentiments at the expense of freedom of expression, to the support for the imposition of majority symbols (the crucifix), and to the banning of minority symbols (the veil) (Solar 2009; Martínez-Torrón 2012). In particular, cases concerning religious symbols from *Dahlab* to *Lautsi* represent instances of the Court's relapse into majoritarianism and a voluntaristic view of the margin of appreciation. While there is no optimal solution in the crucifix case, we have argued that the Court should not have left unquestioned the Italian state's imposition to display the crucifix in a state school.

The recent inclusion of the margin of appreciation in the new, Protocol 15, Article 1 of the Convention may be an opportunity for developing a more consistent and principled view of it along the lines of the RDMA. However, in spite of the Court's palpable merits in challenging the privileged relation between state and majority religion starting with *Kokkinakis v. Greece*, cases such as *Lautsi* raise doubts as to the ECtHR's capacity to protect, in a coherent way, freedom of religion and the growing pluralism in Europe.

Notes

1 In this chapter, we use secularism as a worldview and ideology that is hostile to religion (e.g. to the manifestations of religion in the public sphere). The open secular framework with reference to the ECtHR has different characteristics that can be retrieved from the

Court's jurisprudence itself: first, "open" refers to the acknowledgment of various models of collaboration between the secular state and religious communities/institutions; second, "open" refers to the recognition of the legitimacy and value of public manifestations – either individually or as a group – of religion in the public sphere; third, this framework entails the positive recognition of the value of pluralism in a secular-democratic state. For more details on the principled defence of such an approach, see Bhargava (2007); Taylor (2007a); Bouchard and Taylor (2008) and chapter 1 in this volume.

2 The Court's jurisprudence is available at: echr.coe.int/echr/en/hudoc (accessed 5 May 2014).

3 See Protocol 15, Article 1.

4 *Handyside v. United Kingdom* (1976), paras 48 and 49.

5 For a somewhat similar distinction, see Letsas (2006: 709–715, 720–724).

6 All these articles have a similar structure. They set forth fundamental rights to be protected in their first paragraphs. In the second paragraphs, they provide that state authorities may interfere with the Convention right in pursuit of any of the legitimate aims laid down in the text as long as such restriction is prescribed by law and necessary in a democratic society.

7 On these objections see especially Brauch (2005: 147–150) and Solar (2009: 160–161).

8 For this line of criticism, see Panara (2011) and Zucca (2013).

9 See, for instance, Brauch (2005: 147–150) who insists that the Court must abandon the margin of appreciation and return to the text (on this, see also Martínez-Torrón 2003: 17). In a similar line, the judge De Mayer, in his partially dissenting option in *Z. v. Finland, para. III* (1997), stresses that:

> it is high time for the Court to banish that concept from its reasoning. It has already delayed too long in abandoning this hackneyed phrase and recanting the relativism it implies. (...) But where human rights are concerned, there is no room for a margin of appreciation which would enable the States to decide what is acceptable and what is not. On that subject the boundary not to be overstepped must be as clear and precise as possible. It is for the Court, not each State individually, to decide that issue, and the Court's views must apply to everyone within the jurisdiction of each State.

10 His conception of rights as trumps forces Letsas to be especially distrustful of balances between rights and reasons of public interest. See Letsas (2006: 717, 719–720, 731–732).

11 Weaker conceptions along the lines of Raz's interest theory or Alexy's structural conception of rights as principles could perhaps do a better job in accounting for convention rights. However, as commentators have noted, we need a conception weak enough to allow for balances, but strong enough to justify a general priority of rights over public interest. On this debate, see McHarg (1999); Greer (2003); Kumm (2007); and Legg (2012).

12 On the general functioning of the proportionality test, see Alexy (2002: 66–69); González Beilfuss (2003); Klatt and Meister (2012: Chapter 1); Barak (2012: 243–420).

13 In *Handyside v. United Kingdom*, para. 48, the ECtHR understands "necessary in a democratic society" not as indispensable or absolutely necessary. It refers to a "pressing social need", and holds that it is for the national authorities to make the initial assessment of such a need. As noted by Greer (2003: 409, 428), this requirement allows for a priority of rights over collective goals since it imposes on the state the burden of proof regarding this pressing social need. On the function of the proportionality assessment in the ECtHR's reasoning, see also Arai-Takahashi (2002: 15, 99–100), Spielmann (2012: 22), Legg (2012: Chapter 7).

14 On the relevance of second-order reasons in the assessment of the proper national margin of appreciation, see especially the recent contribution of Legg (2012).

15 As Gabriel Adreescu and Liviu Andreescu (2011: 210–212) point out, this theory allows the Grand Chamber to compensate the concern for neutrality emerging from the fact that crucifixes invest Christianity with greater visibility in Italian schools by other safeguards of freedom of religion and for religious non-indoctrination in schools run by the state.

16 On the relation between consensus and evolutive interpretations, see Dzehtsiarou (2011).

17 For a more critical view with regard to the relevance of the European consensus in the understanding of the ECHR, see Letsas (2004: 204–305). For an opposite opinion suggesting that the Court should generally follow the current consensus at the European level, see Hutchinson (1999: 648–649).

18 Some judges of the Court, Rozakis and Spielmann for instance, stress that the fact that a state is "really" better placed to decide on a given matter is the only reason able to justify a national margin of appreciation, especially when national Courts have already supervised the balance carried out by the state.

19 As noted by Mancini (2010: 25), if the Court grants a broad margin of appreciation in such cases it is in fact playing a counter-majoritarian role, since the European system for the protection of human rights was established precisely to correct some of the major deficiencies of majoritarian democracy.

20 See, for instance, *Kokkinakis v. Greece* (1993), para. 31; *Manoussakis and others v. Greece*, (1996), para. 44; *Serif v. Greece* (1999), para. 49.

21 *Lautsi v. Italy*, para. 60; *Şahin v. Turkey* (2005), para. 107.

22 See *Folgerø v. Norway* (2007); *Zengin v. Turkey* (2007).

23 See www.hri.org/docs/ECHR50.html (accessed 5 May 2014). See *Lautsi v. Italy* (2011), para. 59

24 *Folgerø*, para. 84 and *Lautsi* (2011) citing it in para. 60. They follow *Kjeldsen, Busk Madsen and Pedersen v. Denmark* (1976), the Court argued in para. 53 that:

> [t]he second sentence of Article 2 (P1–2) implies on the other hand that the State, in fulfilling the functions assumed by it in regard to education and teaching, must take care that information or knowledge included in the curriculum is conveyed in an objective, critical and pluralistic manner.

25 Lautsi v. Italy (2011).

26 Ibid.

27 *Lautsi* (2011), para. 72.

28 Ibid.

29 In *Lautsi* (2011), para. 66 the Court says:

> There is no evidence before the Court that the display of a religious symbol on classroom walls may have an influence on pupils and so it cannot reasonably be asserted that it does or does not have an effect on young persons whose convictions are still in the process of being formed.

30 *Lautsi* (2011), para. 74.

31 The Court invokes several times on the margin of appreciation – at paras 68, 69, 70, etc.

32 See also the dissenting option to *Lautsi* (2011), pars. 1. Interestingly, since this case has not been approached following the structure of Article 9.2 ECHR, the Court was not required to assess whether the Italian regulation amounted to a law of minimal quality.

33 *Lautsi* (2011), para. 68.

34 *Lautsi* (2011), para. 72.

35 Surely, there are also situations in which a symbolic image is more powerful than words or even taking part in an activity.

36 We make the distinction between a privileged and a special relationship between state

and religion. Under the ECHR system, the existence of a special relation between state and religion is legitimate (e.g. that a state like Greece has an official religion; or that the educational curriculum in state schools in Norway gives more weight to the majority religion than, say, to Jainism and Confucianism). A special relationship turns into a privileged relationship whenever freedom of religion, minority rights and pluralism as codified in the ECHR are undermined.

37 Suppose that reliable studies in social psychology determined that the presence of the crucifix has a significant indoctrinating effect. If so, then the preferred solution should be, all things considered, banning the crucifix.

38 *Kokkinakis v. Greece* (1993), para. 31. On the relationship between democracy and freedom of religion in the ECtHR, see Nieuwenhuis (2007).

39 This claim was advanced by the High Court of Justice of Castile and the Leon Ruling in its 2009 decision on the crucifix.

40 *Handyside v. United Kingdom* (1976).

41 It is noteworthy that the ECtHR case law is quite flexible in terms of the requirement of state neutrality in the context of freedom of religion. The Court holds that the existence of an established Church does not in itself breach Article 9, and has also admitted a privileged status for the majority religion on taxes, legal proceedings, education and blasphemy laws. Examples of this flexibility are *Darby v. Sweden* (1990), *E. and G.R. v. Austria* (1984), *Wingrove v. United Kingdom* (1996), *Valsamis v. Greece* (1996), or *Folgerø* (2007).

42 *Lautsi* (2011), paras 60 and 62.

43 See, especially, *Folgerø* (2007), *Zengin v. Turkey* (2007), and *Leyla Sahin v. Turkey* (2005).

44 There are important differences between the contextual solutions. In the first case, the decision to remove the crucifix is left to the will of non-Christian parents in a particular school. At the level of principles, the conditional removal solution confers a predominant role to the protection of (non)religious minorities as a central tenet of a fully fledged conception of religious freedom within the meaning of the ECHR. Protection of religious pluralism is certainly a core aspect of what respecting religious freedom means. However, endowing such minorities with the unilateral power to revoke traditional practices coming from a history of Christian predominance is not the only instrument available to protect religious pluralism. In contrast, the deliberation-oriented solution does not grant non-Christian parents a potentially decisive voice. Their views may be debated and confronted in the process of deliberation within the governing body of each school.

45 In other words, the Court could have rejected the uniform imposition of the crucifix, as it did in *Lautsi* 2009, whilst including in the body of its argument a recommendation analogous to the one contained in the concurring opinion of the *Gas and Dubois v. Francia* (2012). In the concurring opinion, the following is stated:

> In reality – and this will be my closing remark – the case-law concedes that there are areas in which the national legislature is better placed than the European Court to bring about change in institutions concerning the family, relations between adults and children and the concept of marriage. Let me give one example. Same-sex marriage is the subject of democratic debate in several European countries. It was mainly for that reason that the Court opted in a recent judgment to exercise limited supervision over national choices (see *Schalk and Kopf v. Austria*, no. 30141/04, ECHR 2010). In my view, the need for consistency in case-law policy calls for an equally restrained approach in the present case, although I find the structure of Article 365 of the Civil Code less than convincing.... It is to be hoped, therefore, that the French legislature will not merely be satisfied with the finding of no violation and will decide, if I may say so, to review this issue.

46 We should underline the fact that there is a difference of opinion between the authors of this chapter. Marisa Iglesias believes that the merits of the deliberation-oriented solutions outweigh their difficulties once the conditions for participatory deliberation at the local level are satisfied and the educational context is, in general, opened up to religious pluralism.

47 *Gorzelik and others v. Poland* (2004), para. 92.

11 Religions and liberal democracies

Final remarks

Ferran Requejo

The human brain is a product of evolution. Over the last 3,900 million years the development and diversity of life on the planet has been spectacular. The first species of the genus *homo* appeared only 2.5 million years ago. And the appearance of this curious animal, which we rather arrogantly refer to as *homo sapiens*, occurred 150,000 years ago – only a moment in evolutionary terms. We do not know exactly when it happened, but with the genus *homo* came a cerebral revolution: the development of symbolic and abstract language. Since then, we have never stopped asking basic questions: What and who are we? What is the universe like? How should we behave? Who should take collective decisions? And so on. And we have continually produced an incredible number of different answers.

Religions are one way of answering these questions and their responses have fascinated humans for tens of thousands of years. Human brains are much given to religious ideas. For as far back as we have evidence, and regardless of their technological development, the different cultures that have existed on the planet have all maintained religious ideas and practices. In fact, humans have displayed great creativity when propounding the existence of gods and spirits. This is a historical and transcultural phenomenon that is present at all latitudes. And contrary to what a number of "enlightened" conceptions of a liberal or Marxist nature have maintained, religions have not disappeared in the modern era, nor are they likely to in the future.

Nobody really knows the reason for all this, although several partial explanations have been put forward, some of which are of an evolutionary or economic nature. The origins of religions are controversial – there have been proposed diverse reasons: functional, psychological, political, moral, biological, subproducts of the improvement of brain abilities to make causal inferences and predictions, etc. For example, the evolution of life and language may have made most human beings believe in religious tenets in order to fit in with the group. It can also be suggested that religions are "economical" ideologies; that is, with a small number of ideas and stories, it is possible to answer a large number of different and profound cosmological and existential questions. First, they provide answers for questions regarding the origin of the world and its relationship with humans. Origin myths and past or future paradises for humanity are created. The proliferation of deities and spirits is useful for building a mental map of the cosmos. Second, they provide answers to existential questions and human needs. We know that we are going to die, and questions about other possible worlds beyond physical death are frightening and disconcerting. And despite the fact that, nowadays, religions may appear to some to be somewhat precarious concepts in scientific and rational terms with regard to what they say about the world, they still appear to provide emotional reassurance for many people. Religions offer "explanations" about the meaning of life, and calm anxieties in the face of danger, pain or death.

On the one hand, religions, in a broad sense of the word, at least to some extent, refer to beliefs in a supernatural world – gods, spirits, etc. (a set of beliefs which sound very strange to non-believers in a specific religion). However, as happens with other common concepts (democracy, nation, ethnicity, state, etc.), "religion" is an elusive concept. There are many definitions of religion and none of them are universally accepted.

On the other hand, religious practices and ideas have been linked with different ways of organizing political coexistence. In fact, religions have turned out to be politically useful, above all since the earliest sedentary and hierarchical societies became established after the "Neolithic revolution" – the most important revolution of them all. The appearance of bureaucratized religions proved to be a good resource for legitimizing the new political orders in increasingly complex and populous societies. And they continue to do so today, even in some liberal democracies.

Thus, religions are an important object of study for scientists, historians, philosophers or political scientists: Why do religions exist? Why do they fascinate so many people? How can we regulate coexistence between different religions? And between the latter and agnostics and atheists? What normative and institutional model can best reconcile liberal democracies and religious pluralism? What are the most suitable multicultural models for this kind of pluralism? How can one reconcile a secular political institutionalization with religious pluralism in the political and social spheres? At the beginning of the twenty-first century, are we moving from a secular model to a "post-secular" one? The questions go on and on. This is a multidisciplinary issue, which involves disciplines such as history, philosophy, political science, biology and the neurosciences. In the next section, I will focus on a number of elements of an epistemological, cultural and political nature that have a bearing on the analysis of religions in contemporary democracies. In the second and third sections we will approach religions as (multi)cultural phenomena and their relationship with liberal democracies.

Epistemology: Prometheus, Gilgamesh and Lear

The ancient Greeks condensed the diverse characteristics of human beings into a variety of myths, among which that of Prometheus and Zeus (included in Plato's *Protagoras* dialogue) stands out. The gods assigned the brothers Prometheus and

Epimetheus the task of handing out skills to the animals and to man so that they would be able to live their lives successfully. Epimetheus asked to be allowed to make the distribution. To some he gave strength, to others speed or wings to flee with, and so on, in such a way that no species ran the risk of being wiped out. When he had handed out all the skills, the human race had still not received its allocation and the day on which the gods' assignment expired had arrived. Prometheus, in a hurried attempt to find a way for humans to protect themselves, stole fire and professional wisdom from Hephaestus and Athena (for which he was later punished). Man now possessed these skills, but still lacked "political science", which was controlled by Zeus. Humans perfected their technologies, but whenever they met together, they attacked each other. Fearing that the human race would become extinct, Zeus sent Hermes – Plato says – to "bring man morality and justice, so that there would be order in the cities".

In view of the development of humanity it would seem clear, with regard to the amount of each skill handed out, that Prometheus was considerably more generous than Zeus. We are better at technology than at politics and justice. This myth clearly illustrates the fact that we humans are prone to do things in a hurry and to improvise. This is an approach that has been shown to be successful by studies into the evolution of life on the planet. Evolution is not based on a plan; rather it is the selection of a series of chance improvisations that have turned out to be effective.

`We know that ideologies of all kinds distort reality. But, together with these ideological distortions, there are others of which we are less aware: those associated with how we think and how we use language when we attempt to analyse and intervene in the world. Let us consider three of them:

1 The tendency to use extremely abstract categories in order to include as many empirical cases as possible. To an extent, this is inevitable. The very act of naming something creates an abstraction. "Talking is an exaggeration", the playwright Thomas Bernhard used to say. But at times we tend towards what could be called the *fallacy of abstraction*: the belief that the more abstract the language we use to describe, explain or transform a given phenomenon, the better we understand or control it. And often what happens is exactly the opposite: the more abstract the language, the poorer and more remote it is from the empirical cases that it attempts to discuss. Hegel knew quite a lot about this. However, some Marxists, for example, were prone to this kind of distortion when, using a small number of categories – "class struggle", "economic base", etc. – they tried to "explain" everything from the Sumerian empire to the technological revolution.
2 The tendency to dichotomously dissect reality. Given the prevalence of this tendency, it would seem that our brain is prone to conceptual contrasts such as inside–outside, near–far, reason–emotions, matter–spirit, genetics–culture, east–west, ying–yang, Eros–Thanatos, etc. This is the spontaneous immersion in a "digital" epistemological perspective, sometimes referred to as the "discontinuous mind" (Dawkins 2011), which has proven advantageous in

the development of evolution. It is very likely that binary contrasts have been useful for ensuring survival in a hostile world, but they are too primitive for understanding phenomena of a political or social nature, for example, in which different variables are interwoven. Despite the advantages we have derived from having this kind of brain, we know that it is a structurally lazy organ that always tries to make as little effort as possible. However, we know that reality is often full of interrelationships, of intermediate areas, of complexities, which force us either to introduce nuances or to directly think in other ways. For example, the desirability of analysing culture *within* genetics, rather than contrasting the two concepts. But this is always more costly in epistemological terms. We need to employ far more words to overcome the tendency towards contrast between terms that are, in fact, often not logically exclusive and can be combined in different ways and with different intensities.

3 The tendency of Western thought not to manage plurality correctly. Nowadays we recognize that political and moral pluralism is not only an unavoidable fact, but also an essential value of contemporary ethics and politics. We know that in any given situation, there is no single way to act correctly in moral terms or that there is no single suitable political decision at any given moment. But in the history of Western philosophy, from Athens to Jerusalem, we have tended to think differently, in "monist" rather than in "pluralist" terms. We have thought in terms of one kind of "man", of a single kind of "moral duty", in a single ideal political system (every ideology has its own version). Hannah Arendt (1958) and Isaiah Berlin (1997) have already pointed out that a lack of pluralism has characterized Western thought since Plato. But despite the fact that we recognize the pluralism of values and of comparable lifestyles, we often continue to believe that there is only one correct answer and that all others are wrong.

Most current theoretical conceptions continue to display these *abstract, dichotomous* and *monist* tendencies. And flawed theories are not the best way to improve practice. One key to thinking and behaving better in human societies is in critically controlling this triad of distortions which live within our languages and our attitudes. This is easier said than done, it requires effort, but it is necessary in order to refine both our analytical abilities and our moral attitudes and political institutions.

Literature sometimes reflects these difficulties. The classic *Epic of Gilgamesh* and Shakespeare's *King Lear* are two of the works that best illustrate the consequences of a lack of practical wisdom on the part of the ruler and the difficult road that must be taken to achieve it. Religion now is no more than a distant reference point. The books' main characters are powerful at the beginning – they are both kings – but are disconcerted by the consequences of their own actions; actions that are expressed through a kind of language that hides rather than reveals reality. They find it difficult to escape from the confusion produced by the contrast between perspectives that they believed to be sound and the practical unfolding of a series of events that have a direct effect on themselves and their societies. In order to do so, they will need to go on a journey, both physical and interior, towards lands that until now were unknown to them and which, in the end, will make them wiser, more tolerant and unhappier. But this will make it possible to "civilize" the government of the city once again and will be of benefit to its subjects.

The Epic of Gilgamesh is the oldest literary work that we know of. The main character is an allusion to the historical king of Uruk in ancient Mesopotamia (approximately 2750 BC). The five oldest extant texts date from around 2100 BC. They are written in Sumerian, the educated language of the period, which is unrelated to any language currently known. The version of the epic currently considered to be standard is based on a later version written in Akkadian.

The "modern" fascination that the main character still exerts is due to the timelessness of the issues he addresses: the city, abuse of power, love, vulnerability overcome and the need to attain lost wisdom by undertaking a difficult and tragic journey that distances him from his past arrogance and sense of security. Gilgamesh is at first an undisputed, although despotic, ruler. To remedy the situation, the gods send Enkidu, a hero who first lives outside the city in a "wild" state, but who becomes "civilized" through the eroticism of a priestess sent by the king himself. He then moves into the city and establishes a close friendship with Gilgamesh after fighting with him. Gilgamesh's desire to acquire immortal fame (in a similar way to Achilles in the *Iliad*) forces the two friends into combat with the monster Humbaba, who was not in fact a threat to the city. The two friends almost lose their lives, but are helped by the gods and, in the end, Gilgamesh reluctantly follows Enkidu's advice and kills Humbaba. Enkidu later pays for this affront by falling ill and dying. Gilgamesh's grief brings him face to face with his own vulnerability, his fear of having to face death. The necessary wisdom to do so cannot be transmitted through words; one must learn it by oneself. Our hero leaves the city and sets off on a journey in search of an impossible immortality. Having overcome all manner of trials and after meeting Utnapishtim, the only man to have attained immortality (the story of the great Flood that inspired the later biblical myth), Gilgamesh accepts human frailty and this makes it possible for him to govern the city of Uruk, to which he finally returns, in a tolerant, balanced and just way. The ingredients are: awareness of one's own limitations, scepticism regarding moral certainties, and the inevitable unpredictability of our actions. In short, the poem speaks of this profound forgotten wisdom, which is ignored by those in power.

Shakespeare's *King Lear* offers one of the greatest versions of the tragedy that envelops all humanity. It is a work that makes no concessions to the appealing moral or religious words of self-deception. The king, when he abandons his throne, begins a journey that allows him to see, through pain and personal degradation, that we are alone in an emotional and cosmological void, in a wilderness of doubts, desires and contradictory thoughts. And beyond this there is nothing: "As flies for wanton boys are we to the gods. They kill us for their sport" (*King Lear*: Act 4, Scene 1). It is difficult to accept that Cordelia dies and the rats do not. The attainment of wisdom is a tragic journey that one can only make on one's own (as Gilgamesh does). It even requires Lear's madness and Gloucester's blindness for them to grasp a truth that they did not see before. "'Tis *the time's plague* when madmen lead the *blind*" (*King Lear*: Act 4, Scene 1 (my emphasis)). At the end, they know that they know very little, but what they do know is more profound than everything that they thought they knew before. Politics should be built on the idea that mankind belongs to nature and that it is small in epistemological and moral terms. Only through the critical wisdom that leads to a weak and tragic nakedness is it possible to act justly. We are a fragile reality. Our only protection from ourselves is a political society that avoids the arrogant arbitrariness of our behaviour. Through Shakespeare, we can hear echoes of Montaigne's sceptical naturalism and the almost-born modern thought of Hobbes and his reflection on the mutual distrust between humans in the absence of effective political institutions.

There are some things that we never stop learning. The history of mankind is like a kind of permanent rebirth of ignorance. In general, it can be said that human societies learn little history, and that they learn little *from* history. And these key epistemological facts have *political* repercussions. Democracies are also systems based on constant forgetfulness; with regard to the question of religion, for example.

Religions and liberal democracies: a renewal of secularism?

Religions as cultural phenomena

Religions are cultural phenomena and can be studied as such. Many historical religions have disappeared and those that are hegemonic today began life as marginal sects. There have been and, there still are, thousands of gods and many religions in the world.

In practical terms, despite the advantages that religions appear to have for their believers, they have also been, and continue to be, one of the main sources of wars and suffering for humanity. Throughout history religions have shown themselves to be prone to acts of terror, dogmatism and contempt for pluralism and human dignity. Religions usually state that they know some kind of fundamental "truth" about the world, and sometimes attempt to impose this on others, but without freedom of religion and thought there is no liberal democracy.

In the majority of contemporary non-democratic societies, religions continue to be an obstacle to freedom, equality and pluralism. They have often shown a perverse side. Bertrand Russell (*In Praise of Idleness*) said the same with regard to Christianity:

> The Jews first invented the notion that only one religion could be true, but they had no wish to convert all the world to it, and therefore only prosecuted other Jews. The Christians, retaining the Judaic belief in a special revelation, added to it the Roman desire for worldwide dominion and the Greek

> taste for metaphysical subtleties. The combination produced the most fiercely persecuting religion that the world has yet known.
>
> (Russell 1935)

And Ernst Bloch (1980) also says it with irony: "the best thing about religion is that it makes for heretics".

Today we know that "sacred books" are usually a poor source of historical information, as they are full of origin myths, invented reconstructions, literary stories taken from other cultures, etc. However, there are two surprising aspects of the social reception of religions by *homo sapiens*: (1) the limited critical spirit in which the stories of one's own religious culture are received – many people believe them to be "historical", and (2) the relatively scant interest that their study awakes from historiographical, archaeological, philological, etc. perspectives among the population, or even among "enlightened" people. It would seem that any critical approach to religious texts must discriminate between historical events and invented stories. Thus, for example, the Bible recounts the story of a group of characters and events that cover a period from the middle Bronze Age – second millennium BC – until the end of the first millennium BC. Most texts, however, are rather recent (most of them date from the period of the Babylonian captivity and the subsequent return to Palestine (sixth to fifth centuries BC). But we would probably find that most Westerners believe that Moses, for example, really existed in the same way and with the same certainty as they believe that Julius Caesar or Alexander the Great were real historical figures.

Biblical historiography agrees on a number of things, although others are still the subject of scientific debate, as archaeological and philological tests, among others, have been inconclusive. There is broad agreement among specialists that some characters and events in the Bible are "invented history". For example, the existence of the patriarchs (Abraham, Isaac and Jacob) and the judges (Gideon, Samson, etc.); the 12 tribes of the Israelites, the story of Moses (one part is a popular tale similar to that of the Assyrians and Persians, and another a story of political leadership subsequent to the period of Babylonian captivity); the exodus from Egypt; the "conquest" of the "promised" land –extermination of imaginary peoples until there is no word about others that really existed in the area; Jericho was abandoned in biblical times and would continue to be so for some time afterwards, etc. A good deal of the biblical story has the structure of a "holy war" (loyalty to a single god would lead to victory over one's enemies and prosperity; misfortune is a punishment for lack of loyalty to this god). In short, the development of a critical culture with regard to the world's religions would help us to understand them better and disassociate them from their mythological side.

It has been empirically proven that people from the highest cultural levels of developed countries account for significantly fewer believers in specific religions when compared with the overall average of the population. However, as mentioned above, and in contrast to the "enlightened" opinion that religions would die out as science spread and countries developed, religions appear to be here to stay. Moreover, we also know that relations between hegemonic religions and individual liberties have historically been somewhat troubled. A quick look at the world today shows that in many places the dominant religions still constitute an ideology that has not been "politically civilized" with regard to respect for pluralism. A report of the US State Department (2010) submitted to Congress in compliance with the international law of religious freedom – which includes the right to defend agnostic and atheistic positions – analyses the state of religious freedom in 198 states. It includes up to five types of violation of this freedom: practices against the collective expression of religious beliefs; the freedom of expression of religious, agnostic or atheistic ideas; the right to change religion; the possession and distribution of religious texts (including books considered "sacred" by their respective believers); and religious education. The countries in which the situation is most serious are (in alphabetical order): Afghanistan, China, Egypt, Eritrea, Iran, Iraq, Myanmar, Nigeria, North Korea, Pakistan, Russia, Saudi Arabia, Sudan, Tajikistan, Turkmenistan, Uzbekistan, Venezuela, and Vietnam.

Liberal democracies and cultural freedom: the debate on multiculturalism

In the United Nations' Human Development Report on cultural freedom (2004), this is considered to be an essential value for the *democratic quality* of a society. It is a type of freedom that forms part of human rights and is decisive for individual development and people's self-esteem. The report suggests five courses of action: (1) multiculturalism: ensure the participation of marginalized cultural groups (electoral reforms, federalism with asymmetric features); (2) policies that ensure religious freedom (including festivals, customs relating to diet and dress, etc.); (3) policies of legal pluralism (a more controversial issue that would, in any case, involve respect for the limits mentioned above); (4) linguistic policies (some democratic states are still monolingual with regard to their institutions and symbols despite their internal multilingualism); and (5) socio-economic policies (minimum wages, education, health).

In general terms, there are two possible approaches to the issue of multiculturalism: (1) to treat it as a practical issue, whose objective is to avoid conflicts in the least traumatic and costly way possible (pragmatic attitude); and (2) to view it as a question of "justice", which requires correct solutions (moral attitude). Both attitudes tend to get mixed up in practical politics. The second attitude, moreover, has produced two contrasting visions: (a) to consider that the "private sphere" (e.g. religion) should be kept separate from the "public sphere" (French republican model), and (b) to accept any kind of privacy in the public sphere as long as human rights and democratic institutions are not questioned (Canadian multicultural model). The other cases would occupy intermediate positions between these two.

The recognition of multiculturalism appeared at the end of the 1960s, mainly in Canada and Australia. In Europe, it was adopted by the Swedish government at the end of the 1970s. Holland adopted it in its "minority policy". The United

Kingdom, a self-styled "multicultural country", has put more emphasis on the fight against discrimination than on the recognition of minority cultures. In Ontario (Canada) – in whose main city, Toronto, over 250 languages are spoken by a population (around 50 per cent) from over 160 countries – the use of the "sharia" law has even been debated (and rejected) as a possible "means of mediation" in family conflicts (marriages, custody of children, inheritances). And also France, with its republican and lay tradition, which rejects ostentatious religious and cultural symbols in the public sphere (e.g. the case of the use of certain items of clothing at school) has opened its doors to multiculturalism in a number of local policies.

One of the conclusions of the debate of recent years on multiculturalism is that cultural freedom is not ensured through the mere application of the civil, participatory and social rights enshrined in democratic constitutions. Until recently, to be in favour of multiculturalism used to be just another "progressive" position, something that did not require too much explanation (like being anti-war, an ecologist or pro-democracy). Nowadays, however, parties, trade unions, the media and opinion polls reflect more cautious positions. This change is in itself a symptom of the perception of the complexity of the issue. Simple positions do not usually fit very well with the growing pluralism of modern-day democracies.

Moreover, the academic world appears to have accepted that cultural problems cannot be reduced to "socioeconomic or social causes". It is true that the two spheres are interrelated, but they are different phenomena that refer to diverse values, objectives, institutions, practices and policies. It is also clear that many cultural identities have been marginalized in the past, and that states always impose their own national, cultural and linguistic features.

While the ethnic and religious composition of societies was highly homogeneous (even when there were internal differences of a national and linguistic nature) it was usually taken for granted that if immigrants arrived, they should "integrate", in the sense of "assimilate", into the cultural patterns of their adopted society. Over time, as the size of immigrant groups increased – something which has always been the case in the United States because of its role as an immigrant country – "integration" came to be understood with regard to the public sphere only, while in the private sphere a multiplicity of customs could be maintained, provided that they did not represent a distortion of democratic values and institutions.

However, Western societies – above all European ones – are nowadays facing something rather different with regard to transnational migrations: a re-politicization of the private sphere. The demand is to be present in the public sphere in a more permanent way, beginning with ways of dressing, food, school curricula and public holidays. It is no longer a case of "integrating" immigrants, but of achieving their "political accommodation" based on their specific cultural characteristics. Thus, it is possible to identify three historical phases in the way that democracies have tended to treat this issue: assimilation, integration and accommodation. The possibilities and consequences of moving from the second to the third phase are still unclear, above all when, in recent years, negative perceptions of multiculturalism have emerged: as a threat to democratic values or national identities; as a source of instability and insecurity; or as a kind of unsolvable conflict.

Behind these perceptions are, obviously, the attacks of 9/11 in New York (2001), 11 March in Madrid (2004) and 7 July in London (2005), as well as phenomena like the violent riots in Paris or the lack of prospects following the hopes awoken on an international scale by the "Arab Spring" (2012). And behind these perceptions is the rise of political parties that associate immigration with threats to "our way of life". Today "integration" is no longer a *magic word*, the very mention of which will ensure a solution to the issue – in the same way that the word "interculturalism" is losing its earlier magical quality. These are terms that have become polysemous – there are different ways to define them and to relate them to different moral and political values. Their practical consequences in the sphere of institutions and public policies have become much more complex and much more replete with contradictions than when they first appeared. Religions belong to this multicultural world. A general question is what kind of institutional model seems more adequate to the current multicultural conditions of liberal democracies.

A renewal of secularism?

Religions have been understood in different ways within democracies, from seeing them as a derivative of individual freedom to associating them with coercion against that freedom. Regardless of whether one believes that the religious dimension represents a valuable aspect of human life, or whether one thinks that it reflects an intellectual and moral immaturity on the part of believers, the fact is that religions are an important part of many people's lives. Nowadays, the pluralism of religious, agnostic and atheistic beliefs is one of the cornerstones of contemporary liberal democracies. Both religious beliefs and their denial are intellectual positions that deserve respect, but both positions must in turn respect the collective political values that we consider fundamental nowadays in liberal democracies: rights, freedoms, and respect for democratic rules, institutions and decision-making processes. This is easy to say, but it is a political institutionalization that has taken thousands of years to establish firmly.

In political terms, the religious wars that devastated Europe in the sixteenth and seventeeth centuries were one of the decisive factors that led to the subsequent establishment of liberal regimes which would make the separation of state and churches (at least to some extent) one of their organizational principles. Political liberalism resulted in the establishment of "civil" limits on Christian ecclesiastical authorities. This "great separation" between the political and religious spheres was quickly seen by Hobbes and the early liberals as essential to avoid the tendency towards "political redemption" of monotheistic religions, as well as being a necessary condition for human emancipation and critical thought (Lilla 2007). From the liberal revolutions onwards, something fundamental changed: the idea gained ground that believing or not believing in gods belonged to the private sphere, and not to the legitimation of political order. The separation of the spheres of religion and politics is one of the most crucial emancipative achievements of the modern age. However, the contextual conditions of current liberal democracies have become more culturally plural and complex than what was usually accepted a few decades ago.

Which specific models of religious pluralism are most in keeping with the values and practices of multicultural liberal democracies? There are several possible answers. On the one hand, there are those models that opt for clear separation between the public sphere and religious expressions. They think that the latter should be present in the private sphere, but not in the public sphere, which belongs to everyone. It is not permitted for a judge, a teacher, a policeman or even students, to display religious symbols. On the other hand, there are the models that allow the expression of beliefs as long as democratic rules are respected (albeit with exceptions).

Broadly speaking, I believe that an updated liberal-democratic secular model should be based on four basic principles: "separation" (of religious and state powers); the state's neutrality (governance); religious freedom; and respect/protection of religious and non-religious minorities. These four principles are interwoven. In current democracies, citizens who are believers in different religions live in close proximity to other citizens who are agnostics or atheists. However, instead of the binary public–private contrast, I think that it is better to distinguish between three spheres of action in the political life of a country: the public sphere, the social sphere and the private sphere. The reason for establishing this distinction is twofold. On the one hand, the public (state) and social spheres do not coincide and, on the other hand, religions have an inherent collective component (they are not only a "private" subject practiced at home or in churches).

Although the borders between these three spheres are porous, in the following pages I will defend the idea that no religion should be present in the public (state) sphere in a twenty-first century liberal democracy. Its place is in the private and social spheres. It is fundamental to continue to insist on the secular model (laicism) especially in contexts of "deep diversity". It has been empirically proven that the decisions of parliaments, governments or courts of law of almost all democracies still display historical habits and conceptual prejudices with regard to the historically dominant religion in each context. In most cases, this contradicts the constitutional precepts of laicism, neutrality and pluralism; conditions practical religious freedom and the protection of religious minorities, agnostics and atheists; and continues to confer an important political role on hegemonic churches. Liberal democracies, out of respect for their own normative principles, ought to be far more secular, even at the constitutional level, than they currently are, although this should not make them hostile to specific religions.

Besides these three spheres of action, I think it is advisable also to distinguish between two general approaches: the expression of beliefs in the private and social spheres and the institutional regulation of the public sphere. The four secular principles pointed out earlier demand a different kind of modulation once these three spheres of action and these two approaches have been taken into account. For example, in the public (state) sphere, neutrality is defined more by what one wishes to *actively* avoid than by the remnants of cultural inertia that a given society still displays. In institutions such as parliaments, governments, courts of law, city councils, hospitals, prisons or schools, which are paid for by everyone, there should be a scrupulous "neutral" respect for (religious and non-religious) pluralism, avoiding symbols or the inclusion of specific religions or atheistic doctrines in education curricula. "Neutrality", as a principle of governance, does not only imply avoiding a hierarchy of religious or atheistic perspectives, but also proactively avoiding them in institutions and public policies.

In fact, to establish the boundaries of neutrality is not a "neutral" subject. However, this is not a majority *democratic* question, nor a question of "customs" or historical culture, but a *liberal* question of the respect and protection of minorities and pluralism. In other words, I think that, generally speaking, what has sometimes been called "open secularism" should mainly be applied in the private and social spheres, whereas "strict secularism" should be applied in the *public* sphere (although some specific matters can be approached as a question of degree and may display specific gradients of limitations depending on the branch of government or the context – wearing religious symbols for some state employees (teachers) or wearing "radical" examples of them, like the burka or niqab, in the social sphere). So, unavoidably, some kinds of religious practices can legitimately be discriminated against in the public sphere of liberal democracies and this could even be the case for a small number of radical cases in the social sphere. In other words, even if we maintain a "weak" conception of the moral foundations of liberal democracies, "neutrality" is not synonymous with passive normative indifference or emptiness. Like other "universal" values, the "moral equality" of individuals is not an absolute value. In practice, it can clash with other "universal" values, such as equality of men and women, security, respect for human dignity, etc.

Broadly speaking, any philosophical attempt to establish the chances of a possible normative "overlapping consensus" between different religious and secular conceptions (Rawls 1995; Habermas 1994) is, in my view, no more than an academic exercise to ornament a theoretical impossibility that will never be able to completely replace pragmatic agreements of a *modus vivendi* type in the framework of pluralism and dissent in present-day democratic societies. Basically, the difference between liberal conceptions that favour "deliberative" consensuses – or those based on "dialogue" or on some kind of "public reason" – and liberal conceptions that are given to agonistic approaches, is how these two perspectives understand "politics".

If we take religious diversity seriously (Taylor 1992), including the agnostic and atheistic perspectives, consensual reconstructions of a Kantian nature will always be in danger of collapsing due to the realistic strength projected by the shadows of the perspectives put forward by natural sciences and by Hobbes, Hegel and Berlin. Consensus on concepts and values is different from consensus on reconstructions of what is reasonable in the public sphere. Consensus on values does not ensure consensus on conceptions of the public sphere. And both are different from consensus on interests and identities. Rationalistic and non-historical Western "humanism" – especially when it lacks scientific knowledge – falls easily in the traps of a bad or narrow anthropology. The most promising kinds of philosophies work on the same side as sciences, on the side of the will of knowledge and the best way of living (again, against ignorance, arbitrariness and superstition).

In fact, possible consensuses based on practical democratic deliberations are more suitable for establishing what is denied than what is affirmed. It is always easier to agree on the evil to be avoided than on the good to be attained. "Cooperation" or "consensuses", however much they are called "overlapping", not only have normative limits, but also epistemological ones. Pluralism of *values*, *objectives*, *identities* and *interests* will always be radical between humans in an "open society". I believe that, regarding this question, the possibilities of practical reason are intellectually more modest than traditional and some "deliberative" current political theories still claim. The result of deep dissent leads to consensuses of a more pragmatic nature (Requeio 2005).

In short, religious and cultural differences are here to stay (and grow) in modern-day democracies. A harmonious world, without antagonisms, as Isaiah Berlin (2001) said two centuries later, is not only impossible but simply inconceivable. Conflicts are inherent in human collectivities. Liberal governments should recognize that all political values will eventually clash, and that all conflicts require negotiation. And the classical Greeks maintained that there were only two ways to overcome the deficiencies of coexistence: *polis* and *paideia*. In other words, *institutional reforms* (which include socio-economic reforms and co-participation in policies of cultural accommodation), and *education* (to promote shared cultural norms of behaviour, based on respect for cultural dissent).

The growing cultural pluralism of contemporary societies coexists with the epistemological tendencies mentioned earlier, to construct *abstract*, *dichotomous* and *monist* conceptions. In our "Western" theories, the risks associated with the *fallacy of abstraction*, the *discontinuous mind* and *conceptual monism* always appear.

Kant (1786) astutely established, although ironically in a more Hegelian than Kantian sense, that the roots of progress stem from humans' natural inclination to want to be social without fully being able to do so. In other words, they stem from their *unsocial sociability*. Our pluralism of values, objectives, interests and identities is always changing, but always constitutes the horizon of our humanity. Humans sometimes desire consensus, but their nature desires other things. Thus, it is advisable to approach human progress from the perspective of the conflicting tendencies of our nature (not against them).

Human brains are well prepared for survival and reproduction. They are very good at emotional responses such as empathy, anger, revenge, shame or gratitude. However, the self-styled *sapiens* are primates that are very prone to deceiving themselves. Evolution has made us gullible. It is always difficult to introduce critical attitudes, as is seeing that scepticism, as Montaigne, Kant and Hegel used to say, is a necessary intermediate step to attaining knowledge. More than "social animals" we are "unsocially sociable" animals (Shakespeare showed this feature in a myriad of small mirrors).

In the political sphere, the crucial thing is to have liberal-democratic institutions capable of resolving conflicts of values, objectives, interests and identities peacefully. The principles of separation, neutrality, religious freedom, and the respect for and protection of minorities are the ones that need updating in contemporary democracies through the practical adjustments of institutions, rights and duties in the public, social and private spheres. I do not believe that it is necessary to talk about a "post-secular" model in contemporary democracies, but to readapt and take seriously the "secular" model that is fundamental for the liberal-democratic emancipation that modernity tried to establish through the "great separation" of the spheres of politics and religion. This occurred about three centuries ago, but we should continue to develop it.

References

Alexy, R. (1993) *A Theory of Constitutional Rights*. Oxford: Oxford University Press.

Alter, P. (1994) *Nationalism*. 2nd edn. London: Edward Arnold.

Andreescu, G. and Andreescu, L. (2011) 'Taking Back Lautsi: Towards a "Theory of Neutralisation"?', *Religion and Human Rights* 6: 207–212.

Arai-Takahashi, Y. (2002) *The Margin of Appreciation Doctrine and the Principle of Proportionality in the Jurisprudence of the ECHR*. Oxford: Intersetia.

Arendt, H. (1958) *The Human Condition*. Chicago: University of Chicago Press.

Audi, R. (1993) 'The Place of Religious Argument in a Free and Democratic Society', *San Diego Law Review* 30(4): 677–702.

Audi, R. (1997) 'Liberal Democracy and the Place of Religion in Politics', in Audi R. and Wolterstorff, N. *Religion in the Public Square*. London: Rowman & Littlefield Publishers, pp. 1–66.

Audi, R. (2000) *Religious Commitment and Secular Reason*. Cambridge: Cambridge University Press.

Audi, R. (2008) 'Rational Disagreement as a Challenge to Practical Ethics', in Smith, Q. (ed.), *Epistemology: New Essays*. Oxford: Oxford University Press, pp. 225–248.

Audi, R. (2011) *Democratic Authority and the Separation of Church and State*. Oxford: Oxford University Press.

Audi, R. and Wolterstorff, N. (1997) *Religion in the Public Square*. London: Rowman & Littlefield Publishers.

Bader, V. (2012) 'Post-secularism or Liberal-democratic Constitutionalism?', *Erasmus Law Review* 5(1): 5–26.

Barak, A. (2012) *Proportionality: Constitutional Rights and their Limitations*. Cambridge, MA: Cambridge University Press.

Barry, B. (2001) *Culture and Equality: An Egalitarian Critique of Multiculturalism*. Cambridge, MA: Harvard University Press.

Barry, B. (2002) *Culture and Equality: An Egalitarian Critique of Multiculturalism*. London: Blackwell.

Beck, U. (2010) *A God of One's Own: Religion's Capacity for Peace and Potential for Violence*. Cambridge: Polity Press.

Bell D. (2000) *East Meets West: Human Rights and Democracy in East Asia*. Princeton: Princeton University Press.

Berg, Th.C. (2010) 'What Same-Sex-Marriage and Religious-Liberty Claims Have in Common', *Northwestern Journal of Law & Social Policy* 5(2): 206–235.

Berger, P.L. (1967) *The Sacred Canopy: Elements of a Sociological Theory of Religion*. Garden City, NY: Doubleday.

Berger, P.L. (ed.) (1999). *The Desecularization of the World: Resurgent Religion and World Politics*. Grand Rapids: Wm. B. Eerdmans Publishing Co.

Berger, P.L. (ed) (2010) *Between Relativism and Fundamentalism: Religious Resources for a Middle Position*. Grand Rapids: Wm. B. Eerdmans Publishing Co.

Berger, P.L., Davie, G. and Fokas, E. (2008) *Religious America, Secular Europe? A theme and Variations*. Aldershot: Ashgate.

Berlin, Isaiah (1969) *Four Essays on Liberty*, Oxford: Oxford University Press.

Berlin, Isaiah (1998) *The Crooked Timber of Humanity*, Princeton, NJ: Princeton University Press.

Berlin, Isaiah (2001) 'My intellectual path', in *The Power of Ideas*. London: Pimlico.

Bernstein, R.J. (1992) *The New Constellation: Ethical-Political Horizons of Modernity/ Postmodernity*. Cambridge, MA: MIT Press.

Bernstein, R.J. (2008) 'The Uneasy Tensions of Immanence and Transcendence', *The International Journal of Politics, Culture, and Society* 21(1/4): 11–16.

Bertolino, R. (1990) 'Obiezione di coscienza', in *Enciclopedia Giuridica vol. XXI*. Roma: Istituto della Enciclopedia Italiana.

Bertolino, R. (1994) *L'obiezione di coscienza moderna. Per una fondazione costituzionale del diritto di obiezione*. Torino: Giappichelli.

Bhargava, R. (2006) 'Political Secularism', in Dryzek, J.S., Honig, B. and Philips, A. (eds), *The Oxford Handbook of Political Theory*. Oxford: Oxford University Press, pp. 637–655.

Bhargava, R. (2007) 'The Distinctiveness of Indian Secularism', in Srinivan, T.N. (ed.), *The Future of Secularism*. New Delhi: Oxford University Press, pp. 20–37.

Bloch, E. (1980) *Atheismus in Christentum*. Verlag: Suhrkamp Wissenschaft.

Bloch, M. (1989) *Feudal society*. 2nd edn. London: Routledge.

Bloom, A. (1987) *The Closing of the American Mind: How Higher Education has Failed Democracy and Impoverished the Souls of Today's Students*, New York: Simon & Schuster.

Bottici, Ch. and Challand, B. (2013) *Imagining Europe. Myth, Memory, and Identity*. Cambridge: Cambridge University Press.

Bouchard, G. and Taylor, Ch. (2008) *Building the Future. A Time for Reconciliation*. Abridged Report. Quebec City: Commission on Accommodation Practices Related to Cultural Differences, Bibliothèque et Archives Nationales du Québec.

Bradatan, C. and Ungureanu, C. (eds) (2014) *Religion in Contemporary European Cinema: the Postnational Constellation*. London: Routledge.

Bradatan, C. and Ungureanu, C., (eds) (2014) *Religion in Contemporary European Cinema: the Postnational Constellation*. London: Routledge.

Brauch, J. (2005) 'The Margin of Appreciation and the Jurisprudence of the European Court of Human Rights: Threat to the Rule of Law', *Columbia Journal of European Law* 11: 113–150.

Brems, E. (2009) 'Human Rights: Minimum and Maximum Perspectives', *Human Rights Law Review* 9(3): 349–372.

Bruce, S. (2002) *God is Dead: Secularization in the West*. Oxford: Blackwell.

Buddhist Scriptures (1959) Translated and edited by Edward Conze, London: Penguin Classics.

Burns, J.H. (ed.) (1988) *The Cambridge History of Medieval Political Thought. Vol. 1: c.350–c.1450*. Cambridge: Cambridge University Press.

Butler, J., Habermas, J., Taylor, C. and West, C. (2011) 'Concluding Discussion', in Mendieta, E. and Van Antwerpen, J. (eds), *The Power of Religion in the Public Sphere*. New York: Columbia University Press.

Calhoun, C., Juergensmeyer, M. and Van Antwerpen, J. (eds) (2011) *Rethinking Secularism*. Oxford: Oxford University Press.

Cappuccio, L. and Gamper, D. (2010a) 'La funzione educativa dello Stato e la copertura costituzionale dell'obiezione di coscienza: il caso dell'Educazione alla cittadinanza nell'ordinamento spagnolo', *Diritto Pubblico Comparato ed Europeo* I: 107–133.

Cappuccio, L. and Gamper, D. (2010b) 'L'educazione alla cittadinanza nell'esperienza spagnola: insegnamento della Costituzione o ateismo di Stato?', *Quaderni di Diritto e Politica Ecclesiastica* XIX 1: 147–158.

Caputo, J. (2001) *On Religion*. London: Routledge.

Cartabia, M. (2011) 'In tema di "nuovi" diritti', in *Studi in onore di Franco Modugno*. Napoli: Editoriale Scientifica, pp. 625–643.

Casanova, J. (1994) *Public Religions in the Modern World*. Chicago and London: The University of Chicago Press.

Casanova, J. (2006) 'Religion, European secular identities, and European integration', in Byrnes T. and Katzenstein, P. (eds), *Religion in an Expanding Europe*. Cambridge: Cambridge University Press, pp. 65–92.

Casanova, J. (2009) 'Immigration and the New Religious Pluralism: A European Union –United States Comparison', in Levey, G.B. and Modood, T. (eds), *Secularism, Religion and Multicultural Citizenship*. Cambridge: Cambridge University Press, pp. 139–163.

Clanton, J.C. (2008) *Religion and Democratic Citizenship: Inquiry and Conviction in the American Public Square*. Lanham: Lexington Books.

Close, C.W. (2009) *The Negotiated Reformation: Imperial Cities and the Politics of Urban Reform, 1525–1550*. Cambridge: Cambridge University Press.

Cohen, C. (1968) Conscientious Objection', *Ethics* 78(4): 269–279.

Cohen, J. (1996) 'Procedure and Substance in Deliberative Democracy', in Benhabib, S. (ed.), *Democracy and Difference: Changing Boundaries of the Political*. Princeton: Princeton University Press, pp. 95–119.

Cooke, M. (2006) 'Salvaging and Secularizing the Semantic Contents of Religion: The limitations of Habermas's Postmetaphysical Proposal', *International Journal for Philosophy of Religion* 60(1/3): 187–207.

Cooke, M. (2007) 'A Secular State for a Postsecular Society? Postmetaphysical Political Theory and the Place of Religion', *Constellations* 14(2): 224–238.

Crouch, C. (2004) *Post-Democracy*. New York: Wiley.

Danchin, P.G. (2008a) 'The Emergence and Structure of Religious Freedom in International Law Reconsidered', *Journal of Law and Religion*, 23: 455–534.

Danchin, P.G. (2008b) 'Suspect Symbols: Value Pluralism as a Theory of Religious Freedom in International Law', *Yale Journal of International Law* 33(1): 1–61.

Davie, G. (2000) *Religion in Modern Europe. A Memory Mutates*. Oxford: Oxford University Press.

Dawkins, R. (2011) 'The tyranny of the discontinous mind', *New Statesman*, Christmas issue.

Delumeau, J. (1991) *Naissance et affirmation de la Réforme*. Paris: PUF.

De Maglie, C. (2010) *I reati culturalmente motivati. Ideologie e modelli penali*. Pisa: Edizioni ETS.

Dennett, D. (2010) *Science and Religion*. Oxford: Oxford University Press.

De Roover, J., Claerhout, S. and Balagangadhara, S.N. (2011) 'Liberal Political Theory and the Cultural Migration of ideas: The Case of Secularism in India', *Political Theory* 39(5): 571–599.

Derrida, J. (2002) *Acts of Religion*. New York and London: Routledge.

Dickson, Ch.W. (2012) 'Inseverability, Religious Exemptions, and New York's Same-Sex Marriage Law', *Cornell Law Review* 98: 181–208.

Dworkin, R. (2013) *Religion without God*. Harvard: Harvard University Press.

Dzehtsiarou, K. (2011) 'European Consensus and the Evolutive Interpretation of the European Convention on Human Rights', *German Law Journal* 12(10): 1730–1745.

Eberle, C. (2002) *Religious Conviction in Liberal Politics*. Cambridge: Cambridge University Press.

Eisenberg, A. (2010) *Reasons of identity. A Normative Guide to the Political and Legal Assessment of Identity Claims*. Oxford: Oxford University Press.

Farr, T. (2008) *World of Faith and Freedom*. Oxford: Oxford University Press.

Feldblum, Ch.R. (2006) 'Moral Conflict and Liberty: Gay Rights and Religion', *Brooklyn Law Review* 72: 61–123.

Ferrara, A. (2009) 'The Separation of Religion and Politics in a Post-secular Society', *Philosophy Social Criticism* 35(1–2): 77–91.

Ferrari, S. (1997) 'The New Wine and the Old Cask. Tolerance, Religion and Law in Contemporary Europe', *Ratio Juris* 10(1): 75–89.

Ferry, J.-M. (2005) *Europe, la voie kantienne*. Paris: Éditions du Cerf.

Ferry, J.-M. (2010a) *La religion reflexive*. Paris: Éditions du Cerf.

Ferry, J.-M. (2010b) *La république crépuscolaire*. Paris: Éditions du Cerf.

Flynn, T. (2010) 'Clarion Call or False Alarm: Why Proposed Exemptions to Equal Marriage Statutes Returns Us to a Religious Understanding of the Public Marketplace', *Northwestern Journal of Law & Social Policy* 5(2): 236–259.

Fraser, N. (1992) 'Rethinking the Public Sphere: A Contribution to the Critique of Actually Existing Democracy', in Calhoun, C.J. (ed.), *Habermas and the Public Sphere*. Cambridge MA: MIT Press, pp. 109–142.

Freeman, S. (2007) *Justice and the Social Contract*. Oxford: Oxford University Press.

Gallagher, M. (2010) 'Why Accommodate? Reflections on the Gay Marriage Culture Wars', *Northwestern Journal of Law & Social Policy* 5(2): 260–273.

Garvey, J.H. (2000) *What are Freedoms for?* Cambridge MA: Harvard University Press.

Gauchet, M. (1985) *The Disenchantment of the World*. Princeton, New Jersey: Princeton University Press.

Gaus, G. (1996) *Justificatory Liberalism*. Oxford: Oxford University Press.

Gerards, J. (2011) 'Pluralism, Deference and the Margin of Appreciation Doctrine', *European Law Journal* 17(1): 80–120.

Glendon, M.A. (1991) *Rights Talk. The Impoverishment of Political Discourse*. New York: The Free Press.

González Beilfuss, M. (2003) *El principio de proporcionalidad en la jurisprudencia del Tribunal Constitucional español*. Madrid: Aranzadi.

Gorski, P.S., Kim, D.K., Torpey, J. and Van Antwerpen, J. (eds) (2012) *The Postsecular in Question*. New York: New York University Press.

Gray, J. (1995) *Enlightenment's Wake: Politics and Culture at the Close of the Modern Age*. London: Routledge.

Gray, J. (2000) *Two Faces of Liberalism*. London: Polity Press.

Greenawalt, K. (1988) *Religious Convictions and Political Choice*. Oxford: Oxford University Press.

Greenawalt, K. (1995) *Private Consciences and Public Reasons*. Oxford: Oxford University Press.

Greenawalt, K. (2007) 'Moral and Religious Convictions as Categories for Special Treatment: The Exemption Strategy', *William and Mary Law Review* 48: 1605–1642.

Greenfeld, Liah (1992) *Nationalism: Five Roads to Modernity*, Cambridge, MA: Harvard University Press.

Greer, S. (2003) 'Constitutionalizing Adjudication under the European Convention on Human Rights', *Oxford Journal of Legal Studies* 23(3): 405–433.

Habermas, J. (1992) *Postmetaphysical Thinking*. Cambridge, MA: MIT Press.

Habermas, J. (1994) 'Struggles for Recognition in the Democratic Constitutional State', in Taylor, Ch. (ed.). *Multiculturalism: Examining the Politics of Recognition*. Princeton NJ, Princeton University Press.

Habermas, J. (2005) *Zwischen Naturalismus und Religion*. Frankfurt: Suhrkamp.

Habermas, J. (2006a) 'Pre-political Foundations of the Democratic Constitutional State', in Habermas, J. and Ratzinger, J. *The Dialectics of Secularization. On Reason and Religion*. San Francisco: Ignatius Press.

Habermas, J. (2006b) 'Religion in the Public Sphere', *European Journal of Philosophy* 14(1): 1–25.

Habermas, J. (2008a) *Between Naturalism and Religion*. Cambridge: Polity Press.

Habermas, J. (2008b) 'Notes on a post-secular society', *Signandsight.com. Let's Talk to Europe*, 18 June. Available at: www.signandsight.com/features/1714.html (accessed 24 April 2013).

Habermas, J. (2010) *An Awareness of What is Missing. Faith and Reason in a Post-Secular Age*. Cambridge: Polity Press.

Habermas, J. (2011) '"The political". The rational meaning of a questionable inheritance of political theology', in Butler, J., Mendieta, E. and Van Antwerpen, J. (eds), *The Power of Religion in the Public Sphere*. New York: Columbia University Press.

Habermas, J. and Taylor, Ch. (2011) 'Dialogue', in Mendieta E. and Van Antwerpen J. eds. *The Power of Religion in the Public Sphere*. New York: Columbia University Press, pp. 56–78.

Herz, J.H. (1957) 'The Rise and Demise of the Territorial State', *World Politics* 9(4): 473–493. Available at: http://blogs.ssrc.org/tif/2008/01/29/inclusion-and-accountability-in-the-public-sphere/ (accessed June 2013).

Huntington, S.P. (1991) 'Democracy's Third Wave', *Journal of Democracy* 2(2): 12–34.

Hutchinson, M. (1999) 'The Margin of Appreciation and the Jurisprudence of the European Court of Human Rights', *International and Comparative Law Quarterly* 48(3): 638–650.

Kant, I. (1786) *Conjectures on the Beginning of Human History* (several editions).

Kant, I. (2001) *Religion and Rational Theology*. Trans. and edited by Allen W. Wood and George di Giovanni (called *Theology*). New York: Cambridge University Press.

Klatt, M. and Meister, M. (2012) *The Constitutional Structure of Proportionality*. Oxford: Oxford University Press.

Kratochvíl, J. (2011) 'The Inflation of the Margin of Appreciation by the European Court of Humans Rights', *Netherlands Quarterly of Human Rights* 29(3): 324–357.

Krisch, N. (2010) *Beyond Constitutionalism. The Pluralist Structure of Postnational Law*. Oxford: Oxford University Press.

Kumm, M. (2007) 'What Do You Have in Virtue of Having a Constitutional Right? On the Place and Limits of the Proportionality Requirement', *Public Law & Legal Theory Research Papers Series* 6–41. New York University School of Law, pp. 1–46.

Kymlicka, W. (1995) *Multicultural Citizenship: A Liberal Theory of Minority Rights*. Oxford: Oxford University Press.

Laborde, C. (2008) *Critical Republicanism. The Hijab Controversy and Political Philosophy*. Oxford: Oxford University Press.

Laborde, C. (2011) 'Political Liberalism and Religion: On Separation and Establishment', *The Journal of Political Philosophy*, 21(1): 67–86.

Laborde, C. (2012) 'State Paternalism and Religious Dress Code', *International Journal of Constitutional Law* 10(2): 398–410.

Laborde, C. (2014) 'Equal Liberty, Non-Establishment and Religious Freedom, in Requejo, F. and Ungureanu, C. (eds), *Democracy, Law and Religious Pluralism in Europe*, London and New York: Routledge, Chapter 2.

Lafont, C. (2007) 'Religion in the Public Sphere. Remarks on Habermas's Conception of Public Deliberation in Post-secular Societies', *Constellations* 14(2): 239–259.

Lafont, C. (2008) 'Inclusion and Accountability in the Public Sphere', in *The Immanent Frame. Secularism, religion, and the public sphere*. Available at: http://blogs.ssrc.org/tif/2008/01/29/inclusion-and-accountability-in-the-public-sphere/ (accessed 9 May 2014).

Lafont, C. (2009) 'Religion and the Public Sphere: What are the Deliberative Obligations of Democratic Citizenship?', *Philosophy & Social Criticism* 35(1–2): 127–150.

Lafont, C. (2014) 'Religious Pluralism in a Deliberative Democracy', in Requejo, F. and Ungureanu, C. (eds), *Democracy, Law and Religious Pluralism in Europe*, London and New York: Routledge, Chapter 3.

Larkins, J. (2010) *From Hierarchy to Anarchy: Territory and Politics before Westphalia*. London: Palgrave Macmillan.

Legg, A. (2012) *The Margin of Appreciation in International Human Rights Law: Deference and Proportionality*. Oxford: Oxford University Press.

Letsas, G. (2004) 'The Truth in Autonomous Concepts: How To Interpret the ECHR', *European Journal of International Law* 15(2): 279–305.

Letsas, G. (2006) 'Two Concepts of the Margin of Appreciation', *Oxford Journal of Legal Studies* 26(4): 705–732.

Lilla, M. (2007) *The Stillborn God: Religion, Politics and the Modern West*. NewYork: Knopf.

Lingua, G. (2012) *Il principio ricostruttivo. Comunicazione ed etica nel pensierio di Jean-Marc Ferry*. Pisa: Edizioni ETS.

López-Sidro, Á. (2009) 'La objeción de conciencia de los jueces a los matrimonios entre personas del mismo sexo en la doctrina del Tribunal Supremo', *Revista General de Derecho Canónico y Derecho Eclesiástico del Estado* 21: 1–18.

Loughlin, J., Allott, P. and Crellin, R. (2012) *The UK Government's 'Big Society' Programme and Catholic Social Teaching*. Cheltenham: Matthew James Publishing Ltd.

Lukes, S. (2005) *Power: a Radical View*. 2nd edn. New York: Palgrave Macmillan.

Luther, Martin ([1517] 1957) 'Luther's Ninety-Five Theses', in *Luther's Works* (Book 31), C.M. Jacobs (tr.), Fortress Press.

McCarthy, Th. (1995) 'Enlightenment and the Idea of Public Reason', *European Journal of Philosophy* 3(3): 242–256.

MacDougall, B., Bonthuys, E., Norrie, K. and Van den Brink, M. (2012) 'Conscientious Objection to Creating Same-Sex Unions: An International Analysis', *Canadian Journal of Human Rights* 1(1): 127–164.

Macioce, F. (2006) *PACS. Perché il diritto deve dire no*. Milano: San Paolo.

Macioce, F. (2011) 'L'objection de conscience dans la post-modernité', *Stato, Chiese e pluralismo confessionale*. Available at: www.statoechiese.it (accessed 5 May 2014).

Maclure, J. and Taylor, C. (2011) *Secularism and Freedom of Conscience*. Cambridge, MA: Harvard University Press.

McGoldrick, D. (2011) 'Religion in the European Public Square and in European Public Life-Crucifixes in the Classroom?', *Human Rights Law Review* 11(3): 451–502.

McHarg, A. (1999) 'Reconciling Human Rights and the Public Interest: Conceptual Problems and Doctrinal Uncertainty in the Jurisprudence of the European Court of Human Rights', *The Modern Law Review* 62: 671–696.

McNeill, J.T. (ed.) (1960) *Calvin: institutes of the Christian religion (vol. 1)*, F.L. Battles (tr.), Philadelphia, PA: The library of Christian classics. Available at: www.ccel.org/ccel/calvin/institutes (Accessed 12 May 2014).

Mahoney, P. (1998) 'Marvellous Richness of Diversity or Invidious Cultural Relativism?', *Human Rights Law Journal* 19(1): 1–6.

Mancini, S. (2010) 'The Crucifix Rage: Supranational Constitutionalism Bumps Against the Counter-Majoritarian Difficulty', *European Constitutional Law Review* 6: 6–27.

Martin, D. (1978) *A General Theory of Secularization*. Oxford: Blackwell.

Martin, D. (2005) *On Secularization: Towards a Revised General Theory*. Farnham: Ashgate.

Martínez-Torrón, J. (2003) 'Los límites de la libertad de religión y de creencia en el Convenio Europeo de Derechos Humanos', *RGDCDEE* 2: 1–46.

Martínez-Torrón, J. (2012) 'The (Un)protection of Individual Religious Identity in the Strasbourg Case Law', *Oxford Journal of Law and Religion* 1(2): 365–385.

Mawhinney, A. (2013) "Religious Accommodation and the Changing Nature of the Right to Freedom of Thought, Conscience and Religion in Human Rights Law', Unpuplished manuscript.

Mendieta, E. and Van Antwerpen, J. (2011) 'Introduction', in *The Power of Religion in the Public Sphere*, New York: Columbia University Press.

Metz, J.B. (1998) *A Passion for God: The Mystical-Political Dimension of Christianity*. NY: Paulist Press.

Metz, J.B. and Moltmann, J. (1995) *Faith and the Future: Essays on Theology, Solidarity, and Modernity*. Maryknoll, NY: Orbis Books.

Micklethwait, J. and Wooldridge, A. (2009) *God is Back: How the Global Rise of Faith is Changing the World*. London: Penguin.

Milbank, John. (1990) *Theology and Social Theory: Beyond Secular Reason*. Oxford: Basil Blackwell.

Modood, T. (2007) *Multiculturalism: A Civic Idea*. Cambridge: Polity Press.

More, Sir Thomas ([1516] 1904) *Utopia*. John Churton Collins (ed.), Oxford: Clarendon Press.

Nagel, Th. (2009) *Secular Philosophy and the Religious Temperament: Essays 2002–2008*. Oxford: Oxford University Press.

Nagel, Th. (2012) *Mind and Cosmos: Why the Materialist Neo-Darwinian Conception of Nature is Almost Certainly False*. Oxford: Oxford University Press.

Nandy, A. (1985) 'An Antisecularist Manifesto', *Seminar* 314(October): 22–25.

Navarro-Valls, R. (2005) 'La objeción de conciencia a los matrimonios entre personas del mismo sexo', *Revista General de Derecho Canónico y Derecho Eclesiástico del Estado* 9: 1–27.

Navarro-Valls, R. and Martínez-Torrón, J. (2012) *Conflictos entre conciencia y ley. Las objeciones de conciencia*. Madrid: Iustel.

NeJaime, D. (2012) 'Marriage Inequality: Same-Sex Relationships, Religious Exemptions, and the Production of Sexual Orientation Discrimination', *California Law Review* 100: 1169–1238.

Nieuwenhuis, A. (2007) 'The Concept of Pluralism in the Case-Law of the European Court of Human Rights', *European Constitutional Law Review* 3: 367–384.

Norris, P. and Inglehart, R. (2004) *Sacred and Secular: Religion and Politics Worldwide*. Cambridge: Cambridge University Press.

Nussbaum, M. (2008) *Liberty of Conscience. In Defense of America's Tradition of Religious Equality*. New York: Basic Books.

Nussbaum, M. (2013) *The New Religious Intolerance. Overcoming the Politics of Fear in an Anxious Age*. MA: Harvard University Press.

Nynäs, P., Lassander, M. and Utriainen, T. (eds) (2012) *Post-secular Society*. New Brunswick, NJ: Transaction Publishers.

Ozment, S. (1980) *The Age of Reform: An Intellectual and Religious History of Late Medieval and Reformation Europe*. New Haven and London: Yale University Press.

Panara, C. (2011) 'Another Defeat for the Principle of Secularism: Recent Developments on the Display of the Crucifix in Italian Courtrooms', *Religion and Human Rights* 6(3): 259–265.

Parkinson, P. (2011) 'Accommodating Religious Belief in a Secular Age: The Issue of Conscientious Objection in the Workplace', *UNSW Law Journal* 34(1): 281–299.

Polanyi, K. [1944] (2001) *The Great Transformation: The Political and Economic Origins of Our Time*. 2nd edn. Boston, MA: Beacon Press.

Porter, J.M. (ed.) (1974) *Luther – Selected Political Writings*. Lanham, MD: University Press of America.

Putnam, H. (2002) 'Norms/Values', in *The Collapse of the Fact/Value Dichotomy and Other Essays*. MA: Harvard University Press, pp. 111–135.

Rawls, J. (1971) *A Theory of Justice*. Cambridge, MA: Belknap Press of Harvard University Press.

Rawls, J. (1985) 'Justice as Fairness: Political not Metaphysical', *Philosophy & Public Affairs* 14(3): 223–251.

Rawls, J. (1993) *Political Liberalism*. Cambridge, MA: Harvard University Press.

Rawls, J. (1995) 'Reply to Habermas', *Journal of Philosophy*, 92(3): 132–180.

Rawls, J. (1996) 'Introduction to the paperback edition', *Political Liberalism*. Cambridge, MA: Harvard University Press, pp. xxxvii–lxii.

Rawls, J. (1997) 'The Idea of Public Reason Revisited', in Rawls, J. *The Law of Peoples*. Cambridge, MA: Harvard University Press, pp. 129–180. Also published in: *The University of Chicago Law Review* 64(3): 765–807.

Rawls, J. (1999) *The Law of Peoples*. Cambridge, MA: Harvard University Press.

Rawls, J. (2005) *Political Liberalism: Expanded Edition*. New York: Columbia University Press.

Raz, J. (1986) *The Morality of Freedom*. Oxford: Oxford University Press.

Renteln, A.D. (2004) *Cultural defence*. Oxford: Oxford University Press.

Requejo, F. (1991) *Teoría Crítica y Estado Social. Neokantismo y Socialdemocracia en J. Habermas*. Barcelona: Anthropos.

Requejo, F. (2005) Multinational Federalism and Value Pluralism. London–New York: Routledge.

Rodotà, S. (1993) 'Problemi dell'obiezione di coscienza', *Quaderni di diritto e politica ecclesiastica* 1: 55–72.

Rorty, R. (2003) 'Religion in the Public Square: A Reconsideration', *Journal of Religious Ethics* 31(1): 141–149.

Ruiz Miguel, A. (2010) 'Educación para la ciudadanía: entre la neutralidad estatal y la objeción de conciencia', *Anuario de filosofía del derecho* 26: 107–146.

Russell, B. (1935) *In Praise of Idleness*. New York: W.W.Norton & Company.

Sajó, A. (2008) 'Preliminaries to a Concept of Constitutional Secularism', *ICON* 6 (3–4): 624–629.

Sajó, A. (2009) 'The Crisis that was not There: Notes on a Reply', *ICON* 7(3): 515–528.

Salvatore, A. (2010) *The Public Sphere: Liberal Modernity, Catholicism, Islam*. New York: Palgrave Macmillan.
Sandel, M.J. (1989) 'Moral Argument and Liberal Toleration: Abortion and Homosexuality', *California Law Review* 77(3): 521–538.
Sandel, J.M. (1998) *Democracy's Discontent: America in Search of a Public Philosophy*. Cambridge, Massachusetts: Belknap Press of the Harvard University Press.
Sandel, M.J. (2005) *Public Philosophy*. Cambridge, MA: Harvard University Press.
Schwartzman, M. (2004) 'The Completeness of Public Reason', *Politics, Philosophy and Economics* 3(2): 191–220.
Sen, A. (2005) *The Argumentative Indian. Writings on Indian Culture, History and Identity*. UK: Penguin Books.
Skinner, Q. (1978) *The Foundations of Modern Political Thought. Vol. 1. The Renaissance–v. 2. The Age of Reformation*. Cambridge: Cambridge University Press.
Smith, A.D. (1998) *Nationalism and Modernism*. London: Routledge.
Smith, A.D. (2010) *Nationalism: Theory, Ideology, History*. 2nd edn. Cambridge: Polity Press.
Smith, D. (2010) 'Bruno Dumont, "Hadewijch"' *Filmmaker*. Available at: www.filmmakermagazine.com/news/2010/12/bruno-dumont-hadewijch/. (accessed 9 May 2013).
Smith, N.H. and Laitinen, A. (2009) 'Taylor on Solidarity', *Thesis Eleven* 99: 48–70.
Solar, J.I. (2009) 'Cautelas y excesos en el tratamiento del factor religioso en la jurisprudencia del Tribunal Europeo de Derechos Humanos', *Derechos y libertades* 20: 117–161.
Somerville, C.J. (1998) 'Secular Society Religious Population: Our Tacit Rules for Using the Term Secularization', *Journal for the Scientific Study of Religion* 37(2): 249–253.
Spielmann, D. (2012) 'Allowing the Right Margin the European Court of Human Rights and the National Margin of Appreciation Doctrine: Waiver or Subsidiarity of European Review?', CELS Working Paper Series, February. Cambridge University, Faculty of Law, pp. 1–30.
Spruyt, H. (1994) *The Sovereign State and its Competitors: An Analysis of Systems Change*. Princeton: Princeton University Press.
Stepan, A. (2005) 'Religion, Democracy and the "Twin Tolerations"', in Diamond, L., Platter, M.F. and Costopoulos, Philip J. (eds) *World Religions and Democracy*. Baltimore: The Johns Hopkins University Press, pp. 3–26.
Stern, M. D. (2010) 'Liberty v. Equality; Equality v. Liberty', *Northwestern Journal of Law & Social Policy* 5(2): 307–317.
Stout, J. (2003) *Democracy and Tradition*. Princeton: Princeton University Press.
Stychin, C.F. (2009) 'Faith in the Future: Sexuality, Religion and the Public Sphere', *Oxford Journal of Legal Studies* 29(4): 729–755.
Szakolczai, A. (2013) *Comedy and the Public Sphere*. New York and London: Routledge.
Talisse, R. (2009) *Democracy and Moral Conflict*. Cambridge: Cambridge University Press.
Taylor, Ch. (1985) 'Interpretation and the Sciences of Man', in *Philosophical Papers: Volume 2, Philosophy and the Human Sciences*. Cambridge: Cambridge University Press.
Taylor, Ch. (1988) 'Le juste et le bien', *Revue de métaphysique et de morale* 93(1): 33–56.
Taylor, Ch. (1989a) *Sources of the Self: The Making of the Modern Identity*. Cambridge, MA: Harvard University Press.
Taylor, Ch. (1989b) 'Cross-purpose: The Liberal-Communitarian Debate', in Rosenblum,

N.L. (ed.), *Liberalism and the Moral Life*. Cambridge, MA: Harvard University Press. Reprinted in Taylor, C. (1995) *Philosophical Arguments*. Cambridge, MA: Harvard University Press.

Taylor, Ch. (1991) 'Comprendre la culture politique', in Hudon R. and Pelletier, R. (eds), *L'engagement intellectuel: mélanges en l'honneur de Léon Dion*. Québec: Les Presses de l'Université Laval.

Taylor, Ch. (1992a) 'Quel principe d'identité collective?', in Lenoble, J. and Dewandre, N. (eds), *L'Europe au soir du siècle: Identité et démocrate*. Paris: Les Éditions Esprit.

Taylor, Ch. (1992b) *Multiculturalism. Examining the Politics of Recognition*. Princeton, NJ: Princeton University Press.

Taylor, Ch. (1998) 'Modes of Secularism', in Bhargava, R. (ed.), *Secularism and its Critics*. Delhi: Oxford University Press.

Taylor, Ch. (1999a) 'A Catholic Modernity?', in Heft, J.L. (ed.), *A Catholic Modernity? Charles Taylor's Marianist Award Lecture*. Oxford: Oxford University Press.

Taylor, Ch. (1999b) 'Comment on Jürgen Habermas. From Kant to Hegel and Back Again', *European Journal of Philosophy* 7(2): 158–163.

Taylor, Ch. (2002a) 'Democracy, Inclusive and Exclusive', in Madsen, R., Sullivan, R., Swidler, W. and Tipson, S.M. (eds), *Meaning and Modernity. Religion, Polity, and Self*. Berkeley, CA: University of California Press.

Taylor, Ch. (2002b) 'Gadamer on the Human Sciences', in Dostal, R.J. (ed.) *The Cambridge Companion to Gadamer*. Cambridge, UK: Cambridge University Press.

Taylor, Ch. (2002c) *Varieties of Religion Today: William James Revisited*. Cambridge, MA: Harvard University Press.

Taylor, Ch. (2004) 'Notes on the Sources of Violence: Perennial and Modern', in Heft, J.L. (ed.), *Beyond Violence. Religious Sources of Social Transformation in Judaism, Christianity, and Islam*. New York: Fordham University Press.

Taylor, Ch. (2005) 'The Immanent Counter-enlightenment: Christianity and morality', *South African Journal of Philosophy* 24(3): 224–239.

Taylor, Ch. (2006) 'Religious mobilizations', *Public Culture* 18(2): 281–300.

Taylor, Ch. (2007a) *A Secular Age*. Boston, MA: Harvard University Press.

Taylor, Ch. (2007b) 'Cultures of Democracy and Citizen Efficacy', *Public Culture* 19(1): 117–150.

Taylor, Ch. (2007c) 'Several Reflections on the Theme of Solidarity', *Thinking in Values – The Tischner Institute Journal of Philosophy* (I): 68–77.

Taylor, Ch. (2008) 'Charles Taylor interviewed, by Ben Rogers', *Prospect Magazine* 143, 29 February. Available at: www.prospectmagazine.co.uk/issue/143/ (accessed 11 November 2013).

Taylor, Ch. (2009) 'John Main and the Changing Religious Consciousness of Our Time', in Freeman, L. and Reynolds, S. (eds), *John Main: The Expanding Vision*. Norwich: Canterbury Press.

Taylor, Ch. (2010a) 'The Meaning of Secularism', *The Hedgehog Review* 12(3): 23–34.

Taylor, Ch. (2010b) 'Solidarity in a Pluralist Age', *Project Syndicate*, 27 September. Available at: www.project-syndicate.org/commentary/solidarity-in-a-pluralist-age (accessed 11 November 2013).

Taylor, Ch. (2010c) 'Afterword: apologia pro libro suo', in Warner, M., Van Antwerpen, J. and Calhoun, C. (eds), *Varieties of Secularism in a Secular Age*. Cambridge, MA: Harvard University Press.

Taylor, Ch. (2011a) 'Religion is Not the Problem. Secularism and Democracy'. *Commonweal* 138(4): 17–21.

Taylor, Ch. (2011b) 'Recovering the Sacred', *Inquiry* 54(2): 113–125.

Taylor, Ch. (2011c) 'Why We Need a Radical Redefinition of Secularism', in Butler, J. Habermas, J., Taylor, C. and West, C. (eds), *The Power of Religion in the Public Sphere*. New York: Columbia University Press.

Taylor, Ch. (2011d) 'Disenchantment–Reenchantment', in Levine, G.L. (ed.), *The Joy of Secularism: 11 Essays for How We Live Now*. Princeton, NJ: Princeton University Press.

Taylor, Ch. (2012) 'Interculturalism Or multiculturalism?', *Philosophy & Social Criticism* 38(4–5): 413–423.

Toft, M., Philpott, D. and Samuel Shah, T. (2011) *God's Century: Resurgent Religion and Global Politics*. New York and London: W.W. Norton.

Troeltsch, E. (1931) *The Social Teaching of the Christian Churches*. Vol. II. London: Allen & Unwin.

Ungureanu, C. (2012) 'Europe and Religion: An Ambivalent Nexus', in Zucca, L. and Ungureanu, C. (eds), *Law, State and Religion in the New Europe*. Cambridge: Cambridge University Press, pp. 307–333.

Ungureanu, C. (2014) 'Dworkin's Last Word: Religion without God', in *Journal for the Study of Relisions and Ideologies*, 13(38): 220–228.

United Nations (2004) *Human Development Report on Cultural freedom*. New York: United Nations.

Weber, M. (2002) (first published in German in 1905) *The Protestant Ethic and the Spirit of Capitalism*. 3rd edn. Oxford: Blackwell.

Weithman, P.J. (2001) 'Religious Reasons and the Duties of Membership', *Wake Forest Law Review* 36: 511–534.

Weithman, P.J. (2002) *Religion and the Obligations of Citizenship*. Cambridge: Cambridge University Press.

Widiss, D.A., Rosenblatt, E. and NeJaime, D. (2007) 'Exposing Sex Stereotypes in Recent Same-Sex Marriage Jurisprudence', *Harvard Journal of Law & Gender* 30: 461–505.

Wilson, R.F. (2010) 'Insubstantial Burdens: The Case for Government Employee Exemptions to Same Sex Marriage Laws', *Northwestern Journal of Law & Social Policy* 5(2): 318–368.

Wittgenstein, L. (2009) *Philosophical Investigations*. 4th edn. London: Blackwell.

Wolterstorff, N. (1997) 'The Role of Religion in Decision and Discussion of Political Issues', in Audi R. and Wolterstorff, N. *Religion in the Public Square*. London: Rowman & Littlefield Publishers, pp. 67–120.

Wolterstorff, N. (2012) *Understanding Liberal Democracy: Essays in Political Philosophy*. Oxford: Oxford University Press.

Zucca, L. (2009) 'The Crisis of the Secular State – A Reply to Professor Sajó', *ICON* 7(3): 509–511.

Zucca, L. (2011) 'Lautsi: A Commentary on a Decision by the ECtHR Grand Chamber', *International Journal of Constitutional Law* 11(1): 218–229.

Zucca, L. (2013) *A Secular Europe*. Oxford: Oxford University Press.

Zucca, L. and Ungureanu, C. (2012) *Law, State and Religion in the New Europe*. Cambridge: Cambridge University Press.

Index